Ladies of the Lake

Ladies *of the* *Lake*

CAITLIN
AND
JOHN
MATTHEWS

Thorsons
An Imprint of HarperCollinsPublishers

Thorsons
An Imprint of HarperCollins*Publishers*
77–85 Fulham Palace Road,
Hammersmith, London W6 8JB

Published by The Aquarian Press 1992
5 7 9 10 8 6

A catalogue record for this book
is available from the British Library

ISBN 1 85538 045 5

Typeset by Harper Phototypesetters Limited,
Northampton, England
Printed and bound in Great Britain by
Creative Print and Design (Wales), Ebbw Vale

Dedication

This book is dedicated to the waterways of our Earth,
that the waters of every spring, river, lake and sea
may flow with their original purity once more.

We see by means of water.
Wolfram von Eschenbach, *Parzival*

also
In Memoriam
the Forest of Broceliande
which suffered the scourge of fire in 1990,
that the sacred groves of the Ninefold may be recreated.

Invocation of the Gifts

For a Ninefold Chorus
Translated from the Scots Gaelic by
Caitlín Matthews

1 2 & 3 We bathe your palms
In showers of wine,
In the crook of the kindling,
In the seven elements,
In the sap of the tree,
In the milk of honey.

All We place nine pure, choice gifts
In your clear, beloved face:

1 The gift of form,
2 The gift of voice,
3 The gift of fortune,
4 The gift of goodness,
5 The gift of eminence,
6 The gift of charity,
7 The gift of pure maidenhood,
8 The gift of true nobility,
9 The gift of apt speech.

1 Dark is yonder town,
2 Dark are those within,
1 You are the brown swan,
2 Going within fearlessly,
3 Their hearts beneath your hand,
2 & 3 Their tongues beneath your foot,
1 2 & 3 No word will they utter to do you ill.

1 You are a shade in the heat,
2 You are a shelter in the cold,
3 You are eyes to the blind,
4 You are a staff to the pilgrim,

5 You are an island in the sea,
6 You are a stronghold upon land,
7 You are a well in the waste land,
8 You are healing to the sick.

1 Yours is the skill of the Faery Woman,
2 Yours is the virtue of Bride,
3 Yours is the faith of Moira[1] mild,
4 Yours are the deeds of the women of Greece,
5 Yours is the boldness of Emer the beautiful,
6 Yours are the features of Darthula's[2] face,
7 Yours is the spirit of Maeve the strong,
8 Yours is the affection of the Sweet Singer.

1 You are the luck of every joy,
2 You are the light of the sun's beams,
3 You are the door of lordly welcome,
4 You are the pole star of guidance,
5 You are the step of the roe of the height,
6 You are the step of the white-faced mare,
7 You are the grace of the swimming swan,
8 You are the jewel in each mystery.

9 Nine waves around you,[3]
Nine winds above you,
Nine paths across you,
Nine fires about you,
Nine wells beneath you,
Nine wisdoms given you,
Nine gifts given you,
Nine skills given you,
Nine strengths given you,
All Ninefold the blessing of the *sidhe*.

[1] *Moira* is Mary.
[2] *Darthula* is Deirdre.
[3] Please note that I have added the last verse, which is not found in the original. C.M.

Contents

PART THREE – THE LANDS ADVENTUROUS

The Grail Maidens

Foreword

There is, or used to be, a truism of the feminist hard line that 'the personal is political'. Well, I'm not much of a feminist, but I can use their slogans to my own convenience; and right now, I'll make that an excuse for telling how I met John and Caitlín Matthews.

A few years ago - I don't know how many, but I was considerably younger and spryer than I am now, at least three strokes and a heart attack ago - I was one of the guest lecturers on a tour of Arthurian magical sites in Britain. The host was the well-known proprietor of the Gothic Image bookstore in Glastonbury, Somerset, Jamie George; and if I were to recount here the series of coincidences by which Jamie and I became acquainted and became friends when I first visited England, I would be accused of expecting my readers not only to suspend disbelief, but to hang it by the neck until dead.

On this tour, there were some exceptionally nice people, and all too few tourists. A tourist to me is the kind of person we had on at least one other tour: we were passing through Glen Lomond, one of the great scenic wonders of the world, in my own opinion the equal or better of the Grand Canyon, and these, these *tourists* sat and played *gin rummy*.

Now, on that long-ago tour, we had several guest lecturers. As everyone who knows me knows, I am not good with names, and one of the guests was the expert on sacred geography and earth mysteries, John Michell. Later I was seated next to one of these guests and he answered when I called him John, so I took him for Mr Michell. Some hours later I found out that the speaker was not John Michell, but that John Michell was one of the other guests, tall, lean – even cadaverous – and soft spoken. So who was this one, young dark-haired and delightfully friendly? I decided it must be our psaltery player, Bob Stewart, and left it at that. It was in fact John Matthews. Eventually I got them straight, and all was well.

When I received a dot-matrix manuscript from the Matthews with a request for a foreword, my heart sank; one of the things I have learned in the interval is to be very chary of such promises. Like Dorothy L. Sayers' character Harriet Vane, 'I'll do anything for anybody except say their beastly book is good when it isn't.' I have lost a number of supposed friends that way, so I seldom promise such things any more.

So I regarded the manuscript without enthusiasm and thought to myself, 'Oh, hell, did I really promise them that? Well, here goes another friendship, dammit!' and sat down to read the blasted thing.

To my surprise and delight, it turned out to be the kind of thing I could read with interest, even fascination. It is a work of substantial scholarship, of the kind which I, as a writer of novels (and fantasy at that, in the sense that everything ancient is fantasy, since when you get more than 200 years in the past, you have to make a lot of it up anyway; existing historical records are something less than complete) could never do – and wouldn't want to. It treats each of the women in the Arthurian legends as the equivalent of one of the Celtic goddess-forms, rather as the late Robert Graves did in *The White Goddess*; and does it with an imagination – rather, an *imaginativeness* – and skill not usually associated with the scholarly work of Graves. Although Graves, himself a poet of no mean stature, would probably approve. (He speaks of one form of research as 'poetic reverie'.)

One of the book's many virtues is an excellent and accessible bibliography; an addition which I could never emulate, but found very useful. Luckily I don't have to emulate it – one of my college professors once told me there were two kinds of knowledge: knowing a thing and knowing where to look it up, and I've always been good at picking other people's brains.

I'll share one more vignette while I'm thinking of that trip. On the last night, all of us foregathered for a farewell meal in a London restaurant; an *Indian* restaurant, meaning that curries so hot were served that I kept wondering why Caitlín - then in the final stages of pregnancy - did not go into labour there and then. It happened to be Jamie George's birthday, and the final item brought in was a marzipan-iced birthday cake. Unknown to Jamie, John had supplied the cake with trick candles, so that when Jamie blew them out, they spontaneously lit again, and Jamie blew them out again - very productive of frustration, and of so much smoke that we set off the fire alarm in the restaurant; not making us, I suppose, very popular with the management.

But it's one of those things I'll always remember about that trip, years later. John and Caitlín are a lot of fun; and so is their book. I wish all of them well.

Marion Zimmer Bradley

Acknowledgements

Special thanks to Marion Zimmer Bradley for writing the foreword to our book.

Grateful recognition to Felicity Wombwell and Helene Hess for many intimate conversations which have helped uncover some more of the drowned lands of Lyonesse.

To Mildred Leake Day and Mette Pors, both distinguished Arthurian scholars, for their advice and companionship.

To all our readers and workshop participants – male as well as female – who have enacted, meditated upon and dialogued with the Ladies of the Lake and shared their magical voyages with us.

To the Company of Hawkwood who together form a Round Table of endless quest, story and adventure.

To the many reformed bands of the Ninefold who are beginning to remember the teachings of the Ladies of the Lake, especially the Sisters of the Sacred College of Aquae Sulis who formed a notable triple Ninefold at Imbolc 1991.

Approaches to this Book

In this book we have discussed the Arthurian tradition as a composite whole, treating each of the strata with respect and with cross-relation between the texts. The Arthurian tradition arose through oral tradition – what we call 'mythology' – and passed into literary transcription. From thence it was given a literary stamp by different authors, in very much the same way as a modern soap opera is generated. The result has been a variegated and complex set of stories, centring around Arthur. Later writers, like Malory, attempted to correlate and codify these often random strands of story into a cohesive whole. Modern Arthurian novelists are either still doing this, or else creating further episodes in the continuing adventures of the Round Table. In attempting to reach through the levels of tradition to contact the Ladies of the Lake, we have tried to show the hand-holds and stepping places, drawing on both medieval text and the underlying Celtic tradition.

A short note on terminology: we have noticed a growing tendency to confuse 'Celtic', 'British', 'Welsh' and 'Gaelic'. As a general note for overseas readers: the word 'British' refers to the people inhabiting the area which is now called 'England and Wales'. This word is also broadly used by us to indicate the folk now called 'Welsh', the Cymru (pronounced '*Cum*-ree'), as they still prefer to call themselves. They were the indigenous people of the island of Britain, before the Saxon and Norman invasions, just as the Picts were the native people of Scotland. The native Cymric or British people spoke a Brythonic Celtic tongue, which survives in the Welsh language. Gaelic is a Goidelic Celtic tongue which was spoken in Ireland and later in Scotland. When we talk about Celtic, we are speaking broadly about the traditions of Britain and Ireland combined, since both countries share many common themes and stories.

Throughout, we have used the word 'myth' respectfully, to indicate 'a sacred story on many levels'. We totally reject the dictionary use of 'myth' to mean 'a fictitious or imaginary person or thing' (*Shorter OED*).

The objection may be raised that the Arthurian tradition is 'just a story', to be enjoyed within its own parameters, and that to make imaginative and magical connections between ourselves and this tradition is to be self-deluded. Our answer to this accusation is that the mythic story is the mirror wherein human understanding and experience is reflected. The Arthurian legends may inform us about our historical, social and spiritual past and give us insight into how our lives may be lived now. These traditions are lively ones which require the reanimation of personal interaction. In this book, we relate modern experience to the Arthurian stories with sensitivity to the stories and their original context; we do not assume a shared consciousness or understanding between modern and traditional knowledge.

This becomes obvious as we examine the Ladies of the Lake, who often represent the most primal aspects of Arthurian tradition. Immediately we are confronted with mythic scenarios which have no day-to-day currency in our contemporary world: sacrifice, ritual mating, second sight, enchantment and shape-shifting. These represent the inner or esoteric levels of the Arthurian tradition. On the other hand we can also find parallels and resonances with our own society: the abuses of power, rape, abduction, sexual politics, family manipulation, relationship dependency, jealousy and disempowerment.

This book chooses to deal with both the inner levels, the teachings the Ladies of the Lake have to give us, and with the outer levels of the stories, for there is an exchange between the two which is not often stressed. The Ladies of the Lake cannot be viewed through the simplistic glass of modern feminist politics, which often distorts traditional archetypes of the inner worlds into disempowered victims of male aggression. They are strong, resourceful lineage-holders of our native tradition who have the persistent endurance of water to affect our world. The context of our nine Ladies and their many sisters is truly an archetypical one.

Read this book once before working practically with it. Write in its margins, start journals, allow yourself to be made thoughtful or be provoked to outrage. React to and interact with the stories and archetypes. We have striven to give you authentic textual sources to work from and any speculation of ours is clearly indicated as such. A full bibliography (pp.225-32) supports this research.

This book has meditations and ideas in it to help give you firsthand experience of the Ladies of the Lake. To many people, myths remain 'just stories' unless they are able to go beyond the text and apply what they are reading to their own experience.

Each chapter ends with a visualization. Many people are not visually oriented and find it hard to concentrate on an image. If you need a little help getting started, there are many suitable images in our *The Arthurian Tarot* (The Aquarian Press, 1990). You might lay down the following cards to represent the women in this book:

	Card title from
Lady	*The Arthurian Tarot*
Igraine:	Grail Queen
Guinevere:	III Guinevere
Morgan:	XI Sovereignty
Argante:	II The Lady of the Lake
Nimuë:	Spear Maiden
Enid:	VI The White Hart
Kundry:	Stone Maiden
Dindraine:	Sword Maiden
Ragnell:	XIII The Washer at the Ford

The exercises given are mostly visualitive in this book, requiring that you put the script on tape or else learn the sequence. (A tape of the visualizations is available, see p.222). Thereafter you close your eyes and go. Whatever experience you have will be your own. The following simple guidelines for such visualitive work will help you find your way safely:

1. Alternative reality and everyday reality are both valid realities which can be explored. Just as you do not confuse dreaming with waking, so neither should you confuse your ordinary state and your meditative state. Give your visualizations a clear beginning and ending and write down immediately what you experienced.
2. Do not attempt visualitive work during intense emotional states; you probably won't experience much in any case. The same applies if you are taking drugs 'for effect': if you want to blow your psyche to blazes, this is the best way of doing it! So please be careful.
3. Show respect when you are encountering beings in alternative reality. Apply the same good manners you would show in everyday life to people you meet. However, do not resign responsibility for yourself and carefully test any advice you are given in your meditations. Thank your guides for helping you.
4. If any being you encounter shows signs of not wanting to go away, but seems to inhabit your head when you don't actively want this, you have not sealed off properly after your meditation. Request the being to go away and visualize it leaving you and passing within through a door to the Otherworld.

Visualitive work is helpful in stimulating contact with the imaginal realms, but it should not become a prop. Apply your findings to your everyday life as practically as possible. The compassionate outpouring waters which nurture the spirit are not your private swimming pool. If, by contact with you, others experience these energies for themselves, so much the better.

Go out into the natural world and commune with the waterways of your land. What do the waters themselves tell you? These arteries of our land are important, not only to allay drought and nourish the countryside, but also as active channels of moving energy. Get involved in campaigns to clean up rivers, streams and lakes in your area. Find out where local holy wells are located and start to clean them up if they are polluted or disused. This is an important task which symbolically acknowledges the Damsels of the Wells, the archetypal guardians of spiritual nurture.

Unless we clean up our waterways, we will have a larger environmental disaster on our hands. Many parts of the world already have drought due to the climactic imbalances which short-sighted humanity has brought about. Unless we seek out and listen for the voices of the wells, our world will also become a spiritual waste land.

Archetypal dependence, whereby we start to lean upon certain stock characters, situations or assumptions, can severely cramp our development as effective human beings. Allow yourself the freedom to explore archetypes within this book which you find difficult or challenging. Do not allow yourself to be defined solely by a small group of self-cosseting frameworks which never stretch your potential. Question, grow and adapt to stay lively.

Live your life to the full and may the blessing of the Ladies of the Lake empower you to fulfil your destiny!

Caitlín and John Matthews
Beltane, 1991

The Initiation of the Lake

No-one should doubt that these adventures took place at that time in Britain and in all the other kingdoms; and many more occurred than I recall, but these are the best known.

Perlesvaus

WOMEN OF THE ARTHURIAN LEGEND

Where are the women in the Arthurian legend? Why aren't they more dynamic? These questions are often asked of us at our workshops, and the reader might indeed also wonder about the role and visibility of women in the Arthurian story.

On the surface, the men go on quest as knights, fighting battles and tournaments, and often acting as extensions of the king himself, while the women stay at home, seeming only to be pawns in dynastic marriages, rescue-fodder or sources of courtly admiration for the knights. But the women of the Arthurian legend do have several roles to play, for theirs is a hidden story. If traditional story-tellers and romancers have not focused upon them very well, it is hardly surprising, considering the times in which these stories were transmitted. Women were an unknown and possibly dangerous country to the clerics; to the singers of courtly love, they were a distant object of attainment, mysteriously hidden, bountiful or cruel by turns. Between this over-romanticized view of women and the fearful distrust with which they were seen by the Church, women in general did not appear in a fully illuminated way.

It is only in our own time that women have begun to speak

for themselves, and it is unsurprising that their voices are often harsh, bitter and frustrated. That they are also singing in celebration, joy and renewal, though, is a sign of a hastening integration of the feminine into a world which has been predominantly masculine in character for too long.

This is also an age when the power of myth as saving story is being fully appreciated and explored. The Arthurian legends are particularly useful in this regard because they synthesize ancient and medieval motifs, drawing on both Pagan and Christian sources. During the Middle Ages this fusion produced the most popular sequence of stories, comparable with the soap operas of our own popular culture, and these stories were read and heard by people both high and low with equal enthusiasm.

Today many people are disillusioned with orthodox spiritualities such as Christianity. Many women in particular view Christianity as a monstrosity which robbed all Western women of their power. Some have sought Pagan revival and reverted to ancient Goddess spirituality to fill the spiritual vacuum. This brings us a diversity of opinions and standpoints, but if we can stand aside and with neutrality observe the power of the saving story and of the myth as primal narrative, we will see that in whatever mode it is cast, it is the *story* not the dogma that lasts. The stories which are told here come from many sources, and some of our subjects - such as Morgan - comprise many levels of myth. We have treated these myths as a totality, for the tradition within each story is a seamless garment, and we have chosen to uncover the women of Arthurian tradition partly because we feel our native myths and stories have as much to offer us as the Classical deities when it comes to discerning our spiritual potency.

In this book we are going to focus upon nine women. We have called them 'Ladies of the Lake', a term which may need clearer definition. The principle Lady of the Lake is known from later medieval Arthurian tradition as the one who gives Arthur his empowering sword, Excalibur, and who is the foster-mother of Lancelot. But her archetype is one which is common to the myths of north-west Europe, and to Britain and Ireland in particular. In this book we have called the Lady of the Lake by one of her many names, Argante, to avoid confusion with our other Ladies of the Lake. All nine women are Ladies of the Lake precisely because they derive their power from the Otherworld which, in Celto-Arthurian tradition, is perceived to be associated with the element of water. Arthur's knights, on the other hand, derive their status and power from the Round Table – at which no woman sits, for it represents an order of knighthood and is thus a male initiatory symbol. Even so, there are indications that certain knights sought initiation at the hands of women.

For women, the symbol of the otherworldly Lake is similarly potent to that of the Round Table. The element of water has feminine symbolism attached to it: it is a flowing, weaving, uncontainable force which invades and moistens. Many primal symbols in north-west European tradition derive from bodies of water, especially the Celtic Otherworld, which often lies across water. This is the case with Avalon and the Irish Tir na mBan (Land of Women). The healing power of natural features such as lakes, cauldrons, wells and springs underlies the later expressions of the Grail. Our ancestors perceived their deities not in human terms, but directly in nature. These sacred places had guardians to protect and tend them, some of which constellated in ninefold sisterhoods. Thus, certain places became imbued with sacred significance, or were found to possess certain energies which became associated with the deities of the land. Whether we perceive our nine ladies about a lake or about a cauldron, the effect is the same. Each of them is magically active to some degree: people with whom they associate are changed, often dramatically. This is a normal effect of a priestess and of a dynamic woman. The element of water is perceived as emotive, dangerous, overwhelming. Our contact with it causes us to change by means of an inner voyage upon the tides and currents of the emotions.

Although there are other women in the Arthurian legend, the ones we have chosen have the strongest resonances to the Lake, that paradigm of otherworldly forces which stems from the

West. The place of the West is associated with water in Celtic tradition. The western seaboard of Britain and Ireland is washed by the Atlantic and – by association – by the power of the Blessed Islands which lie submerged, like Atlantis, in our imagination.

The native faery tradition of these islands underpins and complements the Arthurian lore contained here: the Lady of Llyn y Fan Fach gives medicinal powers to her descendants before returning to her lake;[1] Ceridwen brews a magical cauldron whose wisdom-inspiring draught is stolen by Gwion, and the subsequent liquid is unfit for consumption and poisons the horses of Gwyddno; the monstrous ever-birthing giant mother, Cymeidi Cymeinfoll, emerges from an Irish lake and becomes a productive source of warriors for both Irish and British kings.[2] The maiden Liban outlives her contemporaries by becoming a lake-creature; Meredith, the well-guardian, is raped by Seithenin and the waters overwhelm the land, as they do when the Breton Dahaut drowns Ys.[3] The Damsels of the Wells guard the waters in the Pagan Grail prequel (see Chapter 8) until they are raped and withdraw their services. Without water, the land becomes a waste land. The loss of the Grail or cauldron is at the base of the problems in Arthur's kingdom. The champion of the Lady of the Fountain maintains his watch over the source of the waters. The power of the waters is everywhere in the Celtic world where great treasures have been found, treasures originally thrown into lakes as offerings to the spirits of the gods. The Romano-Celtic Goddess Coventina guards her well, and the waters of Sulis Minerva still flow at Bath.

This otherworldly and faery tradition has been largely overlaid or discounted. But the abilities and status of these figures nearer resemble those we would now designate as goddessly. The devolution of Goddess to the status of ugly witch or diminutive faery has gone side by side with the devolution of women's spiritual potential. Our society sees women as creatures of sexuality or paradox; it discounts women's otherworldly dimension and their sacral nature. The Ladies of the Lake who appear in Arthurian tradition have important or powerful functions which have been long overlooked. They have been too easily discussed in the context of their social roles of wife, sister or daughter of a man, not important in their own right. Women reading this book may have drawn the conclusion that the Arthurian legends are a set of patriarchal myths which tells man's story at the expense of woman's. But, taking a hard look at the material presented here, we clearly have several levels of understanding operating, which we have attempted to uncover. We have chosen to study the women on their own ground, in their own terms, rather than as accessories of men. Each woman appearing in this book is important in her own right and cannot be so relegated.

But let us first take the accusation that the Arthurian women are there to empower men. To be sure, it is the knights who go out on quest and adventure and the women who stay home, save for a few exceptions. The women, however, seem to be remnants of an earlier regime. They appear to be priestesses and empowerers in a specific sense. They bring healing, insight, challenge and difficulty as well as empowerment. Indeed, sometimes they cause disempowerment, as Morgan and Nimuë do. All of the Arthurian knights are empowered by women, and some by faery or otherworldly women: Gawain by Ragnell, Perceval by the Nine Witches of Gloucester and Lancelot by the Lady of the Lake herself.

There is a great deal of objection in feminist circles to this mythic trend of women empowering men, wherever it is found. However, to pretend otherwise is to change the mythic function of men and women. It was the esotericist Dion Fortune who coined an aphorism which we should all take to heart: 'That which is latent on the outer is potent in the inner; and that which is potent in the outer is latent in the inner.'⁴

She further glosses this cryptic statement in the following way: women's natures are latent in the everyday world and potent in the inner realms, while men's natures are potent in the everyday world and latent in the inner realms. This statement does not take into account the circuitry of gay or bi-sexual people, which will sometimes differ radically from this model, but works as an excellent rule of thumb for everyone else. It explains a lot that we have attempted to grapple with in terms of gendural roles and functions. Women are often perceived to be passive in the realms of everyday life and powerful in the magical realms: the many metaphors of women as dangerous, as witches and as enchantresses are scattered throughout world cultures. Men, on the other hand, seem to have their primacy in the everyday world, but be less happy in their relations with the inner worlds of magic, the psyche or the imagination. This statement is not a fixed law but general rule which has many exceptions. Dion Fortune's writing derived from practical and ethical magical experience, an experience which is not commonly shared by many men or women today, because our society has jettisoned its spiritual and psychic values.

We are currently acknowledged to be living within a 'patriarchal' culture wherein the inner world of imagination, art, magic and the psyche plays little or no part. It is so negligible that there are few social structures wherein such practices are considered 'respectable' modes of life. However, the patriarchal world cannot live without the inspiration which the matriarchal world can supply. Women tend to power-house male personalities and institutions without a second thought. They give the necessary moisture to what may be an essentially dry idea. This analogy also works the other way: the instinctive and often unrealized nature of women needs the pragmatism of men. Too much Yin and not enough Yang leaves projects floating aimlessly about.

This is not to say that women are aimless and only men have direction. We also utilize the internal dynamo within each of us to supply this need. A woman may conceive an idea from a dream, but draw on her practical abilities to project and manifest it, just as a man may draw on his imagination to fuel a project he wishes to promote.

In terms of mythology, this schema of inspiration is generally polarized in terms of male and female protagonists. In the *Odyssey*, Odysseus cannot get himself out of scrapes without the aegis of Athene, Leukothea or Calypso; similarly, the innumerable enchanted women of Arthurian and general medieval legend cannot be rescued from imprisonment without the aid of knights. Both men *and* women need the help of each other, but neither is bereft of sources of help within themselves: Perceval's growing sensitivity is aided by his awareness of an internal female figure whom he thinks of as 'the woman he loves best'; Enid's great patience with her headstrong husband, Erec, is based on her strong vision of a complementary partnership of love. The internal help of the feminine can be accessed by men, just as the external pragmatism of the masculine can be accessed by women.

Within the Arthurian legend, however, self-motivating women are hard to find. For the reasons behind this, we must look at the context in which these stories were transcribed. Medieval culture marginalized women's abilities and so their social position was likewise tenuous. Women were considered to be dangerous, because they were unknown, unexplored territory. That there was a wealth of fable connected with women's nature we have full evidence: the medical fable of the errant womb which wandered about in a woman's body giving rise to her changeable moods; the religious fable about her treacherous nature, wherein Eve, and subsequently woman, was the perpetrator of the evils of human existence; the social fable that women were property, to be viewed only in terms of their fathers, brothers or sons.[5] Against this harsh and uncompromising background we have to set our scene.

Briefly viewed, our nine ladies are not typical of the medieval woman: the Lady of the Lake is a totally autonomous being of otherworldly nature, a queen in her own right who possesses no permanent consort; Nimuë is a Pagan woman brought up in the confines of a forest; Ragnell is an otherworldly being of great knowledge, as is Kundry; Igraine is a queen who goes into the realms of Faery; Morgan, her daughter, is a shapeshifter and priestessly woman; Guinevere is a childless queen who takes lovers; Dindraine is a dedicated priestess who goes in quest of the Grail; Enid is an impoverished noblewoman who is acclaimed as substitute queen and who undergoes the trials of a misunderstanding husband in order to reach the inner mysteries of love and sovereignty. They are women who hold 'dual nationality', being movers both in Middle Earth and in the Otherworld.

The major feature of return or withdrawal to an otherworldly state is pronounced among these ladies. The majority return to the Otherworld – Igraine goes to the Castle of Maidens, Dindraine to Sarras, the Grail city; Guinevere becomes a nun. Only Enid remains to mediate the power of love in Middle Earth. But this is as it should be, for there must always be one person to liaise between the worlds. So Bors returns from the Grail quest as the witness to those at court of what has taken place.

The Ladies of the Lake have a strange freedom: they arrive in a story and then often reappear in other guises later on. Some are seen to return to their Lake origins, like Igraine, Morgan and Dindraine; others fade from sight, like visions withdrawing from our consciousness. They each bear distinct traces of the Goddess in her many aspects. The Goddess of the Land, or Sovereignty, as she is called, is one of the great scattered archetypes of British and Irish tradition. When images of the Divine Feminine were cast out of 'official' spirituality, the Goddess fragmented and became subsumed in many stories. When we study each of the Arthurian women, this becomes clear. The Goddess has been put through the mincer and reassembled, so that, in the case of Morgan, for example, we see a veritable 'pantheon in miniature', as R.S. Loomis says.[6]

The Goddess of Sovereignty is the subject of *Arthur and the Sovereignty of Britain*, where Caitlín Matthews has traced her appearances through the stories of *The Mabinogion*. Some of the material from that book overlaps with this, and readers may find it helpful and illuminating to read that study as a companion to this, but we have given a different emphasis here, presenting other material from a wider selection of texts. The role of the knight as the champion of the Goddess can be found in John Matthews' *Gawain, Knight of the Goddess*.

The substitution of the woman for the Goddess is discernible throughout our study. Igraine is priestess-mother of Britain, the destined mother of Arthur. Morgan is the daughter of Avalon and half-sister to Arthur, representative at his court of the otherworldly powers. Guinevere is the Flower Bride, the inspirer of Britain, the royal woman who is sought by many abductors who desire to rule the land. Argante is the inner priestess and instructor of Lancelot. Nimuë is the huntress of the grove who makes Merlin's powers her own. Dindraine is the inspirer of the Grail quest, whose own blood is forfeit for the healing of all. Kundry is the messenger of the deep voice of the Goddess. Enid is almost a substitute for the white hart of love and sovereignty and for Guinevere herself. Ragnell is the transformer of all women.

We should beware of viewing these Ladies of the Lake as analogues of modern or even medieval women. They should be viewed in their mythic context and we should listen to what they have to say without psychologizing them. There may be useful and interesting ways of seeing the Ladies as products of a medieval society which had incorporated earlier aspects of female potential into its literary works, ways of freedom and power which were actually denied most real women at that time. The position of Arthurian women worsens as the stories are further retold in the later Middle Ages; the proto-Celtic underpinning of the stories betrays a stronger, freer line.

The untenable role of the imprisoned damsel is given by Tennyson in his 'Lady of Shalott' poem. Here the Maid of Astolat is translated into an enchanted maiden who is doomed to weave whatever she sees in her mirror, but never to look down upon the world of Camelot in person, let alone enter it herself.

This image of the woman who dreams and dreams and never fulfils her dreams is very important at the present time, for it is a state in which many modern women find themselves. While it is empowering to inhabit our towered imaginations, they can become our self-chosen prison. Even the Lady of Shalott, seeing the figures come and go, sighs, 'I am half sick of shadows.' However, eventually she cannot – even at the cost of calling the curse upon her own head – deny her nature any more:

> She left the web, she left the loom,
> She made three paces thro' the room,
> She saw the water-lily bloom,
> She saw the helmet and the plume:
> She look'd down to Camelot.[7]

She breaks the curse and dies, but at least she has made the attempt to be free of her endless weaving.

Perhaps there are many women who fear this very thing - that the web of their dreaming will prove stronger and more supportive than their imagined lives in the outside world, that without the fuel of their dreams they will soon die. The solution to such fears is to find practical ways to utilize the dreams and still have time to weave. Women who live at the mercy of the everyday world often neglect their dreaming, so that their protective web, like that of the Lady of Shalott's, flies out of the window and the imaginative inner eye cracks from side to side.

This image of the woman weaving in seclusion, who has to be drawn out of her introspective preoccupation, is one familiar from Classical legend where Proserpine weaves a scarf out of the elements of creation for her mother, Ceres. Three goddesses come to tempt her from her task into the outside world where her potential will be useful: Minerva, Goddess of Wisdom and Diana, Goddess of the Moon - both Virgin archetypes - are accompanied by Venus, Goddess of Desire.[8] The sacred drama of Proserpine would never have taken place had she remained in her cave.

In the same way, life does not intend women to remain virgins locked in ivory towers, but to engage in its struggles. The exercise of coping with the struggle of life is a female initiation, just as the battle to come to terms with what lies within is the ultimate initiation of men. These initiatory struggles are not supposed to be easy; the difficulties we encounter are *supposed* to challenge and stretch us.

The popularity of *Mists of Avalon* is founded upon the resonance which modern women seeking empowerment find with Morgan le Fay, as portrayed by Marion Zimmer Bradley.

Morgan's anger at the usurpation of the ancient religion and the magical role of women by the Christianized Arthurian world also lies at the basis of much modern female anger. It has given a new way of looking at the Arthurian legend for women without a story.

It is ironic that the world of myth, now so desperately sought and dearly cherished in our world which has jettisoned the saving stories as 'untrue', should provide women with scenarios which seem to deny them a dynamic or positive role. Do we transform the myth, change it, rewrite it, pretend it never happened that way? Or do we work through it and listen to what it tells us about the way we need to learn from each other? There are many who have taken the first course, in often radical ways, expunging the unwanted elements with all the zeal of a political pogrom. With the second method, we must adopt the role of a restorer of ancient canvases, gently cleaning away the layers of grime and neglect until the original paint shines through in its pristine colours. When we do this, we discover that the world of myth gives us clues and ways of approach we did not first notice.

This book is not only for women who seek inspiration from our native myths and goddesses, but also for men who wish to realign themselves with a dynamic that has been frequently submerged or discounted. The way to the Ladies of the Lake is by means of water; the returning voyager finds him or herself with a set of fully operating emotions which will flow compassionately into a world which is rapidly becoming arid of either water or compassion. To avoid that waste land, we listen to the voice of the waters.

We need to gaze into the Lake as our mirror of inner awareness. Its surface will reflect our own hidden depths. Like the mirror of the Lady of Shallot, it will show us new ways of perceiving our own story.

REFERENCES

1. John Rhys, *Celtic Folklore*.
2. *The Mabinogion*, ed. Lady Charlotte Guest.
3. John Matthews, *Taliesin: The Shamanic and Bardic Mysteries in Britain and Ireland*.
4. Dion Fortune, *Aspects of Occultism*.
5. Caitlín Matthews, *Sophia: Goddess of Wisdom*.
6. R.S. Loomis, 'Morgue la Fée in Oral Tradition', *Romania*.
7. Alfred Lord Tennyson, *The Lady of Shalott*.
8. Caitlín Matthews, op. cit.

The Ninefold Sisterhood

They dance, the nine korrigans,
Crowned with flowers, robed in white,
About the fountain, in moonlight.

> From *The Verses of the Lore*,
> traditional Breton (trans. Caitlín Matthews)

The ninefold nature of this study is deliberate. Ninefolds
constellate in the Celtic tradition as the triple-aspected Goddess
who is three times three. In one of the first quests in Malory's
Morte d'Arthur, the Goddess appears as in her threefold guise as
three women - a maiden, a mature woman and an old woman.
This triplicity is associated in both Classical and European
tradition with the *Parcae* (the Apportioners) or the Fates, of
whom Isidore of Seville writes:

> Three Fates fabricate Fate upon their distaffs and spindles,
> twisting the thread of wool through their fingers: they represent
> the three periods of Time; the past which is already spun and
> divided on the spindle, the present which passes through the
> fingers of the spinner, the future which is the thread wound up
> on the distaff which has passed through the fingers of the spinner
> on the spindle as the present will become the past. We call them
> the Parcae for they spare very few. They are three in number:
> the first to spin the life of man, the second is the weaver, the
> third is the cutter of the thread.[1]

This threefold appearance of the Goddess is sometimes
multiplied to become a ninefold sisterhood to whom come
seekers who need the advice of a sibyl or fay - a word derived

from *fatae* or fate. The number nine has mystical properties: multiples of nine, however they are added up, come to nine. It is thus a number of perfection, completion and culmination.

Gaelic tradition tells us that the faery kind are said to possess nine ages, with nine times nine periods of time making up each age:

> Nine nines sucking the breast,
> Nine nines unsteady, weak,
> Nine nines on foot, swift,
> Nine nines able and strong,
> Nine nines strapping, brown,
> Nine nines victorious, subduing,
> Nine nines bonneted, drab,
> Nine nines beardy, grey.
> Nine nines on the breast-beating death,
> And worse to me were these miserable nine nines
> Than all the other short-lived nine nines that were.[2]

The mathematically-minded will be gratified to learn that the span of a faery's life is 729 which, added together, reduces to $9+9=18$; $1+8=9$.

The Ninefold are consistent throughout Celtic tradition. In Britain, we read of the Nine Witches of Gloucester who provide the weapon-training for Peredur.[3] These are paralleled in Gaelic tradition by the eponymous goddess of the Isle of Skye, Scathach (pronounced 'Ski-ach'). She trains the youthful Cuchulainn in arms and challenges him to overcome her – a feat which Peredur similarly performs for his teacher.

That leaves the sisters of the cauldron, the nine maidens who cool the Cauldron of Annwn with their breath, thus inspiriting its liquor.[4] These women are perhaps nearest to our own Ladies of the Lake, for they have many gifts in their guardianship. The poem in which they appear in person speaks of them blowing upon the waters of the cauldron with their breath, as though inspiring them with their muselike gifts. Like the fairy-godmothers of folk-tale, each has a gift to offer the one who imbibes from the cauldron. Their collective gifts are memory,

psychic omniscience and otherworldly kinship, for those who
have been reborn of the cauldron become initiates in
otherworldly knowledge and therefore have no abiding place in
the earthly realms.

Then there is the Avalonian goddess, Morgen, and her eight
sisters, in Geoffrey of Monmouth's *Vita Merlini*. Avalon is like the
Irish Land of Women, which is itself but one of the Blessed
Islands of the West to which heroes sail on their *immrama* or
wonder voyages.[5]

But did women truly live together in sisterhoods in Pagan
Celtic times, or is this the speculation of fiction? We have two
fine accounts from Classical sources which reinforce the
reality of such sisterhoods.

In *continental Celtic lore*, Strabo relates the following:

> [Caesar] says that there is a small island in the ocean not far
> from the land, lying off the mouth of the Loire; and the women
> of the Samnitae inhabit it; they are possessed by Dionysius and
> propitiate the god with initiations and other sacred rites; and
> no man may land on the island, but the women themselves sail
> out from it and have intercourse with men and then return. It
> is their custom once a year to remove the roof from their temple
> and to roof it again the same day before sunset, each woman
> carrying part of the burden; but the woman whose load falls
> from her is torn to pieces by the others, and they carry the pieces
> around the temple crying out 'euoi' and do not cease until their
> madness passes away; and it always happens that someone
> pushes against the woman who is destined to suffer this fate.[6]

Pomponius Mela in his *De Situ Orbis III - 6* reports that:

> The island of Sein, near the Ossimiens, is known because of the
> oracle of a Gaulish God; the priestesses of that divinity are nine
> in number; the Gauls call them 'Senes'; they believe that,
> animated by a particular spirit, they can by their spells create
> storms in the air and on the sea, take the appearance of any sort
> of animals, cure the most serious illnesses, know and foretell
> the future, but only to those seamen who go over the ocean to
> see them.[7]

There seems very little difference between these women and the Avalonian sisterhood. The ninefold sisters are truly the Celtic muses, with powers more extensive than the Classical sisterhood. The daughters of Mnemosyne were steadily downgraded over the course of time to mere patronesses of the arts. However, there is a strong predilection in Celtic society for the communicative arts as a mode of esoteric transcription. The triple-aspected goddess Brighid was worshipped in Ireland, while in Britain the goddess Brigantia was depicted in Romano-Celtic times with the attributes of Minerva. The poet Taliesin is said to speak 'with the aid and direction of Minerva' in the *Vita Merlini*.[8] Caesar also verifies this: 'Among the Gallic people they hold that Minerva instituted the arts and crafts.'[9] The Christian sisterhood of St Brigit of Kildare, which venerated the saint who had subsumed many of the goddess Brighid's attributes, consisted of 19 or 20 nuns who tended the saint's fire, with St Brigit herself taking the twenty-first watch. However, it is possible that Gerald of Wales, who commented upon this exclusively female foundation wherein no men were allowed, may have been mistaken in his numeration: we may speculate that there may have been two companies of nine, with the saint as the presiding nineteenth sister.

All ancient traditions relating to the Goddess, especially those based on oral lore, tend to lose their subtlety and nuance over the centuries. This is hardly surprising when the guardians of that tradition are suppressed. It is now hard for us to approach the Goddess: we walk along pathways which have become overgrown and neglected. The Goddess who once appeared to our ancestors in garments of rainbow brilliance, now appears to us covered in a formless mantle. The West has been schooled in the narrow constraints of monotheism, allowing Deity no shades or gradations. This has suppressed the richness of true heritage. How can we restore the Goddess and appreciate Her full spectrum of aspects?

In *The Elements of the Goddess* by Caitlín Matthews, a way of comprehending the many aspects of the Goddess is set forth,

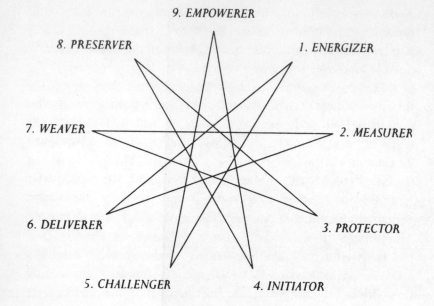

9. EMPOWERER

8. PRESERVER   1. ENERGIZER

7. WEAVER   2. MEASURER

6. DELIVERER   3. PROTECTOR

5. CHALLENGER   4. INITIATOR

Figure 1: Aspects of the Goddess

which is briefly summarized here. The major aspects of the Goddess can be symbolized upon the glyph of a nine-pointed star (see Figure 1).

Each of the numbered points corresponds to the following aspects, which are given non-specific titles which can be applied to any mythology or tradition. The titles are defined first of all by their effect upon us. The examples of goddesses who manifest under these aspects are drawn from world mythology. We have included the Ladies of the Lake, but each has numerous other definitions and cannot be ultimately pinned down under one title.

1. **The Energizer** aspect activates stasis and energizes us, helping us to get things moving. However we see the Goddess, when She first speaks to us, She usually takes this energizing form. We are moved and uplifted by a great, joyful power beyond our intellectual ability to control or understand.

There is great ecstasy in this aspect, a dynamism and a sexual or non-dual response which is felt intensely in the body. Examples: Hathor, Shakti, Guinevere.

2. **The Measurer** aspect shows us the extent of our limitations. This aspect is concerned with patterns, shapes, destinies. We may first encounter the Goddess as the Energizer, but when we have explored the wild horizons, we have travelled to the limits of our destiny, and return to understand and learn the patterns of her cyclic changes. Examples: Mnemosyne, Maat, Kundry.

3. **The Protector** is a guardian who upholds the boundaries which we discovered under the Measurer. She is concerned with transformative protection and merciful love. When we experience this aspect, we become fierce and tender at once towards our spiritual tradition. The Protector makes sure that we find a warrior's balance in our own guardianship and do not seek to create restrictive boundaries which keep our tradition in chains and prevent seekers from finding joy. Examples: Durga, Sekhmet, Argante.

4. **The Initiator** aspect is an opener of doors who is concerned with our rebirth. The way to our first encounter with the Initiator may be paved with difficulties. Practical problems which exemplify our own stagnating psyches will suddenly arise. But our practical solutions become our initiatory encounter. The Initiator gives us new ways and determinations to help reform our lives. Examples: White Buffalo Woman, Cardea, Ceridwen, Nimuë.

5. **The Challenger** aspect may appear at any time. She is concerned to root up whatever is unused and make it useful again. So it is that she manifests in terrifying forms. We know we have met the Challenger when we start to answer the questions we have been avoiding, when we courageously wade into the centre of a problem and face up to our inadequacies and illusions. Examples: Ereshkigal, Kali, Morgan.

6. **The Deliverer** aspect transforms and liberates us. She will not rest until every burden is lifted, every grief effaced. We

know the strength of the Deliverer when we are able to go beyond our selfishness into a wider compassion, when we refuse to pass our own pain onto others. The Deliverer often manifests as a goddess who chooses human form. Examples: Rhiannon, Sophia, Persephone, Enid.

7. **The Weaver** aspect is often seen as a witch or enchantress. She is concerned with appropriate shapes which provoke response. She activates the strange alchemies of our being, blending our life-experiences to produce an individual weave which is our own inimitable signature to the world. The Weaver shows us how to play again and to be sensitive companions of Creation. Examples: Circe, Neith, Ragnell.

8. **The Preserver** aspect sustains and maintains life itself. She is not concerned with bare survival but with intelligent and beneficial methods of living. The Preserver shows us how to inhabit our spiritual tradition and breathe with it. We can then keep the hearth-fire of tradition burning and are able to warm others by our living example. Examples: Brighid, Mary, Igraine.

9. **The Empowerer** aspect bestows mature wisdom. She is concerned with making a bridge between opposites, showing the still-point of beauty and harmony within all things and situations. The Empowerer gives us the confidence to go out and teach, help or instruct in our ways. We know when the Empowerer is at work in us when the deeply-rooted wisdom which lay unguessed within us flows freely. Examples: Isis, Mary Magdalene, Dindraine.

The ninefold sisterhoods which abound in Celtic tradition clearly reflect the face of the Goddess in their own inimitable way. They may once have functioned in a similar way to the nine Greek muses, each having some specific gift or quality to bestow. When we examine the Celtic ninefold sisterhoods, we discover that certain features are reported of them: they are shapeshifters, seers, weather-witches and warrior-women; they are teachers, healers, guardians, skilled in the ritual arts of love, givers of destiny. Their duties may be assigned to the ninefold circle of aspects, as follows. Women who exemplify these gifts and qualities within Celtic tradition are given here.

1. **The Energizer** offers the 'friendship of the thighs' and acts as a giver of inspiration. Examples: Medbh (Maeve), Flidais.
2. **The Measurer** is a weaver of destiny and gives insight into the patterning of life. Examples: The Washer at the Ford, Macha, Arianrhod.
3. **The Protector** is a teacher and foster-mother, giving instruction and laying down the path which her students will tread. Examples: Brighid, Scathach.
4. **The Initiator** is a seer and prophetess whose presence inspires the seeker. Examples: Ceridwen, Boann.
5. **The Challenger** is a warrior-woman and often appears as an adversary. She gives aid in battle and conflicts. Example: Morrighan, Creidne.
6. **The Deliverer** is a healer who opens a pathway to the liberation of love. Example: Brighid, Eriu.
7. **The Weaver** is a shapeshifter and weather-witch. She gives new opportunities. Example: Etain, Fand.
8. **The Preserver** is a fire keeper, a guardian of sacred traditions. She gives stability and continuance. Example: Cessair, Branwen, Goewin.
9. **The Empowerer** is a priestess who makes offerings or sacrifice. She gives deep wisdom and strength. Example: Banba, Queen of the Land of Women, Rhiannon.

This may give us insights into how the roles of the ninefold sisterhood were constellated in ancient times. But how does it help us understand the Ladies of the Lake? The giving of random Goddess examples may help the reader to fix the idea of the aspect in question, but it is soon clear that some goddesses are multi-faceted and do not fit tidily into one category in this way. It is the same with the Ladies of the Lake, each of whom can appear in many ways:

Guinevere is an Energizer, constellating a host of lovers and abductors who desire her, yet she is also a Preserver when she functions as Queen of Britain, and an Empowerer when she is called upon in her role as representative of Sovereignty.

Kundry is a Measurer, demarking the movements of the Grail knights, but she is also a Challenger and Protector when she keeps the quest alive and instructs the seekers in better skills.

Argante is a Protector as foster-mother; she is also an Initiator and a Preserver of ancient traditions.

Nimuë is an Initiator, but she can also be an Energizer, acting as Merlin's muse, and a Weaver, when she operates as an enchantress.

Morgan's chief role is that of Challenger in the Arthurian legends, but she is also a Weaver and a Measurer. Her final appearance is as a Deliverer when she ferries Arthur to Avalon.

Enid is a Deliverer, but she is also a Preserver and Empowerer when she acts as the representative of Sovereignty.

Ragnell is a Weaver, but she is also an Empowerer and Deliverer when she opens the pathways to love.

Igraine is a Preserver, but she can also be seen as an Energizer of Uther and a Protector or Preserver of the ancient traditions.

Dindraine is an Empowerer, but she can also be an Initiator when she instructs her Grail-companions and a Measurer who sees the clear lines of destiny.

These patterns may mean nothing to you until you have read the book and done some meditation of your own. Only hard personal effort and study will enable you to animate this theory for yourself.

Let us also look at some of the patterns which arise in this study. We see that the Ladies of the Lake fall into three collective triads:

A: The Kindred of Arthur, who surround Arthur himself. There are more texts and information about these women than about the others, because they are prime movers in the king's life. Each has her otherworldly retreat as a spiritual touchstone to her earthly existence. Their normal realm is the court.

$$\left.\begin{array}{ll}\text{Igraine} & \text{Mother} \\ \text{Morgan} & \text{Sister} \\ \text{Guinevere} & \text{Wife}\end{array}\right\} \text{of Arthur}$$

B: *The Sovereign Sisters* are the otherworldly women who bring the greatest skill to bear upon Arthur's realm. Stories about them are sparse, confused and ill-reported because we only see the earthly side of their lives. Their realm is the Otherworld.

> Argante   Queen of the Lake, fosterer of Lancelot, giver of the sword
> Nimuë   Spiritual sister of Merlin
> Enid   Wife of Erec/Gereint

C: *The Grail Maidens* are the women who are closely concerned with the transformation of Arthur's realm. Each is a guardian of the Earth's wisdom and so their appearance in texts is played down or viewed as less important than the Grail-quest proper. Their realms are the Lands Adventurous.

> Kundry   Keeper of the Grail's wisdom
> Dindraine   Sister of Perceval, Grail-winner
> Ragnell   Wife of Gawain, transformer of the Grail's love

There are other ways of looking at the Ladies of the Lake. Ancient bardic tradition used to memorize corresponding traditions and stories in collective triads. Our own Ladies may be remembered as follows:

1. The three guardian matriarchs of the land of Britain who illuminate knowledge: Igraine, Argante, Kundry.
2. The three keepers of otherworldly vision who illuminate power: Morgan, Nimuë, Dindraine.
3. The three transformers of the heart who illuminate love: Guinevere, Enid, Ragnell.

We note that Igraine, Argante and Kundry act as mothers or guardians for those in their charge and that they are repositories for arcane knowledge and deep wisdom. Similarly, Morgan, Nimuë and Dindraine are each sisters or companions to prime Arthurian characters; through disciplined concentration of their skills they wield great power. Guinevere, Enid and Ragnell are each wives of important Arthurian characters; they act as transformers whose love flows from an open heart for the benefit of many.

A further means of comprehending these archetypes is their correlation to the wheel of the year. Figure 2 shows how the ninefold Ladies of the Lake may be constellated around the Celtic year.

The following titles may also be given to the Ninefold:

Queen of the Waste Land	Dindraine
Dark Woman of Knowledge	Kundry
Flower Queen	Guinevere
Lady of the Joy	Enid
Hallows Queen	Igraine
Lady of the Door	Nimuë
Queen of the Wheel	Morgan
Dame of the Riddles	Ragnell
Goddess of the Lake	Argante

The titles of their male counterparts may be given thus:

Ragnell
MIDWINTER
21 December

Morgan
SAMHAIN
31 October

Dindraine
OIMELC
31 January

Nimuë
AUTUMN EQUINOX
21 September

Argante
Lady of the Lake

Kundry
SPRING EQUINOX
21 March

Igraine
LUGHNASADH
31 July

Guinevere
BELTANE
30 April

Enid
MIDSUMMER
21 June

Figure 2: The Sisterhood of the Year

Knight of the Grail	Galahad
The Foolish Knight	Perceval
Knight of the Heart	Lancelot
Restorer of the Joy	Gereint
Dragon King	Uther
Lord of the Tower	Merlin
Knight of the Ford	Uriens
The Champion Knight	Gawain
King of the Land	Arthur

Obviously, many other male counterparts might be substituted here: Lancelot and Arthur might transpose, for example, and Owain or Mordred be substituted for Uriens.

This may lead us into a consideration of the interweaving polarities between the Ladies of the Lake and some of the men who interact with them. They are seen to support, promote or partner the following Arthurian men:

Igraine	Uther, Arthur, Gawain
Morgan	Uriens, Owain, Mordred, Arthur
Guinevere	Arthur, Lancelot
Argante	Lancelot, Arthur
Nimuë	Merlin
Enid	Gereint/Erec
Kundry	Perceval
Dindraine	Galahad
Ragnell	Gawain

There are many diverse relationships between each lady and those who come into her ambience. Sometimes it is as though each is the otherworldly analogue of an Earth-bound man, acting as a power-house for the man's quest. Without her influence, the men would not necessarily succeed. The ways of water cleanse the doors of vision, enabling the earthly actors to find the experience that they need. The women archetypically represent these qualities. They are also complemented by the reciprocal quests which the men represent. The following examples may be given:

Lady of the Lake	Her Archetypal Quality	Complimentary Partner	His Quest
Igraine	Nurture	Uther	Establishment
Morgan	Healing	Mordred	Change
Guinevere	Harmony	Arthur	Stability
Argante	Vision	Lancelot	Fame
Nimuë	Inspiration	Merlin	Transmission
Enid	Love	Erec/Gereint	Responsibility
Kundry	Knowledge	Perceval	Enlightenment
Dindraine	Guidance	Galahad	Steadfastness
Ragnell	Compassion	Gawain	Understanding

As there is no space to include a full study of these interrelations, readers might like to read and meditate upon the stories in which these characters appear, finding their own correspondences and polarities.

We leave you with three meditation images to which you may wish to return when you have read the book. Figure 3 shows the ninefold Ladies of the Lake seated about three symbols. Beneath the Round Table is a cauldron which is supported by Dindraine, Kundry and Ragnell. They are the guardians of the cauldron, the earliest analogue of the Grail. The Round Table is supported by Igraine, Guinevere and Morgan. The Round Table is an analogue of the land itself, and its institutions are upheld by the kindred of the three queens. Above the Round Table is a nine-pointed star which is supported by the Lake Lady, Nimuë and Enid. Their otherworldly movements mark out the patterns of the destined dance.

These symbols can be meditated on in combination or isolation and can lead to separate initiations. The Initiation of the Cauldron leads us to the discovery of our inner gifts and strength, to warriorhood and effective living. The Initiation of the Round Table leads to the manifestation of these gifts in our own sphere of influence, to queenship and responsible living. The Initiation of the Nine-Pointed Star leads to the rediscovery of the ancient lore of the Otherworld, to priestesshood and insightful living.

Each of these experiences is detailed with practical instructions on **The Initiations of the Lake** audio tape which is available from BCM HALLOWQUEST, London WC1N 3XX. Send SAE or 2 IRCs for details.

REFERENCES

1. L. Harf-Lancner, *Les Feés au Moyen Age*, our translation.
2. Alexander Carmichael, *Carmina Gadelica*.
3. *The Mabinogion*, ed. Lady Charlotte Guest.
4. Caitlín Matthews, *Mabon and the Mysteries of Britain: An Exploration of 'The Mabinogion'*.
5. Caitlín Matthews, *The Celtic Book of the Dead*.
6. Quoted in J.J. Tierney, *The Celtic Ethnography of Posidonius*.
7. Quoted in Max Gilbert, *The Fairies Melusine, Viviane and Aine*.
8. Geoffrey of Monmouth, *Vita Merlini*, trans. Basil Clarke.
9. Tierney, op. cit.

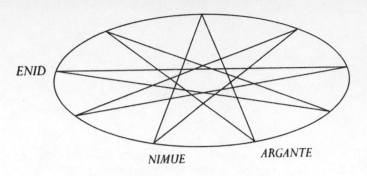

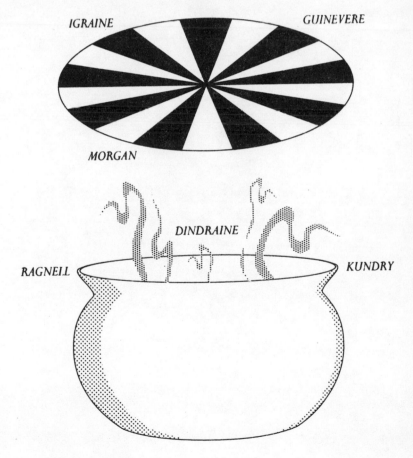

Figure 3: The Initiations of the Lake

ONE

❧

The Court

The Kindred of Arthur

We begin our journey at the court of King Arthur. The court is the meeting-place of all who inhabit the outer world. It is usually a man's world, where affairs of state take precedence. At face value, it is a place of civilization and culture, yet within its structures are subtler layers where the influences of the Lake run deep. The royal lineage is based upon the currency of blood, whereby the matrilineal line supplies a host of genetic influences which are tacitly applauded, yet subsumed and ignored. Thus the contributions of mother, sister and wife are discounted.

Many women today find themselves within such a world, especially within the family or the complex circle of relationships which are analogous to the Arthurian court. Women are not perceived to have an individual social context of their own. The laws of inheritance and heraldry demonstrate this in countless ways. Under such a regime it is imperative for women to understand and show forth their own names and deeds, and to comprehend the power that they truly wield. The search for their innate sovereignty is the quest underlying this predicament.

The kindred of Arthur each have their own destinies to fulfil: Igraine, Guinevere, Morgan.

Igraine

'Men have plucked women out of dragon's lairs,'
King Uther said, 'And I will pluck Ygraine.
O Rose in briars difficult to gain,
Lighten my mind with stratagems to use.'
John Masefield, *The Begetting of Arthur*

Variant Names:
Igerna, Ygerne, Eigr, Ingrene, Igrayne, Arnive.

THE MYTH OF IGRAINE

Igraine first appears in the mainstream Arthurian tradition as Ygerna within Geoffrey of Monmouth's chronicle *The History of the Kings of Britain* (c.1136). Here Uther, recently created King of Britain, invited his nobles to attend his coronation feast in London. Gorlois, Duke of Cornwall, brought with him his wife, the most beautiful woman in Britain - Ygerna. Uther desired her, angering Gorlois, who withdrew his household from court. Uther ordered him back and Gorlois refused, so that Uther began to ravage Cornwall. Gorlois put Ygerna in Tintagel as the safest place in his dukedom, while he took himself to his encampment at Dimilioc. Uther called on his friend Ulfin to advise him. Ulfin conceded the military impossibility of taking Tintagel by arms, as it was surrounded by the sea on a narrow isthmus. He suggested Merlin might know a way to gain possession of Ygerna. Merlin saw the strength of Uther's passion and counselled him that the only way to get Ygerna was to take a potion that would change Uther into the semblance of Gorlois, and Ulfin into the likeness of Jordan of Tintagel, the better to gain entry to the impregnable fortress. The people of Tintagel and Ygerna herself were deceived by this trick, and Uther thus slept with Ygerna and begot Arthur upon her.

Meanwhile at the siege of Dimilioc, Gorlois was overcome and killed. Messengers rode to Tintagel to tell Ygerna the news and were astonished to see someone they took to be Gorlois seated beside her. Uther pretended grief at the sack of his camp and then rode out in order to meet the king in battle. He resumed his own appearance, rode back to Tintagel and claimed Ygerna as his wife.

> From that day on they lived together as equals, united by their great love for each other; and they had a son and a daughter: the boy was called Arthur and the girl Anna.[1]

The daughter, Anna (who gets renamed Morgause in subsequent texts), marries Loth of Lothian, but we hear no more about Ygerna in Geoffrey. Layamon's Ygerne, while imprisoned in Tintagel is 'sorry and sorrowful in heart, that so many men for her should there have destruction'.[2] Layamon's Merlin is full of precognitive knowledge of the result of Uther and Ygerne's union: 'For yet he is unbegot, that shall govern all the people.'[3] It is also in Layamon that we first hear the story of Arthur's upbringing by Argante in Faery.

Chrétien de Troyes' *Perceval* or *Le Conte del Graal* tells of Gawain's adventures and meeting with Igraine. He is led to the Castle of Maidens by a scornful damsel called Orguelleuse or 'the Proud One.' Gawain's adventures parallel those of Perceval, who goes to seek the Grail. Instead, Gawain finds the earthly paradise of Celtic tradition, inhabited by women. This is an important distinction in the story of the quest: Perceval seeks for a transcendent object – the Grail – while Gawain finds his way into the Land of Women.

The Castle of Maidens is inhabited by a queen who had brought much gold and silver with her, as well as her daughter and her daughter's daughter. The place is protected by strong magic created by a magician who accompanied the queen: only knights without a stainless character may remain in its precincts. The rest of the castle's inhabitants are squires awaiting knighthood and widows and orphaned damsels whose inheritance has been taken from them and who await a vindicator. They all await a true knight who will restore them to their rights.

Gawain enters the castle and attempts the dangers of the Perilous Bed. This is a bed so armed and guarded as to keep him well occupied defending himself, but he overcomes its perils, slays a lion and is acclaimed by the one-legged host of the castle. He then learns that being the victorious champion of this place is no sinecure - he is expected to remain therein for the rest of his days. He is understandably annoyed, but the queen comes to speak to him, gently asking about the sons of King Lot (who are, of course, Gawain himself, Agravain, Gareth and Gaheris). She also asks about King Arthur and Guinevere. Gawain is permitted to leave on condition that he will return.

On leaving the castle, Gawain enquires of a knight, Guiromelant, who the ladies he encountered were. The white-haired queen adorned in white with golden flowers proves to be none other than Igraine. Gawain professes astonishment at this, not knowing Arthur's mother was still alive. Guiromelant says, 'When his father, Utherpendragon was laid to rest, it happened that Queen Igerne came into this land, bringing all her wealth, and upon this rock she had the castle built . . .'[4] He then says that the other queen whom Gawain saw was none other than his own mother, the wife of King Lot. And that the maiden was Clarrisant, his own sister.

In the parallel episode to Gawain's visit to the Castle of Maidens in Wolfram von Eschenbach's *Parzival*, which follows Chrétien's *Conte del Graal* closely enough, Gawain finds himself in the Terre Merveile, or Land of Wonders. The Castle of Maidens is called Schastel Merveile, and the lady who rules this place is Arnive - a German variant of Igraine. The castle has a wondrous pillar within it that, like a video camera, records and presents everything that happens within a six-mile radius of the castle. Arnive tells Gawain, who is her grandson, about the enchantments upon the land which have been caused by the evil enchanter, Klingsor. She laments her loss of happiness and looks to Gawain for its restoration.

When Arthur and his mother are reunited later in the text, Kei tartly remarks, seeing Gawain surrounded by Arnive, Sangive, his mother, Itonje, his sister, and Orgeluse, the Duchess of Logroys, Gawain's mistress, 'Who gave Gawain this gaggle of ladies?'

Mother of her People

Igraine is a mysterious matriarch whose nature has been much obscured and overshadowed by her famous son, Arthur. We need to look at her ancient role as the mother of the king, and as royal woman in her own right, for the woman who had the royal blood was she whose children could be rulers, according to the ancient understanding. Maternity, not paternity, was the important thing, as it still is within Judaism which, despite its patriarchal structures, insists that Jewish identity is determined by birth from a Jewish *mother*. The child of a Jewish father and a non-Jewish mother is not and can never be a Jew.

Matrilineal succession was an ancient feature of all native European peoples of pre-Celtic times.

> In the elder days, when the succession passed through the female line, the Sovereignty resided in the person of the queen, who, as high priestess, was also the reincarnation of the Great Earth mother, and chose, from among her warriors, a man to mate with, lead her war-band, and after the cycle of seven years, become the king-sacrifice and die to ensure fertility for the soil and prosperity for the tribe.[5]

Later Celtic tradition generally gives us the patronymics of children, e.g. Branwen ferch Llyr (Branwen, daughter of Llyr), Madawg ap Meredith (Madoc son of Meredith) or Art mac Conn

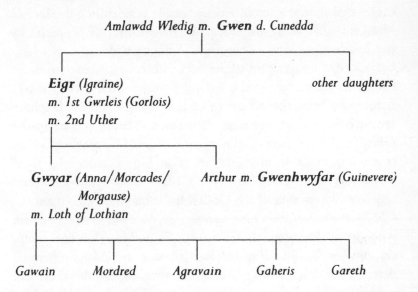

Amlawdd Wledig m. **Gwen** d. *Cunedda*

Eigr *(Igraine)*
m. *1st Gwrleis (Gorlois)*
m. *2nd Uther*

other daughters

Gwyar *(Anna/Morcades/*
Morgause)
m. *Loth of Lothian*

Arthur m. **Gwenhwyfar** *(Guinevere)*

Gawain   *Mordred*   *Agravain*   *Gaheris*   *Gareth*

Figure 4

(Art son of Conn). This is a tradition which we still uphold in Britain. Once a woman has been married and taken her husband's name, her own lineage is automatically forgotten. However, earlier Celtic and pre-Celtic traditions give us a few characters who are remembered by their *mother's* name, e.g. Mabon ap Modron and Conchobar mac Nessa. It is perhaps significant that Mabon's mother, Modron, is a goddess whose name means 'mother', just as his means 'son'. King Conchobar of Ulster is also named after his mother, Nessa, a fierce, combative woman who lived the life of an outlaw before she encountered the druid Cathbad, Conchobar's father.

What line does Igraine spring from? Her antecedents are obscured by the ancient genealogies, but we can reconstruct her lineage as in Figure 4.

The names in brackets are the alternative, later textual names for the characters we know so well. The earliest texts give Igraine two children, Arthur and a daughter who is variously called Gwyar, Anna, Morcades or Morgause. This daughter is, in all cases, married to Lot or Loth of Lothian, to become the mother of Arthur's famous nephews. It is not until the late *Le Mort Artu* that Morgause becomes the mother of Mordred by her half-brother, Arthur, through a chance encounter in which both parties are ignorant of the other's identity. Throughout the earlier tradition, Mordred is Arthur's nephew, the perfect kingly heir, since he is the offspring of the royal woman's daughter. Igraine's father, the legendary Amlawdd Wledig, is said, in the *Life of St Illtud*, to have been King of Brittany. Her mother, Gwen, is an important woman of the royal blood, since she is of Cunedda's line. Cunedda was a fifth-century chieftain and military commander of the Gododdin tribe who came from the Old North to what we now identify as Wales to expel the Irish, who were harrying the Britons. Cunedda's kindred were responsible for founding many dynasties in Wales, indicating that the northern British blood was revered. Igraine therefore comes from an all-round well-connected kindred which is totally British. Her father's people, the Bretons, derive from British colonists who left during the fourth and fifth centuries, while her mother's people derived from the Old North. Gododdin was one of the old British kingdoms, along with Strathclyde and Rheged, which retained its identity quite late into the Saxon period. This region, known as 'the Old North' remained the focus of much medieval Welsh interest, since the ancestors of the Welsh people were believed to have derived from this region. Strong links were retained with both locations.[6]

Igraine is thus associated with two regions of Britain – Cornwall, by virtue of her first husband, Gorlois, and possibly her father, Amlawdd Wledig – and Edinburgh, by virtue of her mother's people and by association with the Castle of Maidens in many texts.

The old name for Edinburgh, or Dunedin, was Castellum Puellarum. It is called so both by Adamnan's *Life of St Columba* and by the chronicler Bede; both write of it as the dwelling-place of nuns. Scholars have taken this to refer to the missionary work of the female St Moninne or Darerca (d.517 AD), but the association of Edinburgh with maidens may well have been due to a more ancient foundation of the ninefold sisterhood. This city on the Firth of Forth was in the Kingdom of Manau of Gododdin, or Lothian. It is significant that Igraine should give her daughter, Morgause, in marriage to the King of Lothian, thus sending her royal-blooded daughter back to her own people. Igraine's mother, Gwen, was of the Old North, after all. So Morgause is a grand-daughter of the Gododdin, and returns thither to continue her family dynasty and raise a family of warriors.

Loth of Lothian obviously held the North for Uther Pendragon, and was honoured by the gift of Uther's own daughter as wife. To the north of Lot's Manau Gododdin was the kingdom of the Picts. Pictish tribal custom was conservative and long-enduring, remaining Pagan long after the rest of Dalriadic and Gaelic Scotland had been Christianized. The juxtaposition of the two peoples leads to an interesting question: why did Igraine call her son Arthur? Was it in conscious remembrance of her own people? There are many Pictish names beginning with the prefix 'Art' or bear, e.g. Artcois (Bear's Leg), Artbranan (Bear King), and Artgan (Little Bear). Scotland retains many traces of Arthur, both of his battles and residential sites associated with him. If Igraine's family were of Lothian, would this not make the idea of Edinburgh as Arthur's Seat more than a topographical fantasy? As son of the royal woman, Arthur would have better claim to Lothian than most, except, of course, his nephews - his sister's sons - with whom he does indeed come into conflict.

Igraine's only son by Uther is roughly taken from her and fostered by Merlin. She is the object of a substitute mating - one of three such which take place in Arthurian legend, for there is also the substitution of Elaine for Guinevere, not to mention the union of Merlin's mother with an otherworldly man. The substitution is probably a remnant of a ritual mating whereby the two kindreds of the royal blood were brought together. Selective mating has ever typified the marriage customs of royal houses. It is only in our own day that princes and princesses are permitted to marry commoners if they chose.

The customs preserved in this manner speak to us of an earlier time. Many commentators have attempted to interpret the marriage customs of the British. Julius Caesar, noted for his sweepingly categorical statements, says: '[British] wives are shared between groups of ten or twelve men, especially between brothers and between fathers and sons; but the offspring of these unions are counted as the children of the man with whom a particular woman cohabited first.'[7] Whatever the reality of this statement – and Caesar was clearly interested in making the British sound as barbarous as possible – there is a germ of truth hidden behind it. Mating took place between certain kindred groups, but the children were those of the woman's body. Caesar is here describing polyandry – still practised in remote regions of our planet, notably in Tibet and Nepal.

If we set this side by side with Pictish customs relating to matrilineal succession, we may find useful ways of approaching Igraine's lineage. The matrilineal succession of the Picts has been a much disputed point. The Picts (who called themselves the Cruithean, Pict being a name given to them by the Romans) left no texts, chronicles or stories, only a few stones inscribed with mysterious tribal and totemic symbols and a form of oghamic inscription which has baffled translators. The history of Scotland is further confused by the incursion of the Gaels into the Pictish homeland. The Gaels told their own stories about the Picts, including a series of legal fictions which enabled the Gaels to assume a stake in Scottish lands and the Pictish succession.

One story tells how Cruitnigh, an eponymous ancestor of the Picts, asked Eremon, one of Ireland's invaders, for suitable mates. The Picts then swore an oath to Eremon: 'By sun and moon that the possession of the kingdom of Cruiteantuath [Picts], which is now called Alba, should be held by right of the female than by that of the male progeny to the end of the world.'[8] This story purports to explain why the Picts only accepted the sons of their queens as rulers.

Matrilineal succession does not entail the rule of a woman in her own right: only her male children are legally entitled to reign. Nevertheless, the evidence for Igraine as a royal matriarch appears strong. Let us consider whether there are any further clues in Igraine's name.

Igraine's Celtic name is Igerna or, in British, Eigr. We believe that both variants are derived from the Celtic title *Tigerna* or Lady. The word *tigern* appears in various Celtic names, such as St Kentigern (Lordly Hound); more particularly, it is the pivotal epithet of the name Vortigern (Strong Lord). Vortigern appears as the predecessor of the Pendragon clan and the story of his downfall is the *enfance* story of Merddyn Emrys or Merlin.

If Igraine's Celtic name, Igerna, really derives from Tigerna, we possibly have a royal title, for, by this reckoning, Igraine would have been *the* Tigerna or Lady. Subsequent evidence discloses that Igraine's role continued to revolve around matters of sacred queenship, even after her own part in Arthur's story was over. In the best tradition of the Celts, she faded from the real world, to become queen in the Otherworld.

QUEEN OF THE LAND OF WOMEN

Throughout Celtic tradition runs the theme of the lost child. This is established in the archetypal legend of Mabon who was taken 'from between his mother and wall' when he was but three nights old. It is the task of the Celtic hero Culhwch to discover him, which he does with the help of Arthur's host in the magnificent sprawling narrative, *Culhwch and Olwen*. We are never told why Mabon was stolen, nor who stole him, though the legend informs us that he was found imprisoned in the wall of Caer Loyw or Gloucester. This is itself interesting, since there is a strong tradition concerning the Nine Witches of Gloucester. This ninefold sisterhood is responsible for training and raising heroes in the venerable manner of Celtic warrior women. They train Peredur, the Celtic Perceval. Significantly, when Mabon is rediscovered and liberated, it is not as a baby but as a strong young hunter. We learn nothing of Modron's feelings or motivations in this myth.

The goddess Rhiannon similarly loses her son by mysterious means – he is snatched by a monstrous hand which comes down the chimney on the night of his birth. In order to indemnify themselves and to account for the lost child, the midwives swear that Rhiannon ate her own child, and scatter the bones of a puppy about the bed to lend verisimilitude to their tale. They are believed and Rhiannon is sentenced to stand at the mounting block for seven years, to offer to bear all comers on her back into the hall and to tell her terrible story to all who will listen. Her son is eventually returned unharmed and is named Pryderi.

The role of Modron's loss returns to many women in Arthurian legend. Igraine loses the childhood of Arthur, Herzeloyde loses Parzival, Elaine loses Galahad. This venerable tradition is a feature of most myths and revolves around the necessity of the mother to relinquish her child for a better or higher destiny. We even see this in operation within the story of Mary and Jesus when he is lost in the temple. This episode played a central part in the myth of St Brighid who, in Celtic tradition, is understood to be the foster-mother of Christ, as well as Mary's greatest friend and companion. Brighid makes an augury to discover where Jesus is and finds him in her vision at the well-side teaching the people.[9]

This augury of motherhood is akin to the destiny which a mother (or her substitute, the foster-mother, nurse or faery godmother) must give her child. To take a child from its mother, as Arthur is taken from Igraine, seems cruel and heartless to us today, yet the custom of fosterage was widespread in the ancient world, especially in tribal societies. It was a means of bonding together groups and factions who might otherwise come to blows. To give fosterage to a child was to take on both responsibility and honour: conversely to give one's child into fosterage was both an act of trust and of honour. In the unsettled reign of Uther Pendragon, the hiding of Arthur in a place of safe fosterage was the best insurance of the child's safety. So Arthur's education, like Lancelot's, was in the realms of the Lake, the magical motherland (see Chapter 4).

Sacred motherhood is not a cosy option. The sorrows of the

mothers of heroes are terrible and bitter, and often the subject dies of sorrow like Herzeloyde, Parzival's mother, who breaks her heart waiting to hear from her son.

Arnive, in *Parzival*, also laments the loss of her child and the happy condition of motherhood: 'Exile chills my heart,' she says to her grandson, Gawain. 'May He who numbered the stars guide you in leading us back to happiness.'[10] It is almost as though she greeted her own son, Arthur, in the person of Gawain, his nephew. In Chrétien, Igraine asks wistfully after her son: 'How goes it with King Arthur now?' On hearing of his good health, she says, 'That's not surprising, for he's still a child, King Arthur. If he's a hundred, he's no more; he couldn't be a day over that!'[11]

Arnive asks Gawain a riddle: ' "Which mother bears progeny that becomes its mother's mother?" From water there comes ice, and from this, without fail there comes water again! When I reflect that I was borne of happiness, if happiness is ever seen in me again, one progeny will have borne another!'[12]

Both Chrétien and Wolfram follow a similar course in their characterization of Arnive/Igraine: she is given to mantic utterances that make her sound fond, senile or quietly mad. The obsessions of a mother who has lost her child are not those of Igraine, however. She is shown as fully in charge of herself and her faculties, a remote matriarch still fulfilling her destiny, however humanly hard.

The Celtic tradition of a woman who holds the destiny of a man in her hands is a strong one, producing some powerful figures. Initiation within the confines of the Goddess's temple is alluded to frequently. Taliesin and many others speak of being 'three periods in the Castle of Arianrhod'. To enter the circle of the Goddess is to undergo three initiations. A man encounters the first enclosure when he is conceived of the mother's womb and nourished there, as young Gwion is conceived of Ceridwen's womb. The second enclosure is when a man penetrates a representative of the Goddess and enters into sexual union with her, as when Urien ap Rheged lies with Modron at the Ford of

Barking (see Chapter 3). The third enclosure is when a man enters the sanctuary of the Goddess's temple at death or initiation, as when Taliesin enters the mysteries of Caer Sidi and is possessed of the secrets of the goddess Arianrhod.

Arianrhod is an interesting figure, because she manifests many aspects of the Goddess of Initiation. When the virgin foot-holder of King Math is raped, Math's nephew, Gwydion, suggests Arianrhod as her substitute. The role of virgin foot-holder is the proper task for a maiden who can represent the peaceful nature of the land and Arianrhod seems the right candidate. Math tests all claimants for the title by making them step over his druidic wand. Arianrhod steps over it and immediately upon the floor appear two things which cause her disgrace: one is a fully-formed baby, and the other is an incompletely-gestated baby. The myth gives us no background or clue as to the appearance of these children. Arianrhod's prior sexual activity is not indicated, and we are left wondering whether or not she has been impregnated by the desires of man or men unknown, or whether her own desires have caused the children to be suddenly manifest in this manner.

Math takes the fully-formed baby and calls him Dylan, whereupon he takes to the waters of the sea, like one borne to its inner nature. He is subsequently killed accidentally by his uncle Gofannon. The incomplete child is magically incubated by his uncle Gwydion and brought up. Great obstacles however lie in the way of the child's upbringing. According to law, the mother should be the one to name, arm and give a destiny to her child, and Arianrhod refuses to perform any of these traditional tasks, because of the disgrace which these twin children have caused her. Without these three gifts, the child can have no name, no deeds and no lineage. So Gwydion tricks Arianrhod into naming her child Llew Llaw Gyffes, and further tricks her into giving him weapons. But she draws the line at the last, and swears a terrible destiny upon him: that he shall only marry a woman who is not of human stock. To obviate this last obstacle, Gwydion and Math conjure a woman out of nine kinds of flowers, whom they call Blodeuwedd. She marries Llew

Llaw Gyffes, but subsequently disdains her husband in favour of Gronw, her lover.[13]

This story parallels Arthur's own in many ways. He is initially denied a name, since he is raised apart from his parents and not identified as the child of Uther and Igraine until he draws the sword from the stone. This sword, however, does not serve as his own weapon, for Excalibur is given him by the Lady of the Lake. Lastly, he acquires a wife who is the epitome of an otherworldly flower maiden, Gwenhwyfar or Guinevere, who spurns his love in favour of another.

The loss of the child, his initiation into manhood and responsibility and his subsequent departure into the realms of the Goddess are also all features of Arthur's own story. He is taken from Igraine and given in fosterage, usually to an otherworldly or faery woman. He is initiated into sexual activity by his own half-sister, Morgause, according to some traditions. He is wounded at the Battle of Camlan and translated to the otherworldly sanctuary of Avalon by Morgan, there to be healed. Beneath this complex story lurks a pattern of initiation into the Goddess.

There is a mysterious triad concerning Arthur which has long exercised the imaginations of scholars. These terse triple mnemomics were short compendiums of stories and traditions, memorized by bards; they garner together the earliest information we have on some Arthurian characters. Triad 52 is entitled 'Three Exalted Prisoners of Britain'; it speaks of Llyr Half-Speech who was imprisoned by Euroswydd, Mabon, son of Modron, and Gwair, son of Geirioedd. But there is, says the triad, 'one Prisoner who was more exalted than the three of them [who] was three nights in prison in Caer Oeth and Anoeth, and three nights imprisoned by Gwen Pendragon, and three nights in an enchanted prison under the Stone of Echymeint. This Exalted Prisoner was Arthur. And it was the same lad who released him from each of these three prisons - Goreu, son of Custennin, his cousin.'[14]

The three prisoners instanced in this triad are all men of the royal clan who undergo astounding difficulties in establishing themselves: they are each imprisoned in the Otherworld until released. Arthur is therefore established as one undergoing a similar initiation.

This mysterious triad may perhaps be attempted in the light of the evidence which we have garnered here. Caer Oeth and Anoeth (Fortress of Wonders) might well be the Castle of Maidens, or Castle of Wonders, as it also called. The only Gwen in Arthur's pedigree is his maternal grandmother, Gwen, daughter of Cunedda. The same Castle of Maidens has within it a perilous bed (Chrétien) and a mysterious seeing-stone (Wolfram) – is this the Stone of Echymeint? This tantalizing tradition cannot be proven and must remain speculative, but what if this triad really referred to the matrilineal mysteries of Arthur's mother? Do we have evidence of a triple initiation which Arthur undergoes at the hands of the Ninefold? Three nights in the Castle of Maidens or Land of Women; three nights learning the lore of his grandmother, Gwen ferch Cunedda; three nights upon the Perilous Bed or perhaps looking, like Macbeth, into the mirror of the Three Witches at the line of Banquo's dynasty, into the seeing-stone of the future. Certainly, later tradition has Arthur and his (half-)sister Morgause lying together to produce the ultimate royal heir of the blood-clan, Mordred – an event which takes place outside of time and custom.

Each of the triad's three famous prisoners is released by the same person – Goreu, son of Custennin. Goreu means 'the best'; Custennin is Welsh for Constantine. The name belongs to a character within *Culhwch and Olwen* who does indeed help liberate Mabon in the story, but it is also a bardic kenning for 'the best son of Constantine', perhaps indicating the most worthy descendant of the royal line, since Constantine is the progenitor of the Pendragon line. In the liberation of Arthur from imprisonment, the 'best son of Constantine' is Gawain, Arthur's own nephew. It is Gawain's quest to enter the Castle of Maidens and to liberate all that he finds there, so that the maidens may receive husbands, the squires their knighthoods and the widows their inheritance. It is Gawain who overcomes the test of the

Perilous Bed, and who encounters, without knowing it, all his female relatives and ancestors, including his own grandmother, sister and mother. In *Diu Cröne*, he encounters the figure of Fortuna and transforms her from hideousness to beauty, while in the subsequent debacle of the Round Table, it is Gawain, the good nephew, who supports his uncle against Mordred, the bad nephew. It is Gawain who upholds the lineage of the mother and the status of women throughout Arthurian legend, and who acts as champion of the Goddess of the Land.[15]

As we have seen, the Celtic tradition of the Land of Women remains a strong theme. It could be argued that such a concept was a wish-fulfilling male fantasy, but it appears too often in sacred tradition for this. Real power is invested in the Celtic Otherworld. It is the sacred place to which mortal men are drawn in spirit, to interact with its mysterious ever-living delights.

The return of Igraine to the Otherworld, to the Castle of Maidens where she becomes a Queen Mother, is a very important feature of the Arthurian tradition. The castle's otherworldly nature is clear from the fact that Igraine inhabits it as Queen Dowager: it is a place of the ancestors and matriarchs. Igraine remains in touch with court life while exercising an otherworldly role. Like Arianrhod, she achieves a solitary and powerful seclusion within her own fortress.

It is also significant that the role of the Queen Mother plays so large a part in tradition. There is no parallel tradition of a 'King Father'. 'The king is dead, long live the king!' goes the cry. Kings come and go, but queens stay to set the stage.

The Castle of Maidens occurs many times in Arthurian tradition: in Chrétien, we hear how Gawain proves to be a worthy knight who comes to answer the needs of all women within the Castle of Maidens, since the prophecy goes that 'If such a knight were to come there, he could rule in the hall and return their lands to the ladies and bring many wars to their ends. He could marry off the maidens, confer knighthoods on the squires and in quick succession rid the hall of its magic spells.'[16] This is a task of heroic virtue which Gawain actually accomplishes while Perceval is seeking the Grail. It is easily seen that the two quests are interrelated and that the transcendent vessel is an analogue for the vessel of feminine kind. Gawain, in entering the Castle of Maidens, returns to his own matrilineal kindred which, like a return to the womb, enables and empowers him to realize his high destiny, which is to free women. As we shall see when we consider Ragnell, this is a quest which he pursues to its very end.

Like the Celtic hero Maelduin, Gawain enters the Castle of Maidens and is told he may never leave it. The Queen of the Island of Women, where Maelduin finds himself, tries every ruse to restrain him, but Maelduin, like Gawain, breaks free of the primal enchantment of the woman's realm. We see the lands of the Lake exercising their power here, just as the Lady of the Lake restrains Lancelot from developing too hastily. The dream-like state of womb-life is heightened.

Like the Celtic Land of Women, so too the Castle of Maidens exercises a fascination within the Arthurian stories. In *Ywein* it appears as the place where a kind of medieval sweat-shop operates – the maidens are kept spinning by an ogre or tyrannical knight. This task of spinning is significant, for the spinning goddess is an originating one: the tapestry of life is the handiwork of the ninefold maidens who underlie Arthurian tradition. Like Arianrhod, they give destiny to all who enter their castle. Arthur must enter the confines of the Underworld to steal the cauldron of Annwn, which is 'warmed by the breath of nine muses'.[17] In later Arthurian tradition, the Castle of Maidens becomes a place of testing for the knights on quest. The true Celtic nature of the Land of Women is forgotten and it becomes instead a place of female demons who demand sexual gratification or else threaten to destroy themselves. Both Bors and Galahad have their chastity tested in this way. But the test of the Perilous Bed which shoots missiles at its occupant may indeed have originated in another way. Could the perils of that bed might have been of a more sexual nature in ancient tradition?

MISTRESS OF ENDLESS LINEAGE

The role of engendering the king was a task of great preparation. The old system of arranged and dynastic marriages seems to us heartless, but it has tribal custom behind it and we should consider it in its historical context. The choosing of the correct woman and man in partnership to produce children for the tribe was immensely important. Seers would have been employed in the matter and ancient men and women of the tribe whose one purpose was to guard the lineage would have trained the young people in the usages of engendering.

So Merlin tells Uther: 'If you are to have your wish . . .you must make use of methods which are quite new and until now unheard of in your day. By my drugs I know how to give you the precise appearance of Gorlois, so that you will resemble him in every respect.'[18]

This ruse, so transparent in the medieval chronicle as a memory of older practices, may be read as analogous of the daemonic mating of woman with god, as happens in the myth of Psyche and Eros, and in that of Merlin's own mother. By medieval standards, Igraine was blameless of adultery because of the substitution. But the dubious paternity of a child of a recent widow falls upon Arthur, which is sometimes given as a reason for his fosterage elsewhere.

Igraine has many correlatives with other Arthurian women, notably Elaine of Corbin, mother of Galahad. Galahad is conceived by a ruse which is already familiar to us from Arthur's conception. Lancelot comes to stay with King Pelles, a man of ancient lineage and antique lore, in whose family is a prophecy that their bloodline will engender the Grail-winner. In order to bring about this prophecy, Pelles and Brisen, Elaine's nurse, cold-bloodedly prepare a trap for Lancelot. Knowing that his desire is fixated solely upon Guinevere, they send Lancelot a ring and message saying that Guinevere is in a pavilion nearby. Lancelot falls for the trap and visits the place where Elaine lies in darkness. Befuddled by a potion and the darkness, he believes himself to be lying with the queen; he is potent and begets

Galahad upon Elaine. On waking, he realizes the deception and runs mad in the forest.[19]

Elaine, like Igraine, is not consulted about her own wishes: she is an instrument of her family's prophetic urge. The conception of Galahad then, like that of Arthur upon Igraine, focuses around the fact that one partner is in ignorance of the other's true identity: but that very identity is the key factor in the imprinting of one life upon another.

We are dealing here with sacred or destined conception and with the desires of the heart which, like the wind, cannot be pinioned. Elaine's sole function is to bear a child who will be better than all other knights, just as Igraine's is to bear the king who will be sovereign of all kings. There is a distinct element here of dreaming the desires of the heart – a function which is borne by the archetype of Igraine. Its earliest correlative in Celtic tradition is that of the goddess Elen, Elen Lluddog, Elen of the Ways. She appears in *The Dream of Macsen Wledig* in the *The Mabinogion*. The Emperor Magnus Maximus dreams of her and desires her love, sending messengers far and wide to discover her. She is eventually discovered in Caer Seint, (Roman Segontium or modern Caernarvon) by his messengers, but refuses to come to Rome. Magnus must come to see her. He comes, marries her and espouses the land of Britain. Elen is remembered for the roads – the *sarnau Elen* which still track parts of Wales.[20] But the roads which desires walk are those of the dream-ways.

It is not for nothing that Igerne rules over the Castle of Maidens which has within it a perilous bed, for only one who is valiant and determined can undergo its testing, only the dream-lover truly appointed by deeds of arms and a virtuous heart may sleep with the mother of heroes. Chrétien does not understand the imagery which underlies the Celtic tale which he embroidered, yet he incorporates its elements. Gawain meets the host of the Castle of Maidens – a man with an artificial silver leg who is whittling an ash stick. This character is taken from Eudaf, father of Elen, in *Dream of Macsen Wledig*, who whittles chess-pieces. This character is the prime mover of the mother of heroes' destiny – he is Merlin arranging the union of Uther and Igraine, he is Pelles arranging the union of Lancelot and Elaine, he is the father of the Celtic Igraine, the Tigerna herself, perhaps, Amlawdd Wledig. He is the arranger of destinies, an otherworldly man.

Amlawdd is the Welsh equivalent of the Norse Amlothe (from which Hamlet derives) and of the Irish Amlaide. The medieval *Hanes Gruffydd ap Cynan* also gives an alternative: Avloed. Is Igraine thus a daughter of Afallach, the mysterious King of Avalon? The role of the otherworldly man or stranger-father is well established in folk tradition. It was also once part of ancient mystery cults, where maidens would sleep out of doors and offer their virginity to the first stranger they encountered as a sacred duty to their ancestors.

The story of Arthur's conception may be paralleled by that of the Celtic hero Mongan. In this, Fiachna leaves his wife, Kentigerna, to go into Alba to fight in a battle. In his absence, Kentigerna is visited by an unknown stranger who tells her that Fiachna's life is endangered and that if she would save him, she must sleep with her mysterious visitor. He then promises to go *in the shape of Fiachna* and perform in the life-endangering combat. She complies and Mongan is conceived. The next morning, the stranger announces his identity as none other than Manannan mac Lir, the Irish God of the Otherworld. The subsequent history of Mongan is interesting: he is taken, after weaning, into his father's otherworldly kingdom until he is 12, there to be raised in the magical lore of that wondrous land. The Irish *immram* story, *The Voyage of Bran mac Febal*, buttresses the tradition of Mongan's wondrous semi-mortal condition in a poem which states that Mongan will die young and be taken back to Manannan's realm.[21] This gives us parallels between Mongan's mother and Arthur's which are very significant: both women are visited by an unknown man; both visitors assume (or are capable of assuming) the shape of the woman's husband; both the children of this one night of love are destined to have heroic careers of a fixed or fated duration; both are raised in otherworldly confinement. Both women share a common source for their name – Kent*igerna*, Ygerna.

Manannan and Merlin share similar roles, although Merlin himself does appear to have shared the Irish god's reputation as a night-visitor of women (that tradition is, however, present within Merlin's own conception, whereby his mother lay with a daemon). Merlin acts as a prime mover in the conception of Arthur. Looked at in medieval terms, Merlin is a dubious individual: the illegitimate product of a daemonic father and a cloistered mother. He is reduced to the stature of Uther's pander. If we uncover the Celtic roots of the story, however, another pattern emerges – one not based on Christian morality. Merlin then becomes the priest of a sacred rite of engendering, bringing together the royal sovereignty-bearing woman, the Tigerna, and the land's defender, the Pendragon.

So the experience of Igraine, although described in medieval terminology, is that of the ancient priestesses of this land who opened a pathway in their bodies to the ingress of the child's spirit. This ancient practice, part of Europe's native tantra, saw the priestess lie with a man anonymously in order to receive the man like a god; she herself enacting the part of the Goddess.

Igraine's encounter with Uther takes place mysteriously. He shapeshifts to the appearance of her husband, for a woman should be chaste in her heart and Igraine is here medievally absolved of any guilt. However, the ancient encounter is still there. Uther comes to her unknown and begets Arthur. This is a wonderful and terrifying moment for any woman – that of conception.

The role of Igraine is that of Measurer and Preserver, one who is concerned with the weaving of destiny, with the provision of the right lines and patterns for the unfolding soul. Her power can be invoked to co-ordinate one's energies to plot a project – whether it be the conception of a child, or a creative idea which you wish to bring to birth. Like faery-godmothers, she can help divine its shape and destiny. As mother of the endless line, she keeps the tradition and is the lineage-holder for the Ninefold.

In the Castle of Maidens

Leaving the places that you know, visualize a lake within which is an island. It is shrouded in mist. A slender, glassy tower rears up from it. You wish to cross the lake and come to its secret places. As you make this wish, a one-legged ferryman approaches you poling a small barge. He bids you step within the boat and promises to take you to the other side if you will grant him one wish in return. He asks that you offer one night's sleeping and dreaming to the Lady of the Castle of Maidens. This seems a strange request, but he assures that it is made with no evil intent. You must decide whether you accept this or not . . .

He ferries you across the lake and you are able to disembark upon the island. Here the mist is less dense and you follow the pathway to the door of the castle. A maiden greets you as you approach the gate and gives you welcome in the name of the royal lady. Who is this person, you enquire? The maiden tells you that the royal lady of the Castle of Maidens is the Tigerna, none other than the one whom we know as Igraine. The maiden tells you to be respectful to the Tigerna, and to address her as you would a revered grandmother, full of tradition.

As you enter the hall you find a place of beauty and refreshment of spirit. Here sits Igraine as a great queen with her court about her. There are no men here, only women and boys. She is a matriarch of great power and you make a respectful courtesy before her.

She raises her hand and the musicians cease their playing. Until that time you were unaware of the ongoing beauty of the sound which winds its way into the soul of all who come here. Igraine speaks.

'Welcome, traveller from the courts of men. I see that you are wondering why my ferryman asked you to offer me one night's worth of your sleeping and dreaming. The Castle of Maidens is a place of guardianship and power to which few journey. All who come here are asked to offer me the hospitality of one night's dreaming - only so may the ancient otherworldly traditions be transmitted to your world. You think of this place as a Tower of Glass, as a realm of illusion, yet your own world lives without the deep perceptions and ignores the beauty of the Otherworld. Within the sleep of one night, you will gain communion with the Castle of Maidens and be enabled to understand many things which lie yet unknown within you. To men, I send my maidens; to women, I send my champion. To those in whom the two sexes are mixed, I send my messenger, who can take whatever form I chose. Thus all may know the way of the Otherworld from a soul-friend.'

She indicates that you may sit and refresh yourself at the table which stands forever ready for visitors. Here is the food you like best, the most refreshing of drinks and a bounty which is never found in your world . . . When you are refreshed, maidens bring you fresh clothes to wear. You are being prepared. When Igraine rises, all her retinue rise also. Two maidens accompany you and together you follow the Tigerna.

The royal lady, Igraine, takes you to her to her secret tower up a winding stair. Here is a small room in which there is a shrine with a single flame burning before it. She carefully folds back the doors of the shrine-cupboard and there you look upon an ancient statue of the Mother of the Earth. Before it is a small jar which Igraine handles with reverence. She speaks to you.

'Daughters and Sons of the holy earth, I hold the seed-jar of the most precious grain. The grain of life's seeding is more precious than gold and cannot be made by woman or man's devising. You are also granaries of the sacred seed. You each hold within you the future seeding of the earth.

'Guard the seed-grain well and sow it with intention. Children are a wealth that cannot be estimated. To call into this world the souls of children, let your bodies be ready, bring your minds to the star-source of the seeding. Men of the sacred seed, your duty is to keep your seed well guarded, yet to be generous for the sake of the children yet unborn. Make provision and take responsibility for the fields you have sown. Give shelter to your harvest and give it proper training. Women of the sacred grain, your duty is to kindle the flame of the oven that the seed may be properly parched and take root and grow. In your bringing forth, call upon the deep places of the dark stars, that the grain may be gifted with great soul. Guard the seasons of growing with nurture, feed with loving care and with the water of play.

'Daughters and Sons of the sacred clan, teach these ways to your children and the granary of the stars will be replenished.'

She places the seed-jar before the Mother upon the shrine with an inclination of her head. Then she takes up the flame. It burns with scintillating brilliance, piercing the crystalline lamp with a myriad refracting sparks. She speaks again.

'I speak also to those who have no children, but whose offspring is of the spirit. I am the kindling of the ancient fires and preserve the star-seeds beyond the generations. You who do not pass the blood-seed from age to age are yet tradition-holders, for in you runs the single passion for the stars themselves. Like the unicorn, the pure one apart, your task is of this Otherworld. Welcome indeed are you within this house of soul's keeping! Seek the blessing of the flame which I hold, and know its warmth of inspiration within you.'

Igraine sits in a throne beside the shrine and veils herself. The maidens indicate that you may approach the shrine and ask what blessing you will upon your life. If you wish to have a child, ask for the blessing of conception and lay your hand upon the seed-jar. If you have a family, ask the Mother's protection upon it. If you have a project that you wish to bring to birth, bless yourself with the warmth of the flame by laving your hand across the flame and then across your head. Whatever need is within your life, you may ask for abundant blessings here. All petitioners to this shrine may lay a small stone or crystal upon the altar in token of their need.

Igraine rises, unveiling her face, and puts away the holy images. With hands raised in blessing she says: 'I bless you in the name of Star-Sisters and the Earth-Mother! You will find welcome in this shrine, whenever you have need. Let your need become your pathway hither.'

She leads the way downstairs and bids you farewell. The maidens take you to the barge and you are ferried over once more to your own world. The mists close round the Castle of Maidens and you return to your own time and place, treasuring all that you have learned.

REFERENCES

1. Geoffrey of Monmouth, *History of the Kings of Britain.*
2. Wace and Layamon, *Arthurian Chronicles*, ed. E. Mason.
3. Ibid.
4. Chrétien de Troyes, *Arthurian Romances*, trans. W.W. Kibler and C.W. Carroll.
5. Caitlín Matthews, *Arthur and the Sovereignty of Britain.*
6. *Oxford Companion to the Literature of Wales*, compiled and edited by Meic Stephens.
7. Julius Caesar, *The Conquest of Gaul*, trans. S.A. Handford.
8. Geoffrey Keating, *The History of Ireland*, vol 2..
9. Caitlín Matthews, *Elements of Celtic Tradition.*
10. Wolfram von Eschenbach, *Parzival*, trans. A.T. Hatto.
11. Chrétien de Troyes, op. cit.
12. Wolfram von Eschenbach, op. cit.
13. *The Mabinogion*, ed. Lady Charlotte Guest.
14. *Trioedd Ynys Prydein*, trans. Rachel Bromwich.
15. John Matthews, *Gawain: Knight of the Goddess.*
16. Chrétien de Troyes, op. cit.
17. Caitlín Matthews, *Mabon and the Mysteries of Britain: An Exploration of 'The Mabinogion'.*
18. Geoffrey of Monmouth, *History of the Kings of Britain.*
19. Sir Thomas Malory, *The Morte d'Arthur.*
20. Caitlín Matthews, *Arthur and the Sovereignty of Britain.*
21. Caitlín Matthews, *Elements of Celtic Tradition.*

2
Guinevere

Variant Names:
Wenhaver, Wenor, Gwenhwyfar.

THE MYTH OF GUINEVERE

Since Guinevere is one of the chief characters within the Arthurian legend, we will only be examining her major appearances within tradition.

Her earliest appearance as a distinct character in Celtic tradition occurs in the early British story *Culhwch and Olwen*, where she is called Gwenhwyfar and paired with her sister, Gwenhwyfach. Arthur promises to give his nephew, Culhwch, any boon he wishes excepting only his ship, his mantle, his sword, his lance, his shield, his dagger and, last, but no means least, his wife.

Gwenhwyfar is also listed five times in the *Triads*. Triads 53 and 80 deal with the blow which Gwenhwyfach struck upon Gwenhwyfar, which caused the Battle of Camlan to take place. Triad 54 occasions the ravaging of Medrawd (Mordred) who came to Arthur's Cornish court, consumed all the food and drink, and then dragged Gwenhwyfar from her throne and struck her. Triad 56 tells of the Three Great Queens at Arthur's court: all three are listed as Gwenhwyfar, by three different fathers. Triad 80 instances Three Faithless Wives of the Island of Britain, then calls Gwenhwyfar the most faithless of all, 'since she shamed a better man than any of the others'.[1] The consistency of these themes is explained below.

Gwenhwyfar also appears three times in the Arthurian romances of *The Mabinogion*. In each case, she is gravely insulted: by the Knight of the Sparrowhawk in *Gereint*, inadvertently by Cynon in 'Lady of the Fountain', and by a knight who splashes wine in her face and strikes her in *Peredur*.[2]

In the life of St Gildas, the *Vita Gildae*, written by Caradoc of Llancarvan, we hear about the first abduction of Guinevere, by a certain Melwas of Glastonbury. St Gildas is instrumental in having her returned to Arthur.

This abduction story was clearly one of the earliest features of Guinevere's career, since it is the subject of Chrétien's *Knight of the Cart*. In this story, a knight called Meleagant (clearly drawn from Melwas) came to Arthur to say that he had captured knights and ladies of the court but that he would release them on one condition. He demanded that Arthur allow Guinevere to go into the woods with a knightly escort. There Meleagant would challenge the escort and determine whether the captives should be set free. Guinevere was entrusted to Kay and they rode out. Later, Kay's horse was discovered riderless, so Gawain rode out to seek the queen. He met Lancelot, whose horse had been killed, travelling in a cart, such as was used for public executions. Lancelot and Gawain both discovered the identity of the queen's abductor and that his kingdom was accessible only by two perilous bridges – one over and one under water. Gawain attempted the underwater route and was discovered days later, half-drowned, while Lancelot passed over the over-water bridge which was sharp and narrow as a sword.

After many adventures, Lancelot fought against Meleagant and gained entrance to the castle. He discovered the queen imprisoned behind a grating with the wounded Kay. She urged him to enter her prison and make love to her. Lancelot broke the bars and bloodied his hand thereby. Meleagant, entering the next morning, accused the queen of adultery with Kay, an accusation they denied. Lancelot was captured and forced to fight in a tournament called by the unmarried maidens of Logres. Guinevere recognized Lancelot and first bade him fight poorly, then as usual. Lancelot did his best, routing the opponents and disappearing from the field. This caused great disappointment among the spinsters of Logres. Finally Lancelot overcame Meleagant.

Geoffrey of Monmouth relates that Guinevere was the daughter of a noble Roman family, brought up by Cador. At her coronation, she was attended by four queens: the queens of Albany, Cornwall, Demetia and Venedotia. Guinevere presided at a feast with all the married women of the land 'for the Britons still observed the ancient custom of Troy, the men celebrating festive occasions with their fellow men and the women eating separately with the other women'.[3] During the Roman wars, she was left in charge of the defence of Britain with Mordred, Arthur's nephew. But Mordred took the crown for himself and Guinevere became his mistress. (It is not clear whether this was against her will or not.) When Arthur returned to fight Mordred, Guinevere fled from York to Caerleon and there took the veil at St Julius the Martyr.

Wace embroiders Guinevere's adultery, making the implications obvious: 'For Mordred her name was a hissing. Her lord she had shamed, and set her love on her husband's sister's son.'[4] Layamon also makes her guilt clear: 'Mordred was to her dearest of men.'[5] Arthur dreams that Guinevere pulls down his hall with her hand. He wakes, hears the truth and promises to have her pulled in pieces by horses. As in Geoffrey, she enters the convent at Caerleon.

In Chrétien's *Conte del Graal*, Guinevere is highly praised by Gawain. She is, he says, the most courteous, beautiful and wise woman – the paragon of Eve.

The fullest picture of Guinevere and the best known is

supplied by Malory's *Morte d'Arthur* which was based, but by no means slavishly, on the Vulgate *Lancelot*. Guinevere first appears when Arthur is enjoined by his people to take a wife.[6] He seeks Merlin's counsel, favouring Guinevere, the daughter of Leodegrance of Cameliard for 'This damosel is the most valiant and fairest lady that I know living, or yet that ever I could find.' She is desired, we note, for her bravery and beauty, not for her goodness. Merlin counsels Arthur not to chose her and warns him about Lancelot's destined love for her. But Arthur has set his heart on Guinevere and she is sent to court, along with a wedding gift of the Round Table, which Uther had given to Leodegrance. There follows the Quest of the White Hart, which is described on pp. 48-50.

Guinevere accompanies Arthur on his early campaigns,[7] and it seems that Lancelot loved Guinevere first, for she is totally bound up in her affection for Arthur, though she favours Lancelot.[8]

The major falling out of Guinevere and Lancelot occurs when Lancelot sleeps with Elaine of Corbin. When Elaine comes to court, Guinevere bids Lancelot come to her own room, but Brisen, Elaine's nurse, tricks Lancelot into sleeping with Elaine once more. Guinevere overhears them together and rebukes Lancelot who immediately runs mad. In the subsequent search for him, Guinevere spends £20,000.

After the Grail quest, Guinevere exhorts Lancelot to spend more time with her, but he counsels caution because of the rumours circulating about the court concerning them. At a private dinner, called by Guinevere, a knight called Pinel poisons an apple intended for Gawain. It is eaten by Patrise, who dies. His cousin, Mador, accuses the queen of treason. Arthur judges that Guinevere's knight shall defend her in a course of arms against Mador, or else suffer burning. Not knowing that Guinevere has sent him away, Arthur asks, 'What aileth you . . .that ye cannot keep Sir Lancelot upon your side?' Bors reluctantly agrees to champion the queen, but Lancelot appears in time and defeats Mador, thus vindicating her.

Later Guinevere falls out again with Lancelot over his

championship of the Fair Maid of Astolat, but they are speedily reconciled.

When Guinevere rides out Maying, Sir Meliagrance captures her in an incident that parallels Chrétien's *Knight of the Cart*. Guinevere stands a second time in danger of being burnt, until Lancelot is able to come to her vindication.

The final denouement is planned, with Agravain and Mordred persuading Arthur to lie away from Camelot, so that they may have leave to apprehend Lancelot and Guinevere together. They are discovered and Arthur sentences Guinevere to be burned at the stake. Lancelot saves Guinevere a third time from burning by rescuing her from the very pyre, though he slays many unarmed knights in the procession, including Gareth and Gaheris, Gawain's brothers.

Filled with hatred because of this, Gawain persuades Arthur into going to Joyous Gard to lay siege to Lancelot. A papal bull commands Arthur to take Guinevere to wife once more and to accord with Lancelot. However, Lancelot is banished to France, where Arthur and Gawain take up the siege once again and, in combat with Lancelot, Gawain is wounded.

During his absence in France, Arthur leaves Guinevere with Mordred. Mordred summarily takes the queen for his own wife, but she fortifies herself in the Tower of London. Later, after the last battle, Guinevere becomes a nun at Amesbury, where Lancelot visits her and determines to become a hermit likewise. A year later, Lancelot visits the nunnery and finds Guinevere dead. He himself dies shortly after.

FLOWER MAID AND FAERY QUEEN

The disempowerment of Guinevere is gradual, but ruthlessly portrayed. In many modern fictional retellings, she has become a poor thing, weak and without substance, a pious platitude rather than a woman. Indeed, the false Guinevere, a character who appears in the *Vulgate* text as a substitute for the queen, has almost triumphed. The medieval tradition favoured a repentant Guinevere, enclaustrated in her convent at Amesbury, praying for the two loves of her life - Arthur and Lancelot. This picture sits ill upon the real Guinevere. Looking back to the earlier, Celtic tradition we can see the fiercely beautiful and energizing woman who is loaned to us from the world of Faery. Medieval tradition has left a changeling in her place. If such a queen as Gwenhwyfar entered Amesbury it would be rather as Heloise entered the convent of the Paraclete after the castration of Abelard - a queen whose prayers were addressed to a God who was framed like her lover. The true Guinevere welcomes abduction from such a scenario, and tradition has not been slow to supply her with rescuers, as we shall see.

Guinevere's name is rooted in an ancient mystery. In *Gawain and the Green Knight*, Lady Bertilak is called 'more wener than Wenore', 'fairer than Guinevere'. This comparison gives us a significant clue to Guinevere's nature. The Indo-European, proto-Celtic root word is *gwena*, meaning 'woman'. *Gwena* is related both to Greek *gyne*, 'woman', and 'queen'. So the etymology of Guinevere's name leaves us in no doubt that she is all woman to the core. Or is she? If Guinevere appears more womanly than most women it may be that she has an otherworldly tinge to her nature. In a tradition that does not go in for Classical goddesses of love, Guinevere is virtually the British Venus. She has many correlatives in Celtic tradition, but perhaps none so clearly delineated as Guendolena, the wife of Merlin.

In the *Vita Merlini* by Geoffrey of Monmouth, Guendolena is abandoned after Merlin has run mad. Her lamentations are relayed to Merlin by a messenger who says, 'There was not among the Welsh a woman more beautiful than she. She surpassed in fairness the goddesses, and the petals of the privet, and the blooming roses and the fragrant lilies of the fields. The glory of spring shone in her alone, and she had the splendour of the stars in her two eyes.'[9] This might be a description of Guinevere in her Venus mode. It is also a description of a well-established archetype in Britain and Ireland.

Celtic tradition does not endorse the Classical model of

pulchritude and amorous behaviour. All its famous love-stories feature women who are beautiful and perilous in their own right. Few are complacent Helens, content to be fought over by the men. The figure who exemplifies this trend has been identified as the Flower Maid or Flower Bride. The Flower Maid herself often proclaims her nature through her name: Blodeuwedd, Fflur and Blanaid all mean 'Flower'. This figure usually stands between two men who fight over her possession. Their combat takes place within a seasonal context, with one man representing winter and the other representing summer. This combat obviously featured largely in seasonal rituals throughout the British Isles if mythological evidence is to be trusted. Let us enumerate a few examples.

Abduction Stories in Celto-Arthurian Tradition

Woman	Combatant Suitors	Textual Source
Rhiannon	Pwyll and Hafgan	*Pwyll, Prince of Dyfed*
Blodeuwedd	Llew and Gronw	*Math, Son of Mathonwy*
Creiddelad	Gwyn and Gwythyr	*Culhwch and Olwen*
Essyllt (Isolt)	Mark and Drustan (Tristan)	*Drustan ac Essyllt*
Blanaid	Cuchulainn and Cu Roi	*Aided Cu Roi mac Daire*
Gwenhwyfar	Arthur and Melwas	*Vita Gildae*
Gwenhwyfar	Arthur and Medrawd (Mordred)	*Trioedd Ynys, Prydain* and *Chronicles*
Fflur	Caswallawn and Julius Caesar	*Trioedd Ynys Prydain*
Guendolena	Merlin and the Bridegroom	*Vita Merlini*

With one exception, all these stories are drawn from British tradition. Each triangular relationship pivots around the woman in question. She usually has an established relationship, as Guinevere does with Arthur, but an outsider – usually younger,

stronger and more handsome than her husband - appears and
either carries her off or wins her favour. The other feature of
the abductor is that he is of faery stock, as Melwas is, or else
possesses attractive accomplishments which rank him with such
a man - as Tristan and Cuchulainn both do, the first possessing
the skills of a musician and poet, and the second being the
strongest hero of Ulster.

Sometimes the stranger comes from overseas, as in the case
of Julius Caesar, who may sit strangely in this list to some
readers. Yet the ancient *Triad* tradition speaks of him as being
a contender for the hand of Fflur, the woman who represents
the land of Britain, and whose very name means 'Flower'. Caesar
'abducts' Britain from its ruler, Caswallawn, and steals its
favours. This takes the mythology of the Flower Maid onto a
subtler level, and hints at the power which she possesses.

Creiddelad is a central figure in this consideration. Her name
and persona are equivalent to that of Cordelia, daughter of Lear.
Culhwch and Olwen informs us that 'Creiddelad the daughter of
Lludd Llaw Ereint . . .was the most splendid maiden in the three
Islands of the Mighty, and in the three Islands adjacent, and for
her Gwythyr the son of Greidawl and Gwyn the son of Nudd
fight every first of May until the day of doom.'[10]

How this came about is described later in the story. Gwyn
abducted Creiddelad, the betrothed partner of Gwythyr, and
created great havoc in the land. Arthur went north to arbitrate,
making the judgement 'that the maiden should remain in her
father's house, without advantage to either of them, and that
Gwyn ap Nudd and Gwythyr ap Greidawl should fight for her
every first of May, from thenceforth until the day of doom, and
that whichever of them should then be conqueror should have
the maiden.'[11]

It should be noted that Arthur's judgement protects the
inviolability of Creiddelad - an important factor in the role of
the Flower Maid, who hates to be constrained to any one course
of action. We also note that a seasonal combat is instituted
between the two men. Gwyn ap Nudd (White Son of Night),
is an Underworld deity whose realm stretches from the vale of

Neath in South Glamorgan to the tor of Glastonbury in Somerset, which is one of the entrances to the Underworld. Gwythyr ap Greidawl (Angry Son of the Skilful One) is the wronged party. His name suggests the fury and grief experienced by the stable partner of the Flower Maid triangle, putting him in line with Mark and Arthur, who both lose their queens to otherworldly men.

The combat of Gwyn and Gwythyr over Creiddelad was enacted as a seasonal folk-custom on May Day in South Wales until the last century. The young men divided into two sides of summer and winter. Summer always won and then a May Queen was chosen.[12] Such customs tend not to derive from textual sources; rather they are survivals of early belief.

The Flower Bride choses her own partner, sometimes artfully, as Blodeuwedd and Blathnait do – selecting their lovers and inveigling them to help slay their husbands – or else by skilful judgement, like Essyllt, the later Isolt. In the early British *Drustan ac Essyllt*, she goes to Arthur for judgement with King Mark, her husband, and Drustan (Tristan) her lover. Arthur sagely rules that Essyllt shall be with Drustan when the leaves are on the tree, and with Mark when the trees are bare. Essyllt claps her hands with glee, crying: 'Blessing be the judgement and he who gave it! There are three trees that are good of their kind, holly, and ivy, and yew, which keep their leaves as long as they live.'[13] By this means, she can live with Drustan the whole year round.

A mythological pattern is suggested by this:

Archetype	Season	Arthurian Character
Flower Maid	Beltain	Guinevere
Lady of the Wheel	Samhain	Fortuna/Ragnell
Knight of Summer	Midsummer	Melwas/Medrawd/ Lancelot/Gawain
Knight of Winter	Midwinter	Arthur/Green Knight

The Flower Maid traditionally makes herself manifest at Beltane or May Eve. She is fought over by two seasonal knights, the Knights of Summer and Winter, who stand at the opposite solstices. Polarizing the Flower Maid is the Lady of the Wheel who acts as a giver of destiny.

Many characters represent this archetype in Arthurian legend. The end of Arthur's career is marked by his dream of Fortuna, the Goddess of the Wheel; he dreams of himself whirled high and then overturned. Dame Ragnell appears when Arthur's reign is in danger of toppling due to the magical challenge of Gromer (see Chapter 9). She gives the answer to the question 'What is it women most desire?' and so saves Arthur's life. The Knights of Summer and Winter are numerous. Arthur stands at the still-point of winter, king of diminished kingdom, powerless to act on his own behalf. As he does not engage in arms on his own behalf, he is represented by one of his knights, usually Lancelot or Gawain, to rescue Guinevere from the depredations of the abductor, who is Melwas in one of his many forms or else Medrawd/Mordred. In the story of *Gawain and the Green Knight*, Gawain exemplifies the Summer Knight, for his powers wax at midday; his combat is with the Green Knight who makes his beheading-game challenge at midwinter. There are many complex seasonal combats hidden within this pattern.[14]

In Celtic tradition, the otherworldly gates are open for acts of love at May and for acts of magical reprisal at Samhain, so that there is a distinct and separate pattern, depending on whether the myth centres on the Flower Bride or upon the Lady of the Wheel. We note that, in this pattern, the women relate to the two main Celtic festivals while the men relate to the solstices.

Guinevere's career consistently speaks of her as a woman who stands between two men. The earliest traditions speak of Melwas as her abductor. He goes on to become Chrétien's Meleagant and Malory's Meliagrance. When Lancelot becomes the queen's lover, this pattern of abduction is overlaid somewhat. Guinevere's many abductions, some 14 in all, are dealt with in Caitlín Matthews' *Arthur and the Sovereignty of Britain*. If we examine all these episodes, two figures significantly recur: Melwas and Mordred. By studying the nature of these men, we may come to the heart of the mystery.

First of all, we will examine Mordred. In Celtic tradition he is Medrawd, son of Lleu ap Cynfarch (Lot) and Gwyar or Morcades (Morgause). He is the nephew of Arthur, not his son, and therefore, according to matrilineal descent, the man most likely to be king. He exemplifies the role of the king's *tanaiste* or appointed successor. Arthur trusts Mordred with the protection of the realm when he is absent, and it is during one of these absences that Mordred steals Guinevere to be his own wife. The point underlying this abduction is that the queen is the sovereignty-bestowing woman; by marrying her, Mordred strengthens his claim a hundredfold among the Celtic tribes. Mordred fulfils many of the criteria necessary for being the Knight of Summer. He is the son of Lot, often called Lot of Lochlan. *Lochlan* is the Gaelic word for 'Scandinavia' and is often used to denote 'a stranger from overseas'. In Celtic tradition Lochlan was associated with the Otherworld. This gives Mordred his necessary faery quality as an abductor.

If we turn to Melwas, we see the otherworldly pattern most markedly. The *Vita Gildae* calls Melwas 'the Lord of the Summer Country' and bases him at Glastonbury. The Celtic name for Glastonbury is *Ynys Wtrin*. It lies in modern Somerset which is still called in Welsh *Gwlad y Haf*, 'the Summer Country'. The French romancers were obviously aware of this tradition, for they make Meleagant Lord of the Isle of Gore or Voirre. *Voirre* or *Verre* is French for 'glass'. This location has always been associated with the Otherworld, with the realms of faery. *Glas* is Gaelic for green, the colour of faerykind.

Melwas went into Welsh poetic tradition as an otherworldly lover. This is how he was described by Dafydd ap Edmwnt:

> Alas that a bachelor's sigh avails not
> For me to invoke the art of Melwas:
> The thief that by magic and illusion
> Took the fair one to the world's end:
> To the green wood that juggler went,
> To the leafy rampart of a bough –
> And to climb tonight aloft like him.[15]

Like Robin Hood, who likewise figures in May Day customs, 'Melwas dressed himself in leaves, to lie in wait for Gwenhwyfar and her attendants, who, according to custom, were to come on May morning to gather birch for garlands to welcome summer; by means of that disguise he ran away with her.'[16] As already mentioned, Melwas becomes Meleagant and Meliagrance in the later texts, but he retains his otherworldly castle, from whence Lancelot attempts to rescue Guinevere.

Lancelot usurps the role of abductor/lover from Chrétien onwards, but if we look at him, we find that he fulfils the same criteria as both Mordred and Melwas. Guinevere falls for Lancelot because he is of otherworldly fosterage (see Chapter 4). He is the best, strongest and most invincible knight of the Round Table, and is also from overseas, from the region of Benoic in France.

With all these otherworldly abductors surrounding her, we have to consider another possibility. Does Guinevere have a faery provenance herself?

Scholars give the etymology of Guinevere's Celtic name, Gwenhwyfar, as 'White Shadow' or 'White Phantom'. It is a meaning she shares with the beautiful daughter of Queen Medbh, Finnabhair. Many characters of otherworldly stock have names which dazzle or shine, e.g. Gwawl (radiant), Gwyn (white), Taliesin (radiant brow), etc. Guinevere may indeed be a palimpsest of her faery self, for her earthly acts and disposition may reflect a faery origin. Wherever the White Shadow is, there is an ambiance of otherworldliness, of a freedom which mortal women do not enjoy. Guinevere is the focus of otherworldly disruption for, countless times, faery lovers or suitors invade Arthur's peace to obtain her for themselves. Her polarized nature - beautiful woman yet faithless wife, respected queen who is yet insulted in court - is increasingly played upon by the later romancers who take this as their warrant to portray Guinevere as a noble slut.

We postulate that Guinevere's true nature is based on the mores of the Otherworld, which permit 'all acts of love and pleasure' without guilt. This Celtic basis underlies the later texts which, where they are not painting Guinevere as an adulterous woman, usually stress her ability to move smoothly in the field of courtly love.

The myth of Guinevere places her firmly at May-time, the most suitable time for the Flower Maid to be manifest, when she is at her most beautiful. Significantly the Queen of Faery is to be met with at the two major Celtic festivals, at Beltane (May Eve) and at Samhain (Hallow'een), where she is most often encountered as the Queen of Destiny. These two great festivals mark the times of year when the otherworldly gates stand open ready to allow the visitation of the faerykind to Middle Earth. It is at Beltane that Guinevere is abducted.

The triple nature of Guinevere is noted in Triad 56. Arthurian scholars have been quick to point to the supposed parallel between the queen and the triple Etain who appears in the Irish love-story *Tochmarc Etain*, and to make a case for Guinevere's faery origins. However, it becomes clear from the evidence examined above, that Guinevere does have a mortal existence, but that she exemplifies the role of Creiddelad – *she is the eternal May Queen, with all the privileges that that role entails.*

Guinevere is a dangerous woman – one who is totally aware of the effective nature of her sexuality. Many young women have this deadly power, and exercise it to the full. They can pull the heart-strings and play cat and mouse with their men. Like Blodeuwedd of earlier Celtic tradition, Guinevere is capable of extreme cruelty, putting her men on the rack.

The seemingly treacherous nature of the Flower Bride is such that she is universally rejected by the respectable. This happens to Blodeuwedd, called out of her otherworldly nature by Math and Gwydion for their convenience, to be the wife of Llew. When she shows a will and desire of her own, she is turned into an owl. The refrain of Alan Garner's reworking of this story, *The Owl Service* – 'She wants to be flowers and you make her owls' – is a telling criticism upon womankind. Many women are now so convinced of their owl-dom that their essential flower-self remains obscured. The woman of flowers is presently equated with a debased perception of womanhood: to let her petals show is virtually to invite rape and accusations of whoredom. Women themselves can and must resist such definition while retaining their femininity. The power of the Flower Maid is theirs, the power to energize and to transform dullness and lethargy into vibrant beauty. The power to find and fulfil one's inner nature is the lesson of Guinevere.

Guinevere follows her true nature when she accepts other lovers than her husband. She has a free, otherworldly quality, which is truly as hospitable as any of the ancient ninefold sisterhoods who offered 'the friendship of their thighs' to all comers. She has no children to further humanize her and bring her to reality. Like Blodeuwedd, she answers to another nature. She cannot be expected to be faithful to the contract with one husband when her brief is to be faithful to the inner harmonic of the Goddess of the Land. The Flower Bride is the beautiful face of the land, to be eternally fought over, as Creiddelad is fought over in her eternal triangle. The law of the Goddess of the Land is that she must be guarded by the most worthy knight and by he alone. When the man whom she has made king fails in his duty, she is at liberty to find another, more worthy champion. It is this aspect of the Flower Maid that causes most trouble.

SOWER OF STRIFE

One of the earliest and most consistent features of Guinevere is her ability to stir up strife. This is a quality within the mythic role of Flower Maid who mantles her thorns between the lovely petals so skilfully that the one who picks her never knows of his wound until it is too late. In Malory, Guinevere causes the downfall of the Round Table by her adultery with Lancelot, since during her rescue from the pyre, Lancelot slays Gareth, brother of Gawain and nephew of Arthur, thus causing an irreparable wound to the order of chivalry and involving Arthur in Gawain's blood-feud on Lancelot.

Similarly the early *Triads* speak of Gwenhwyfar causing the Battle of Camlan, the last battle in which Arthur is mortally wounded. The cause of this battle is the blow that Gwenhwyfach struck on Gwenhwyfar. The tale of *Culhwch and Olwen* informs us that the mysterious Gwenhwyfach is the sister of Gwenhwyfar. The meaning of these two names turn around the suffixes attached to them. *Fach* is the mutated Welsh suffix meaning *bach* or 'small'; the *far* part of Gwenhwyfar's name is probably derived from the Welsh *fawr* or 'big'. The similarly named pair of sisters might therefore be called 'Little Gwen and Big Gwen'.

But does the tradition support a pair of sisters? One of the triads enumerates three Gwenhwyfars as the queens of Arthur, while the alleged grave-marker of Arthur found at Glastonbury reflects that here lies Arthur with his *second* wife, Guinevere! There is also a traditional Welsh saying: 'Gwenhwyfar, daughter of Ogfran the Giant, bad when little, worse when big'. This directly involves the Little Gwen and Big Gwen discussed above. When we examine later tradition we find that Guinevere does indeed become polarized into two distinct modes: the fair, courteous queen and the underhand adulteress.

The *Vulgate* cycle tells the story of a false and a true Guinevere – both daughters of Leodegran. The false Guinevere is sired upon the seneschal's wife, the true Guinevere upon Leodegran's queen. The false Guinevere arranges for the banishment of her sister and attempts to substitute herself as Arthur's wife. Thus, the true queen is sentenced to have the skin removed from her head, cheeks and palms for traitorously attempting to be queen. The deception is discovered when the false Guinevere suffers a stroke and the true Guinevere is restored.[17]

We have suggested in *Arthur and the Sovereignty of Britain* that there may be two possible solutions to the Gwenhwyfach/far triads. The first is that Gwenhwyfach is Gwenhwyfar's brother, not sister. In Triad 54 Medrawd is said to strike the queen – a tangible feature of Guinevere's career is the number of insults that she has to bear and the number of abductions to which she is submitted. Wace records that Guinevere and Mordred are sister and brother, thus making their adultery even more heinous. This is a twisted supposition that may have an element of truth in it: Mordred is consistently supposed to abduct Guinevere and set the stage for the last battle.

The second possible solution is that Elaine is the one who strikes the bitterest blow to the queen, through her substitution for Guinevere in a supernaturally-arranged encounter with Lancelot. Guinevere is childless, while Elaine conceives the destined Grail-winner Galahad, by deceiving Lancelot into believing that she is the queen. In Malory – admittedly a long way from the *Triad* tradition – the whole *Morte d'Arthur* episode is laid down by this very deception, for the love of Lancelot and Guinevere is only strengthened by this setback.

But there is another factor which causes the end of the Arthurian saga. There is a way in which the Grail itself is an instrument of the Round Table's downfall. The Grail quest is undertaken in order 'to free the waters' – to cause the lustral waters of the spirit to flow in the land. However, after its achievement, the waters flow only too readily: emotions run high, quarrels break out, jealousy is plumbed and the fall of the Table is brought about. Guinevere is most closely associated with the prelude to the *Morte*, for she is the land incarnate and here the battle over the sovereignty is fought out between Mordred and Arthur.

This reminds us of the tradition which speaks of a knight spilling a cup of wine into her lap, which seems to be such an overt Grail reference that we must explore it further. This incident occurs in *Peredur* where a page is serving Gwenhwyfar with a golden cup.

> Then the knight dashed the liquor that was therein upon her face, and upon her stomacher, and gave her a violent blow on the face and said, 'If any have the boldness to dispute this goblet with me, and to revenge the insult to Gwenhwyfar, let him follow me to the meadow, and there I will await him.'[18]

The untrained squire, Peredur, then avenges the queen by overcoming the knight and taking his armour.

What is the implication of this incident? In the context of the Grail tradition, a terrible blow is struck which renders the land barren and waterless. This is usually struck upon the King of the Grail Lands, who thereafter becomes the Wounded King. Such a blow affects not just the man, but the land over which he rules, for the king and the land are as one, according to the laws of the Goddess, Sovereignty. At the achievement of the Grail, the Wounded King and the land are simultaneously healed. But it is not Arthur who is struck here, though doubtless the knight meant to wound his honour, it is Gwenhwyfar who takes the blow, indicating that, in this tradition, she represents the land and the honour of Arthur.

This implication is strengthened if we look closer at Triad 54 which deals with the Three Unrestrained Ravagings of the Island of Britain. In the first of them, 'Medrawd came to Arthur's court at Celliwig in Cornwall; he left neither food nor drink in the court that he did not consume. And he dragged Gwenhwyfar from her royal chair, and then he struck a blow upon her.'[19] This dual insult seems related to the Celtic origins of the Grail legend which deal with the reaving of a cauldron from the Underworld or the wasting of the land by an otherworldly entity.

If we look at the story of *Lludd and Llefelys*, we will see a similar incident. In this story, King Lludd has several problems besetting his kingdom, one of which concerns the theft of provisions from his own court. Even if a year's worth of supplies is brought in, nothing is left after the first night. Lludd keeps watch and discovers a huge man who creeps in with a hamper into which he starts to put all the food. They grapple together and Lludd overcomes the giant. This story may seem to have little to with the Grail tradition until we learn that the *mwys* or hamper of Gwyddno Garanhir was one of the Hallows mentioned in the list of the Thirteen Treasures of Britain. The quality of this hamper is that if food for one person is put inside, food for a hundred persons can be taken out again. This is a gift of great importance in Celtic society, which was largely based upon the obligations of hospitality. Like the Grail, the hamper dispenses miraculous food and is therefore a hallow which represents the land's bounty.

In the case of Arthur's provisions, it is Mordred who comes to waste his substance. The fact that Mordred also strikes Guinevere strengthens her association with the land's bounty. This dolorous blow upon the goodness of the land and its representative seems like an otherworldly attempt to remove the grace of the Grail from this world. The Grail is itself an object of otherworldly privilege which is bestowed upon Middle Earth. Its removal from these realms causes such grief, want and hardship that many knights go on quest for it.

The theft of the Flower Bride and the removal of the Grail are interrelated themes. Even in *Aided Cu Roi mac Daire* (The Tragic Death of Cu Roi mac Daire), we see the abduction of significant items from the Otherworld by Cu Roi – the three cows of Tuchna and the three birds which sing in their ears causing them to give the milk of 30 cows into a cauldron. Cu Roi also takes a faery woman, Blanaid, whose subsequent story is as like Blodeuwedd's as makes little difference.[20] This tradition shows us the association between the food-bestowing hallow and the woman who likewise represents fruitfulness and fertility. In Chapter 7 we will hear of the Damsel of the Wells and King Amangons who took her golden cup: that particular theft takes a cup from the Otherworld and causes waste land in Middle Earth. Amangons not only steals the cup but rapes the maiden – again, a dual insult involving both food-bestowing cup and woman.

Many folk stories instance a faery woman who comes from the Otherworld and the condition of her staying with her earthly lover is that she will never be struck. The lady of Llyn y Fan Fach is a good example of this. She comes from the lake with magical cows and remains with her lover, bearing him children, for many years. He must not strike her, however, even accidentally. At the third inadvertent blow which he gives her, she returns to the lake, taking the cows with her.

What is the mythological pattern underlying this? Clearly the Flower Bride and the food-bestowing object are intimately connected. It would seem that when either woman or cup is abused, attempts are made to remove them from the realms to which they have been lent. When the Flower Bride is cherished, the land is bounteous. When she is cheated or ignored, she retaliates by opening up the otherworldly gates for a challenger to beset her husband's realm. If a king is not careful, he can lose both queen and kingdom.

Guinevere starts by being a much-loved queen. But things do not remain harmonious. Just as Arthur delegates his adventures and active kingship to his knights, so too does Guinevere become the object of their rivalry. When unjustly accused of Sir Patrise's death, she needs a champion to fight her cause. Arthur says: 'I may not have ado in this matter, for I must be a rightful judge; and that repenteth me that I may not do battle for my wife . . .'[21] He cannot champion her himself, for he is the king, the figure of justice in the land.

The passive nature of Arthur, as we have proved elsewhere, is due to his sacral kingship. Guinevere is an open target, the queenly representative of Sovereignty, so Mordred steals her when Arthur temporarily gives him sovereignty. Nevertheless, the breaking of the Round Table fellowship strikes Arthur more nearly than the loss of Guinevere, for he says, in Malory: 'And much more I am sorry for my good knights' loss than for the loss of my fair queen; for queens I might have had many, but such a fellowship of good knights shall never be together in any company.'[22] Like the Arthur of *Culhwch and Olwen*, who remembers to mention Guinevere last of all his possessions, Malory's Arthur finds that the toys of boys and men have more lasting power for him.

Many blows are struck against Guinevere. She is frequently tested, just as Arianrhod at the court of Math, for her chastity – a test which she always fails. But it is not a test which can be applied to a faery woman. The point about the testing of Arianrhod by Math is that Math is a king who does not go to war as long as his feet are in the lap of a virgin foot-holder. This curious appointment of *troedawc* or foot-holders is not just a quaint legend, but an actual role borne out by various British law-tracts; the position of *troedawc* carried certain privileges and its holder was in a post equivalent to lady or gentleman of the bedchamber in the royal household.[23] While Math has his feet in the lap of Goewin, the land is at peace. Gwydion provokes war between Gwynedd and Dyfed solely in order that his brother Gilfaethwy may enjoy Goewin. When Math arms himself for battle, Gilfaethwy rapes Goewin, singularly disqualifying her from continuing in her position. As already related, Arianrhod is brought forward as a suitable candidate for Math's footholder, but when she steps over Math's wand, twin babies appear.

Guinevere is subject to many such tests at court. The French romances of *Lai du Cor* and *Conte du Mantel* instance tests when a horn and a mantle are brought to court to test the ladies there. The horn spills its contents upon an unfaithful wife, while the mantle will only perfectly fit the chaste wife. Guinevere, as we are aware, already has several incidents of having a cup spilled in her lap or its contents splashed in her face: both *Peredur* and the *Triads* mention this tradition. These two articles of testing both appear in the lists of the Thirteen Treasures of Britain; they are of otherworldly origin and possess magical abilities. Also in the *Triads*, the Horn of Bran dispenses the liquid of one's choosing, while the Mantle of Tegau Gold-Breast will not cover a woman who is faithless.

Chastity tests in literary tradition reflect the medieval preoccupation of keeping women in line: we see the operation of the good old double standard by which men may take mistresses, but women must remain faithful wives, whatever the provocation. Guinevere does not fit this bill, any more than Arianrhod is suitable foot-holder material. Both women retain their Celtic independence which carries a different kind of inviolability. The medieval chastity test which involves the horn which spills its liquid has strayed from its true context. It was perhaps once the cup which only Guinevere could dispense to the most worthy, after the fashion of the ancient priestesses of Sovereignty.

Like Igraine, her mother-in-law, Guinevere is a royal woman. The gift of the Round Table that comes as her dowry is a late hint at her regal nature, for the Table is analogous to the land itself. Whoever partners her holds the land. With possession being nine tenths of the law, it is no wonder that so many would-be abductors come to remove her from Arthur. Significantly, it is the prerogative of the Flower Bride to make her own choice of partner: a choice which often breaks the rules of society, but which accords with her deep inner nature.

QUEEN OF THE COURT OF WOMEN

Where the Flower Bride dwells, there gather many tales of judgement. One of these, Marie de France's *Launfal*, recounts the story of Guinevere's choice of lover. Here we read of the knight, Launfal, who strays into the Otherworld and becomes the lover of the Faery Queen. On his return to mortal realms, she warns him never to speak of her, or he will lose her forever. Launfal is then accosted by Guinevere, who offers him her love: 'You may receive a queen's whole love, if such be your care.' When pressed for reasons for his refusal of her favour, Launfal compares Guinevere unfavourably to the meanest of the Faery Queen's maidens. Arthur is incensed at this insult to Guinevere and puts Launfal on trial. The court decide that Launfal must seek the lady of his heart and bring her to Camelot that everyone might judge for themselves. At that moment two faery women appear, followed by their queen. 'Now the judges were about to proclaim their sentence when, amidst the tumult of the town, there came riding to the palace the flower of all the ladies of the world.'[24] The court agrees that the Faery Queen surpasses Guinevere and Launfal returns to the Otherworld with his mistress.

This story appears to belong to the genre which insults Guinevere, but another pattern is established here. These are the courts of love, wherein criminal concerns are outweighed by matters of the heart. The secret identity of the faery mistress is an established theme in folk tradition, where the one who boasts unwarily of the faery woman's abilities or qualities stands to lose her. Guinevere merely reflects the Flower Bride archetype: when the real thing turns up, she appears indeed as a 'White Shadow'. Guinevere may not be able to hold her own against the Faery Queen, but many texts accord her supreme place in the judgement of women upon men. This theme recurs in both the stories of Nimuë and Ragnell.

Guinevere may cause havoc in the world of men, yet she comes into her own when she enters the emotional and imaginal realms where the writ of law ceases to run. She shows herself confidant and assured, a true Lady of the Lake. Standing as she does in the role of the May Queen, she is best qualified to arbitrate in the courts of love.

Let us turn to the events which surround Guinevere's marriage to Arthur in Malory, to the Quest for the White Hart, in order to see Guinevere as judge of the courts of love in action.

When Guinevere was married to Arthur, Leodegrance, her father, gave him the Round Table as a gift. Arthur bade Merlin go and seek 50 good knights to fill the seats at the Table, but he returned with only 28, their names appearing in gold at their places. To fill another place, Gawain begged to be knighted on Arthur's wedding day.

As they returned to the Table to eat the wedding breakfast, a white hart appeared in the hall pursued by a white hound which was pursued by 30 pairs of black hounds. A knight sitting at the Table was knocked over by the white hart and he picked up the white hound and took it away with him. A lady on a white palfrey then rode in and loudly demanded the return of the white hound. A strange knight then came in and snatched her away. Arthur was rather glad she was gone 'for she made such a noise'!

Merlin, however, bade Arthur attend closely to this adventure and not withdraw from it, else he would suffer dishonour. He then bade Gawain fetch the white hart, Tor get the white hound and the felonious knight or else slay him, and King Pellinore bring the lady and the strange knight back to court.

Gawain set out with Gaheris as his squire and they met with Sorlouse and Brian of the Forest, two brothers who fought to

decide who was the better to become a knight of the Round
Table. He saw the hart crossing water and was there stopped
by Allardin of the Isles who made him joust with him. Gawain
overcame and killed him.

Gawain and Gaheris then followed the hart into a castle and
killed it in the yard. Ablamar of the Marshes came out and slew
two of Gawain's hounds and then made complaint: 'O my white
hart, me repenteth that thou art dead, for my sovereign lady gave
thee to me, and evil have I kept thee . . .'[25] They went within
and fought and Gawain beat Ablamar to his knees where he
asked mercy, but Gawain was angry about the loss of his hounds.
As he was about to behead Ablamar, a lady came from the
chamber behind and threw herself under his sword so that he
beheaded her instead. Gawain was so shocked by this mishap
that he spared Ablamar and sent him back to court to abide
Arthur's judgement.

As Gawain lay down to sleep at the castle, four knights
appeared and berated him for slaying the lady. He fought them
all until four ladies appeared and asked mercy for their knights,
and Gawain spared them because he was wounded by an arrow
through his arm. They gave him the white hart's head to take
back to Camelot, according to his quest, and made him carry
the dead lady's head about his neck and her body over his horse's
neck. So he returned to Camelot.

> And there by ordinance of the queen there was set a quest of
> ladies on Sir Gawain, and they judged him for ever while he lived
> to be with all ladies, and to fight for their quarrels; and that ever
> he should be courteous, and never to refuse mercy to him that
> askest mercy. Thus was Gawain sworn upon the Four Evangelists
> that he should never be against lady nor gentlewoman, but if
> he fought for a lady and his adversary fought for another.[26]

Tor retrieved the white hound and Sir Abelleus who had taken
it, while King Pellinore neglected to help a damsel bemoaning
the dead knight in her lap, and subsequently discovered her half-
devoured by beasts so he brought her head back to court. She
had been his own daughter, Merlin revealed. Pellinore also

brought the lady on the white palfrey, who was Nimuë, a Lady of the Lake.

This story presents Guinevere as a judge of men and supreme arbiter of courtly love. It also establishes the importance of the queen since the subject of the quest is one of sovereignty. The white hart is the prime totem of sovereignty and is often a shapeshifting device of faery women, who lead the unwary into the Otherworld (see Chapter 6). It is also an image of divine and erotic love. It is the symbol of chastity, yet it is also one of guiltless love, such as is enjoyed in the Celtic Otherworld. This story confirms the long tradition of Gawain as a knight of the Goddess, one who reveres all women and acts as their champion above all other knights.[27]

Guinevere's role in Malory and other late texts is to act as an arbiter of morals, a praiser and encourager of knights. She keeps what is perfect bright in the Round Table's realms. She rules affairs of the heart and is harsh in judgement upon men who act in a criminal or unconsidered way. This is further borne out in Chaucer's 'Wife of Bath's Tale', a reworking of an old theme which we shall encounter again in Chapter 9.

In this story we hear how one of Arthur's young knights raped a maiden and was brought before Arthur's court to be sentenced to be beheaded for his crime. However, Guinevere and the ladies begged Arthur to let them be the sole judges in the case. Guinevere brings the miscreant before her and says:

> I grante thee lyf, if thou canst tellen me
> What thing is it that wommen most desiren?[28]

She gives him a twelvemonth to find the answer. The knight's list of answers soon grows apace but he does not have a definitive one. Finally, he comes upon 24 women dancing in a ring and approaches them to ask the question. They vanish, leaving behind them an ugly old woman. She promises to give him the answer in return for his promise to do whatever she next bids him. In the courtroom:

Ful many a noble wyf, and many a mayde,
And manye a widwe, for that they ben wyse,
The quen hir-self sittinge as a justyse,
Assembled been.

The knight gives the answer he has learned from the hag:

Wommen desyren to have sovereyntee
As wel over hir housband as hir love,
And for to been in maistrie him above.[29]

The hag comes forward and demands the redemption of her promise, asking him to marry her. They are married, to the knight's great disgust. In bed, she puts a question to him: Will he have her fair by day and foul by night, or foul by day and fair by night? The knight, on the horns of a dilemma, cannot respond other than by leaving the choice with her. She turns into a beautiful maiden, to remain that way. Thus he learns from his own experience the truth of the answer he was schooled to repeat. By handing over sovereignty to his wife, the knight has learned the lessons of the Lady of the Wheel who stands at the other end of the year from Guinevere as Flower Bride.

The precedent of Guinevere presiding over 'the Queen's court,' is taken up in later Celtic tradition in Bryan Merryman's *The Midnight Court*, where an errant man who disdains women and sexual relations is brought before the critical court of Aoibheall, Queen of the *Sidhe*, the lordly ones of faery in Irish myth. His judges are women, and they find him severely wanting. This is essentially the mythic nature of Guinevere. She sits in judgement over men, testing their virility for the good of the land. The Classical testing of the goddesses by Paris is reversed to its ancient mode in Celtic tradition. It is Guinevere as Queen of the Court of Women who tests the lover. True to the heart, she tests both our intrinsic womanhood and manhood.

The memory of Guinevere needs to be restored to reverence, for she is the true green life within us, enticing us out of our dim, shuttered lives into a more adventurous and rapturous mode.

The Green Lady
ॐ

It is May and you step out to take the country air, walking
along a road that is white with blown blossom. The fields
on either side look welcoming and you wish you could step
more lightly on the grass than upon the road beneath your
feet.

A foolish face peers out at you from among the branches of
a tree, mocking your serious progress when all the world is
bright. It is the sweet, sardonic face of a fool. He makes a
rude noise at you, leaps from the tree, and walks ahead,
imitating your own gait.

You were disposed to be relaxed until the fool came to spoil
your solitary walk. He is a thin fellow with a supple body
that echoes your own movement with cruel exactness. He is
dressed in multi-coloured rags and patches and behind him
is pinned an ass's tail which wiggles very rudely from his
tight, mocking behind. Now he pretends to be a holy man
and intones meaningless drivel in mockery of your
studiously calm annoyance.

Suddenly you catch the drift of merry drums and pipes
coming from your left. What the hell! What cost dignity?
You turn yourself around and leap over the wall into the
field, and away into the green-misted distance. As you get
closer, you pick up other sounds: the sweet psaltery and the
blaring shawm, the intricate bowing of the rebec and the
bright-toned voices of many people.

Over the dip in the ground you see a procession of people
winding away over the fields and woods. They are dressed in
their best comfortable clothes and are dancing along to the
sound of the music, singing a joyous song about spring. Your
own feet begin to dance along and your body is animated
by the beat of the drum. As you join the throng, the fool
joins you and, without acrimony, you take his hand and
enjoy his japes as he somersaults and jigs along. The people
behind you have no compunction about joining in his fun,
and they pull his tail and crack crude jokes which are
innocent of offence.

You are entering into the spirit of the thing at last - which
is why you set out this May morning in any case - when the

music stops in one jagged moment. People stop singing and
crane their necks to see why. The whisper is passed back
through the crowd: 'Follow the flowers!' 'The trefoil blooms
again!'

The mood of the crowd changes in a moment from joyous
celebration to intense expectation. Progress quickens into a
fast walk. You are swept along too, puzzled by the change.
The fool, your companion, points out the thing that has
caused this to come about. Evenly paced, like footprints, are
three white trefoils growing in the ground. The fool behaves
like a dog with the scent of the most toothsome bone in
the world in his nose. He capers round the flowers and
kisses the ground with joy; yet there is also something
strangely reverent in his attitude.

'What does it mean?' you ask him. For answer, he pulls you
along so fast that you are suddenly at the head of the
procession. Ahead of you is a ring of hawthorn trees. The
leaders of the procession stop and signal to the fool. He
comes to them, like a soldier about to be given orders. They
deck him with green garlands and mark his forehead and
arms with white streaks of clay. The effect is ghastly and
hieratic at the same time. Then he is crowned with a
garland of young oak leaves, some still tightly furled in their
curly buds. He takes a pipe from his belt and begins to play.
The music is like a bird calling over and over to its mate - a
sad yet joyful sound.

Then the fool goes forward into the ring of hawthorn trees
and is lost to view. The procession reforms and surrounds
the green bower. The musicians take up the bird-like piping,
the drums are laid aside and the dancers take out their
bells, which are wound on wrist and ankle. All that is heard
is the jingle of bells and the soft piping. The people circle
the bower nine times until a shout goes up. You see a bird
hurtling into the sky from the centre of the copse of
hawthorns. The drums are brought out once more and the
noisy instruments create a din like a horn-call at the end of
a hunt.

The leaders of the procession come and place a posy of
flowers into your hand: 'Go and greet the May!' They direct
you to enter the bower. With some trepidation, you obey
them, passing between the close-set hawthorns with their

creamy blossom. You blink within the clearing. The scent of
hawthorn is overpoweringly strong. Within, is a green dais
upon which reclines a woman dressed in green. She is the
most beautiful and desirable woman you ever seen. Her
heart-shaped face is framed for joy and delight. But you
realize that this is no mere woman; her eyes hold
knowledge that was ancient before the world was made. You
drop onto one knee and give her the offering of flowers,
saying, 'Greetings to the Queen of the May.'

The queen takes them graciously and raises you to your
feet. Her breath is sweet as the hawthorn and her touch
cool. 'Would you know who I am? Queen of the Wild
Lands am I truly, Queen of the May Blossom. Under my
boughs, the tryst of all true lovers, the secret woodlands
hide their mystery. In courts am I also Queen, Queen of the
Round Table, Queen of the Wide-Wheeling World. In the
wilderness I am the White One, Queen of the Night
Hunting, Queen of the Solitary Banquet.'

Her words send shivers through you. It is then that you
notice a man lying beside her on the dais, like one
exhausted. His garments are those of the fool and you
suddenly feel irrational fear for your simple friend. The
queen sees your fear and smiles. 'Well do you shiver. It is a
brave man who enters the bower of the Green Lady on her
own day. Only a fool could join me here. And see . . .' She
touches him with a wand of carven hawthorn and he stirs
slowly like one waking from sleep.

His movements are languid and slow. You notice a ewer and
basin nearby and help him wash his face clean of the white
clay. As the ashen earth falls from his face you nearly drop
with surprise. Here is no fool but the most handsome man
you ever saw. The water clears his wits and he rises, taking
the Lady's hand with trust and love which match the look
in her own eye when she gazes upon him. She lifts the
crown of oak buds and places it upon his head. 'Be king of
my realm this day,' she breathes. As she places the crown
upon his head, the oak buds open and the new king is filled
with the power of the Green Lady's love.

Such sights are not for you and you begin to withdraw, your
duty done. The Green Lady steps towards you, to stay you,
and you see where the trefoils come from. Each step she

takes leaves a white flower. Your fear turns to awe. She
stoops, picks the sacred flowers and touches them with her
wand. They weave themselves into a garland which she
places about your neck.

'Be merry and joyful of heart! My gifts are joyous love and a
light step. Go forth into the world and know me as I am.'
She picks a twig of hawthorn and presses it into your hand.
Under the creamy blossom you feel the prick of the thorns
and understand that the Green Lady is the fullness of life:
she is both the blossom and the leaves' falling, the fruit and
the bare bough. Yet there is no lessening of joy on this
sunny day. You bow to the Green Lady, leaving her and her
consort to their love-making.

Outside, the people have begun their picnic and they shout
at sight of you. Behind you step the Queen and King of the
May to celebrate with their people the full delight of the
season. You stay and feast with them and at twilight depart
softly to your own time and place. In your dreams you can
return here and bring your own partner to share the love
and delight of the Green Lady.

REFERENCES

1. *Trioedd Ynys Prydein*, trans. Rachel Bromwich.
2. *The Mabinogion*, ed. Lady Charlotte Guest.
3. Geoffrey of Monmouth, *History of the Kings of Britain*.
4. Wace and Layamon, *Arthurian Chronicles*, ed. E. Mason.
5. Ibid.
6. Sir Thomas Malory, *The Morte d'Arthur*, Book 3.
7. Ibid, Book 4, ii - iii.
8. Ibid, Book 5, iii.
9. R.J. Stewart, *The Mystic Life of Merlin*.
10. *The Mabinogion*, op. cit.
11. Ibid.
12. R.S. Loomis, *Arthurian Tradition and Chrétien de Troyes*.
13. Caitlín Matthews, *Arthur and the Sovereignty of Britain*.
14. John Matthews, *Gawain: Knight of the Goddess*.

15. Loomis, op. cit.
16. Ibid.
17. Peter Korrel, *An Arthurian Triangle*.
18. *The Mabinogion*, ed. Lady Charlotte Guest.
19. *Trioedd Ynys Prydein*, trans. Rachel Bromwich.
20. Caitlín Matthews, *Mabon and the Mysteries of Britain: An Exploration of 'The Mabinogion'*.
21. Sir Thomas Malory, *The Morte d'Arthur*, Book 18.
22. Ibid, Book 20, ix.
23. Caitlín Matthews, *Mabon*, op. cit.
24. Marie de France, *Lays*, trans. Eugene Mason.
25. Malory, op. cit.
26. Ibid.
27. John Matthews, *Gawain*.
28. Geoffrey Chaucer, *The Canterbury Tales*.
29. Ibid.

Morgan

So great is the people's need –
There are cornfields that must grow
There are deer that must be brought
Within range of the bow
There are fish to be tempted into the net –
There are all our starved daughters
Whose secret furrows cry aloud for seed –
We look for a new King to make fruitful the land.

John Arden and Margaretta D'Arcy,
The Island of the Mighty

Variant Names:
Morgen, Morgain, Feimurgan, Morgue, Morgayne,
Morgana, Morgan le Fay.

THE MYTH OF MORGAN

Morgan is perhaps one of the most complex characters within our ninefold sisterhood. She appears at different levels of the tradition as goddess, enchantress and political woman. While her incorporation from Celtic origins into medieval text is gradual, it is nonetheless complete. She starts life as a shapeshifter, but we dare not blink here, or we will miss her transmogrifications. The transitions which she undergoes are bewildering for the general reader, so we have outlined only the major texts here.

Geoffrey of Monmouth does not mention her at all in his

History of the Kings of Britain, the style of which is strictly that
of a chronicle. Rather, Morgan appears in his more imaginative
novelesque *Vita Merlini*, a fact that gives us an immediate clue
to her real nature. Morgan is not the stuff of sequential history,
but rather part of the interior mythos of the Celts. The *Vita
Merlini* informs us that Morgen dwells with seven or eight sisters
on the island of Avalon. She is noted for her healing powers,
her shapeshifting and her learning. After the Battle of Camlan
she received Arthur and undertook to heal him.

Chrétien mentions her in his *Erec* as Morgan le Fay, and notes
that Guingamar, Lord of the Isle of Avalon, is her friend. She
is said to have made an ointment which heals wounds for her
brother, Arthur. In *Yvain*, she is called Morgan the Wise, the
maker of a soothing unguent. Hartman von Aue calls her a
goddess, an appellation which is repeated in the Middle English
text *Gawain and the Green Knight* (which is considered below),
and again in *Diu Cröne* by Heinrich von den Tulin, while Etienne
de Rouen calls her 'an eternal nymph'.

There are many texts independent of the mainstream
Arthurian tradition in which Morgan figures as a major
protagonist. These established her reputation as a woman of
enchantment into whose faery realms she guides the man whom
she desires as her own. *Alisander l'Orphelin*, *Ogier le Danois*, and
numerous other minor texts tell of Morgan's lovers and their
retention by her in faeryland. Each of these texts stresses
Morgan's independent faery character and none of them are
specifically concerned with the Arthurian world at all. Many of
them derive from Norman sources; Norman settlers in Calabria
brought parts of the Arthurian tradition with them, and it is by
this means that Morgan is transplanted into Sicilian and Italian
texts such as *Tavola Rotunda*, finally becoming the Fata Morgana
of *Orlando Furioso* and *Orlando Innamorato*.

The *Vulgate Cycle*, which forms the basis of Malory's story, gives
us a portrait of Morgan in the *Estoire de Merlin*:

> She was the sister of King Arthur, very gay and playful; she sang
> agreeably; though dark in the face, very well made, neither too

fat nor too thin, with beautiful hands, perfect shoulders, skin softer than silk, engaging of manner, long and straight in the body: altogether wonderfully seductive and, besides all that, the warmest and most sensual woman in all Britain. Merlin had taught her astronomy and many other things, and she studied them so well that she became an excellent scholar and was later called Morgan La Fée because of the marvels she wrought. She expressed herself with gentleness and delightful sweetness, and was more good-natured and attractive than anyone else in the world, when she was calm. But when her anger was roused against someone, she was very difficult to appease.[1]

In Robert de Boron's *Merlin*, she is called Morgue la Fée because she is learned in the seven liberal arts, especially astronomy and physic.

The incident of the theft of the scabbard, also related by Malory, appears first in *Suite du Merlin*. Here Merlin tells Arthur that the scabbard of Escalibor (Excalibur) is more precious than the sword, since it preserves the wearer from loss of blood. Arthur gives it to Morgan to preserve for him, but she makes a duplicate to give to her lover. He warns Arthur to beware, but Merlin, who loves Morgan, warns her and she accuses her lover of having stolen the scabbard, for which Arthur beheads him. From then onwards Morgan bears malice towards Arthur.

In *Lancelot*, 'Morgain' appears as an adversary to Guinevere because of Lancelot, whom she seeks to imprison in her otherworldly Valley of No Return. She created this valley, from which no knight false in love can return, because of a former lover of hers, Guinevere's cousin, from whom the queen separated Morgain. All who enter the valley have to undergo perilous adventures. Lancelot enters and, aided by the ring given him by the Lady of the Lake, destroys the place, rescuing the many knights imprisoned there. Morgain attempts to imprison Lancelot once again, decoying him to a tower by means of a maiden. While languishing there, he paints the Lady of the Lake and Guinevere – the two women of his life. Morgain keeps him imprisoned because she loves him and wants to change his affections from Guinevere to herself, but Lancelot finally escapes her clutches. Morgain appears here very much as a foil to the Lady of the Lake.

But the Morgan whom everyone knows is the character created by Malory. He drew her out of the earlier texts, notably the *Vulgate Cycle*, but changes her character considerably, subsuming her earlier goddessly stature in a welter of enchantment and sorcery. In the following breakdown of Morgan's appearances in Malory, we have given the textual references:

1. ii: 'And King Lot of Lothian and of Orkney then wedded Mawgawse that was Gawain's mother, and King Nentres of the land of Garlot wedded Elaine. All this was done at the request of King Uther. And the third sister Morgan le Fay was put to school in a nunnery, and there she learned so much that she was a great clerk of necromancy. And after she was wedded to King Uriens of the land of Gore, that was Sir Ewain le Blanchemains' father.'

4. vi – xvi: Morgan sends a black barge of 12 lake maidens to dine with Arthur, Uriens and Accolon. After the meal, Uriens wakes up in bed at home, Arthur wakes in a prison and Accolon wakes by a well-side with a fountain nearby. Morgan suborns him to take Excalibur, which she has stolen, to kill a knight for her. Arthur is brought to fight, with a replica of Excalibur. Accolon and Arthur fight and Arthur is wounded by Excalibur, his own sword breaking. The Lady of the Lake then causes Accolon to drop Excalibur so that Arthur can kill his opponent. Accolon confesses: 'Morgan le Fay sent it me yesterday . . . that I should slay King Arthur her brother . . . [for he] is the man in the world that she most hateth, because he is most of worship and of prowess than any of her blood.'

Thinking Arthur dead, Morgan goes to slay Uriens, but the maidservant warns Owain, who stops his mother. 'Men saith that Merlin was begotten of a devil but I may say an earthly devil bare me.' Morgan then steals Excalibur's scabbard while Arthur is sleeping in a nunnery and casts it into a lake.

However, she is pursued. 'Then she rode into a valley where many great stones were, and when she saw she must be overtaken, she shaped herself, horse and man, by enchantment unto a great marble stone.' She takes Manessen, Accolon's cousin, to be her lover.

Later Morgan sends a maiden bearing a richly-decorated mantle to Arthur. The Lady of the Lake warns Arthur not to wear it until he sees its effect. Arthur commands the bearer to put it on and she bursts into flames.

6. iii: While Lancelot lies sleeping, four queens come to him: Queen Morgan le Fay of Gore, the Queen of Eastland, the Queen of Northgalis and the Queen of the Out Isles. They fall to squabbling over Lancelot, and Morgan puts an enchanted sleep upon him so that he may be removed to her castle, the better to make his choice of them. Lancelot refuses them all, choosing death rather than the betrayal of Guinevere, his true love. He is helped to escape by a damsel.

9. xli: Tristan lodges at Morgan le Fay's castle and she gives him a shield of gold which shows a king and queen with a knight standing with either foot upon their heads. It signifies Arthur and Guinevere with Lancelot, but Tristan is not made aware of this. He bears the shield in a tournament where it is seen by Guinevere, who realizes its significance. Arthur is told the meaning by one of Morgan's women and is very angry.

10. xvii: Palomides and Dinadan come to Morgan's castle where the custom is that all Round Table knights must fight Morgan's champions. The castle, given to Morgan by Arthur, is impregnable.

10. xxxv - xxxviii: Mark hated Alisander l'Orphelin and charged 'Queen Morgan le Fay and ... the Queen of Norgalis, praying them in his letters that the two sorceresses would set all the country on fire with ladies that were enchantresses, and by such that were dangerous knights', so that Alisander should be captured. Morgan heals Alisander's wounds from a tournament, and gives him a sleeping potion.

On waking, she makes him swear never to leave the castle for a year, but Alisander escapes and marries Alice.

11. i: We learn that Morgan enchanted Elaine for five years, by locking her in a tower wherein she lay in scalding hot water. Lancelot rescues her.

21. v – vi: 'There received him three queens with great mourning; and so they set them down, and in one of their laps King Arthur laid his head. And then that queen said: "Ah, dear brother, why have ye tarried so long from me? Alas this wound on your head hath caught over-much cold." Arthur was led away in a ship wherein were three queens: that one was King Arthur's sister, Morgan le Fay; the other was the Queen of Northgalis; the third was the Queen of the Waste Lands. Also there was Nimuë, the chief lady of the lake.'

To this list of texts, we must also add the fictional retellings which further develop the myth of Morgan, Parke Godwin's *Firelord* and Marion Zimmer Bradley's *Mists of Avalon*, both of which make Morgan the mother of Mordred by Arthur. This recent fictional development is now so widespread throughout the reading world that few now credit Morgause with the motherhood of Mordred. As we can see from the texts above, this is not borne out anywhere else, though, as we will see below, there are plausible reasons why this addendum to the myth of Morgan may be upheld.

MORGAN, AVALONIAN LADY

Morgan is an ancient figure who maintains the magic of the Lake while simultaneously fulfilling her role as (half-)sister to Arthur. The role of Celtic Goddess has not translated well into medieval tradition where the position of women did not allow an autonomous and unmated figure like Morgan freedom to roam at will. The necessity for her energetic and inspiring presence meant that the respected Goddess figure had to be reframed as enchantress for her to have the requisite freedom.

That Morgan started life as a goddess is in little doubt. Even though Giraldus Cambrensis (Gerald of Wales) in his *Speculum Ecclesiae* ridicules the British for considering Morgan as *dea quaedam phantastica* (some kind of fantastic goddess), calling her 'a noble matron', a blood relative of Arthur's, who took him to Glastonbury for the healing of his wounds, Morgan does not appear as a member of Arthur's family until Chrétien's romances.

The etymology of Morgan's name has been much disputed by scholars. Some have instanced *Muir gena* (sea-born) as a possible derivation. But more likely is Morrighan – *Mor rigan*, 'Great Queen'. Morgan shares many attributes with this Irish goddess, as we shall see. The Welsh goddess Rhiannon similarly derives her name from the proto-Celtic title *Rigantona* or 'Great Queen.' Regan is a name of British tradition. Shakespeare called one of Lear's unrelenting daughters Regan: a suitable queenly name for one so carrion of her father's legacy. *Morgan* is always a male name in Welsh, but then Morgan was never one to follow the orthodoxies of accepted tradition. During her long reign, the Great Queen has borne and worn out many names.

Morgan is truly one of the paramount Ladies of the Lake. She rules the land of Avalon, which lies over an unnamed lake, on the margins of this world with the other. Let us look more closely at the *Vita Merlini*, where we find the following description of Avalon:

> The island of apples which men call 'the Fortunate Isle' gets its name . . . because it produces all things of itself; the fields there have no need of the ploughs of the farmers . . . Of its own accord it produces grain and grapes, and apple trees.
>
> There nine sisters rule by a pleasing set of laws those who come to them from our country. She who is first of them is more skilled in the healing art, and excels her sisters in the beauty of her person. Morgen is her name, and she has learned what useful properties all the herbs contain, so that she can cure sick bodies. She also knows an art by which to change her shape,

and to cleave the air on new wings like Daedalus; when she wishes she is at Brest, Chartres, or Pavia, and when she wills, she slips down from the air onto your shores. And men say that she has taught mathematics to her sisters, Moronoe, Mazoe, Gliten, Glitonea, Cliton, Tyronoe, Thitis, Thetis best known for her cither.

Thither after the battle of Camlan we took the wounded Arthur, guided by Barinthus to whom the waters and the stars of heaven were well known. With him steering the ship we arrived there with the prince, and Morgen received us with fitting honor, and in her chamber she placed the king on a golden bed and with her own hand she uncovered his honorable wound and gazed at it a long time. At length she said that health could be restored to him if he stayed with her for a long time and made use of her healing art.[2]

Morgan rules over an Island of Women like the one to which heroes sail on their *immrama* to the Blessed Isles. Geoffrey of Monmouth's *Vita Merlini* draws upon many established features of the Celtic sisterhood tradition, outlined on p.xxxi. The Fortunate Isle on which so many apples grow is an earthly paradise. The apple, which in Judaeo-Christian tradition is the fruit of the fall, is the fruit of restoration in Celtic tradition. The unnamed faery woman in the orchard who appears in many Arthurian romances is a remembrance of Morgen, the Avalonian lady.

As we saw in the Introduction, British tradition abounds in Ninefolds; they appear again in the sisterhood of the cauldron of Annwn, who breathe over the cauldron and cool it with their breath; or the ninefold sisterhood called 'the Nine Witches of Gloucester' who, as already noted, give Peredur, the Celtic Perceval, his weapon-training. While Classical tradition also has its ninefold sisterhood of the Muses, Celtic tradition has its nine sisters each of whom has a special quality or gift. In the case of the sisterhood of the Underworld cauldron which will not boil the food of a coward, they each bestow a gift of inspiration upon the food within. Geoffrey is annoyingly terse in his enumeration of the Avalonian sisterhood, but the main features of Morgan remain constant within later legend: her ability to heal, her shapeshifting, her great learning. Although she loses her ability to fly, her ubiquity throughout many of the texts is remarkable.

Morgan makes her first appearance in mainstream Arthurian tradition as Arthur's chief physician. This is apparently derived from the *Vita Merlini* where Morgen heals Arthur of his wounds in Avalon - a feature which is notably consistent, even in Malory's twisted picture of Morgan. After all her attempts to deprive Arthur of his kingship, she is finally concerned about the wound which afflicts him.

Healing comes from the waters of the Lake in many instances within Celtic tradition. One of the primary stories in Welsh tradition is the Lady of Llyn y Fan Fach, whose half-faery, half-human lineage is similarly comprised of healers, establishing the famous family, the Physicians of Myddfai. The Lady herself, as related in the previous chapter, vanishes back into the Lake after having been struck three times by her earthly husband, but she leaves her children and the legacy of her skill behind.[3]

Although Geoffrey of Monmouth gives us the first textual source for Morgan, her influence in Celtic tradition precedes his writing, for behind the figure of Morgan stretches a venerable Celtic lineage. As the Celtic and native understanding of Morgen broke down, she became the high queen enchantress of literary tale and reverted to Queen of Faery among the unlearned - Argante, the figure whom the Saxon writer Layamon made into the faery-godmother and receiver of Arthur. In this role, Morgan and the Lady of the Lake are fused into a single entity. We may say that the characteristic which differentiates her from the Lady of the Lake - her independence - derives from her mortal persona as Arthur's half-sister.

The German and Italian Arthurian romancers brought the myth of Morgan into contact with that of the Sibyl. Morgan, like Merlin, became the mouthpiece for assorted prophecies, both becoming incorporated into local stories as token Arthurian characters. The popularity of both Morgan and Merlin testifies to their otherworldly natures, which allows them to appear at will, under most shapes and guises.

Morgan becomes closely associated with the land over which she rules in German tradition. In *Parzival*, we hear that Parzival's uncle, Trevirizent, travelled in his youth to the land of Feimurgan (Morgan le Fay), guided there by a faery called Terdelaschoy (Land of Joy). This sounds as though Wolfram, the author, was ignorant or confused, having transposed the woman for the land and vice versa.

It is possible to see Morgan as Avalonian lady in the many Arthurian romances, although as Arthur's sister she has mostly thrown off her otherworldly entitlements, and other faery maidens exemplify this role of otherworldly guardian. The figure of the Apple Woman, for example, is clearly derived from Morgan: in the *Vita Merlini*, a companion of Merlin's youth appears to him, in a deranged state. Merlin recalls how they had both come upon some apples which his companion ate greedily, falling thereafter into madness. The poisoned apples were put there by a woman whom Merlin had spurned and were intended for him.[4] R.J. Stewart has identified this figure as the Apple Woman. We will immediately note from Chapter 2 that Guinevere herself is falsely accused of poisoning apples in order to kill a knight of the Round Table. But how does this archetype of Apple Woman relate to Morgan?

Many times in Arthurian legend the Apple Woman appears as the mistress of an orchard or enchanted enclosure to which it is difficult to gain entry and from which no man may return. In *Gereint and Enid* from *The Mabinogion*, she rules over the Enchanted Games from her tent, on which hangs the horn of joy. Her champion repels all comers and sets their heads on the fence surrounding the orchard.

Meanwhile in *Peredur*, also from *The Mabinogion*, the young untried Peredur meets three knights of who are on quest for 'the knight who distributed the apples in Arthur's court' - they are Gwalchmai (Gawain), Gwair and Owain.[5] We have no further details of this incident, but can only speculate that the knight of the apples is indeed an otherworldly messenger, bringing faery apples to stimulate the otherworldly journey or quest in much the same way that faery women bring the silver branch to initiate a quest to the Blessed Isles.

Apples bring health, in our symbology, but they are paradisal fruit belonging to the Lady of Avalon: any who have eaten them die to the 'real world' and become travellers in Faery. Thus Merlin's companion runs mad after eating one; the subject of the Scottish ballad, 'Thomas the Rhymer', is exhorted by the Faery Queen not to eat of the tempting apples because they contain all the ills of the Underworld; Sir Patrise falls dead of a poisoned apple so that Guinevere is blamed and likely to be burnt. The apple which heals may also hurt. What is the meaning of this dichotomy?

MORGAN, RAVEN QUEEN

In Western society we have grown used to perceiving archetypes as 'good' or 'bad', so that when we come across a divergently polarized manifestation by the same archetype, we grow confused. This is due to the dualistic philosophy of the West, which has a tendency to polarize everything in this way. Before we read on we should contemplate the manifestations of many native and Eastern deities who may have both compassionate and wrathful appearances. Neither quality negates the other, for the wrathful face of a goddess like Kali may warn and admonish us for our own good, while the compassionate face of Tara may give us healing and encouragement.

Morgan has the power to heal or harm; she seeks lovers only to destroy them; she has an island paradise to which few come, but she does not let visitors out again. Such features continually recur in her mythos and it seems difficult to reconcile them. Celtic tradition supplies the answer in Morgan's prototype, Morrighan, from whom Morgan inherits her role as raven queen.

The Morrighan and her sisters, Badbh and Macha, collectively known as the Morrigna, are a triplicity of Irish goddesses who represent the important functions of victory, battle and prophecy. They were the daughters of Ernmas (Death by Iron), and frequently appear at battlefields in the shape of crows. With the triple Brighid, responsible for healing, poetry and smithcraft, and the major goddesses of Sovereignty, Eriu, Fodla and Banba, the Morrigna form a ninefold sisterhood of goddesses within Irish tradition. The character of the Morrighan is more distinct than either of her sisters, and she herself appears more often in an independent way.

Although the Morrighan is more often identified as a battle goddess, she actually spends an equal amount of time in the pursuit of a suitable mate to be her champion. Her association with the Tuatha de Danaan, whom she enables to win the Second Battle of Mag Tuiread, begins with her union with the Dagda. The Dagda is a titanic Irish deity rather like the British Bran the Blessed. He is the father of the Tuatha de Danaan, a god of great knowledge who possesses a cauldron. The Morrighan met the Dagda on Samhain Eve at the River Unius in Corann, County Sligo. He had just finished eating a mess of porridge from his cauldron, while she was washing herself, one foot upon the south, the other on the north bank. Their conjoining took place over the river, which was thereafter called 'the Bed of the Couple'.

This union at a fording place is very significant for it occurs in other texts related to Morgan. The ritual unions of Celtic and Arthurian tradition are always significant in that they happen in the realms between the Otherworld and Middle Earth, at cross-roads, fords, at the times when the festival of Samhain or Beltane are in force, or when strong magic is in the air. The following examples may be instanced:

Woman	Man	Place/Circumstance of their Union
Morrighan	Dagda	at a ford at Samhain
Modron	Uriens	at a ford, as fulfilment of a quest
Rhiannon	Pwyll	at a magical hill of vision
Igraine	Uther	as a result of shapeshifting, during a battle
Elaine	Lancelot	as a result of an enchanted drink
Ragnell	Gawain	as fulfilment of a quest

Morgan's partnership with Urien of Rheged is one which is well established in British tradition, though within the mainstream Arthurian tradition it is not until 'The Huth Merlin' that Morgan is formally given in marriage to Urien, King of Garlot, whom Malory calls Urien of Gore. Yet Morgan has an earlier association with him which is very significant. The following story was recorded in North Wales in the seventeenth century:

> In Denbighshire there is a parish which is called Llanferres, and is a Rhyd y Gyfartha (Ford of Barking). In the old days the hounds of the countryside used to come together to the side of that ford to bark and nobody dared to go to find out what was there until Urien Rheged came. And when he came to the side of the ford he saw nothing there except a woman washing. And then the hounds ceased barking, and Urien seized the woman and had his will of her: and then she said, 'God's blessing on the feet which brought thee here.' 'Why?' 'Because I have been fated to wash here until I should conceive a son by a Christian. And I am the daughter to the King of Annwn, and come thou here at the end of the year and then thou shalt receive the boy.' And so he came and he received there a boy and a girl: this is Owain, son of Urien, and Morfydd, daughter of Urien.[6]

This story may seem to have little bearing on Morgan, but let us follow the story carefully. Urien comes to the Ford of Barking to investigate this place of dread. Baying hounds are frequently associated with the Dark Goddess, being a strong feature of the Greek goddess Hecate's symbolism, she who similarly haunts crossing places. He finds no dogs, but a woman, with whom he sleeps, as though by prearranged custom, since she does not cry rape, but rather welcomes him with a ritual blessing. She is none other than the daughter of the King of the Underworld, and she brings forth twins.

The story by itself may yield us nothing until we consider the evidence of the *Triads* which tell us more of the parentage of Owain ap Urien: 'Owain Son of Urien and Morfudd his sister, who were carried together in the womb of Modron, ferch Afallach.'[7] So we have a name, or rather a title, for the mysterious woman at the ford, who seems to have changed her father: no longer daughter of the King of Annwn, but of the King of Avalon. Modron, whose name means 'mother' is the British goddess who gives birth to Mabon, the Divine Celtic Youth. As as been proved in *Mabon and the Mysteries of Britain*, the title of Mabon has been accorded to many Celtic heroes. What concerns us here is the identity of the mother.

The *Gesta Regnum Britanniae* (c.1235) kindly provides us with an answer, for it tells us that Morgan's father is none other than *Rex Avallonis*, the King of Avalon. But what does this imply?

The Morgan of later Arthurian tradition is indeed the mother of Owain, by Urien. Following the evidence above, we see that Morgan is cognate with Modron and that she undergoes a ritual union at a fording place. There are many scholars doubtful of Morgan's associations with the British goddess Modron, but we believe that the evidence leads us inexorably to one conclusion: that Morgan undergoes the initiatory ritual of the Blessing of the Mothers, coming purposely from her otherworldly fastness to mate with a mortal man. In the oral Llanferres story, Modron addresses Urien with 'God's blessing on the feet which brought thee here.' This salutation is the first part of the fivefold greeting which is still used in the Old Religion, and which is of great antiquity.[8] This fivefold salutation calls blessings upon the feet, knees, genitals, breast and mouth. Anyone armed with such a blessing receives the benefits of the Otherworld.

The mortal man who encounters the Great Mother, Modron, at the ford comes bringing the gift of generation, the mixed gift of mortality. Modron brings the gifts of sovereignty, like many another woman who stands at a ford, spring or well guarding the primal waters (see Chapter 9). Only by a mixture of the immortal and the mortal can a blessed being come into incarnation and complete the cycle of sovereignty. In the case of Arthur, it is Igraine and the shapeshifted Uther who meet. The union of Morgan/Modron and Urien produces Owain, a figure whose importance wanes in later tradition, though his half-immortal nature shines through.

We are unused to thinking of Morgan as any kind of mother-figure, so fixed has the enchantress persona become. Later tradition has nothing to say of her relationship with her son, Sir Yvain or Uwain, as Owain becomes in the French romances. Yet the French remembered the fact that Morgan was one of the *Bendith y Mamau* (Blessing of the Mothers), as the Welsh call the faerykind. The Bretons likewise remember her as a midwife and faery-godmother as Margot and Morgan,[9] while the French non-Arthurian romance *Huon de Bordeaux* makes Morgain the mother of Auberon, whose horn Auberon used to heal the sick.[10]

Owain inherits his mother's otherworldly nature and attributes to some extent. He acquires a troop of otherworldly warriors called 'ravens', who actually fly in his defence in *The Dream of Rhonabwy*, where he plays a game of *gwyddbwyll* (a board game similar to chess) against Arthur, possibly in an attempt to win the land.[11] In *The Lady of the Fountain*, Owain enters the Celtic Otherworld and becomes the consort and champion of the Lady of the Fountain. In *Gereint and Enid* (and its alternative text, *Erec and Enide*), he is the Lord of Brandigan or Raven Castle, where he is master of the Enchanted Games. Within a magical enclosure is a faery champion who has overcome all challengers, whose heads are displayed upon stakes around it. Gereint/Erec overcomes this champion (see Chapter 6).

From these stories we may deduce that Owain was indeed the son of Morgan, an otherworldly woman, and Urien, Lord of Rheged, and that he combines both mortal and faery natures, winning a faery-woman for his wife and becoming the master of his own otherworldly castle where only the best knight can overcome his champion. His raven-troops are famous in British tradition, accompanying him victoriously wherever he goes.

If we turn to the *Didot Perceval*, we will find further confirmation of these connections. Here Perceval encounters a knight called Urban of the Black Pine whom he fights at a ford and overcomes. Urban had previously been a Round Table knight, but had followed a maiden on a mule, whom he could not overtake, and fallen in love with her. He promised to hold the ford for her for a year and then hoped to win her love. Perceval does not wish to hold the ford himself - the privilege of overcoming Urban. As he says so, a mysterious voice cries out: 'Accursed may you be by whatever we women can contrive, for you have caused us the greatest sorrow.'[12] Hundreds of black birds begin to attack Perceval and he wounds one. It falls to the ground and becomes a woman. Urban explains, 'The voice that you heard was she who called to me, and when she saw that I could not escape from you she changed herself and her damsels into the semblance of birds and they came here to oppress you . . . This one whom you wounded, she was the sister of my lady, but she will suffer no harm, for within the moment she is in Avalon.'[13]

Urban of the Black Pine is none other than Urien, the husband of Morgan. This episode is perhaps one of the clearest instances of Celtic shapeshifting in the whole of medieval literature, showing that one of the major personas of Morgan is indeed the raven or crow. Again, this story focuses upon the defence of a ford - the very place where Morgan and Urien consummate their relationship in the oral Welsh story. We see here the Morgen of Geoffrey's *Vita Merlini*, the Goddess who can fly where she wills.

The raven, crow or rook is a scavenger and predator. It will prey on smaller animals and will eat carrion, helping to keep infection and the evidence of unsightly death at bay. This is also one of Morgan's functions, her heritage from Morrighan. This role of the Goddess is very much overlooked, for she reprocesses all that is outworn or dying, transforming it by her subtle alchemy into something fresh. As the Great Raven, Morgan is the ultimate scavenger of the battlefield taking Arthur to Avalon with as much zeal as the Valkyries bore away the courageous combatants to Valhalla.

And what is the shape of Arthur in Middle Earth, while he dwells in Avalon? Tradition says it is as a chough, that relative of the crow family distinguished by its red legs and beak, that Arthur survives still. The sixteenth-century Spanish poet Cervantes was aware of this, for he mentions it in his *Don*

Quixote. The laws of the Welsh King Hywel Dda (d.950) forbade the killing of crows - generally fair-game elsewhere - and these laws were remembered as late as the eighteenth century when a Welshman reproached a hunter for killing a raven at Marazion Green, since it might have been King Arthur.[14]

So Arthur stands in the tradition of the great god Bran the Blessed, whose name means 'raven'. In *Bran, Son of Llyr*, after the battle in Ireland to reclaim his sister Branwen from a loveless marriage, Bran is mortally wounded. He commands that his head be cut off and borne to the White Mount (the Tower of London), there to act as a palladium for Britain. Like Arthur, Bran does not die, but his head continues to speak and entertains his followers in a timeless otherworldly retreat for 87 years. Unfortunately, a forbidden door is opened and the men then take their lord's head to London to inter it. That site remains associated with ravens: legend tells that if the ravens leave the Tower of London, then Britain will fall to invasion. The *Triads* also relate how Arthur dug up Bran's head in a fit of hubris, wanting no other protection for Britain other than his own. Well, it is all one now. Arthur, like Bran, remains in his otherworldly fastness. Morgan comes at the last battle to bring Arthur from Camlan to Avalon: the Queen Raven taking her lawful mate, the King Raven, into otherworldly seclusion and healing.

The *Gesta Regnum Britanniae* (c.1235) confirms Arthur's true relationship with Morgan in Avalon: 'Wounded beyond measure, Arthur took the way to the court of the King of Avalon, where the royal virgin, tending his wound, keeps his healed body for her very own and they live together.'[15] The modern fictional retellings which make Morgan the secret mate of Arthur unerringly follow this Avalonian tradition.

The many lovers of Morgan can be viewed as her champions. Like the Apple Woman in the tent, or like the Lady of the Fountain, she needs a guardian to keep her secret place safely. Anyone who can overcome the champion is therefore more worthy than the current guardian and so acceptable to her. This shows the inhuman and goddessly mores of Morgan, whose criteria for love are based upon fitness by combat. But the tests of Morgan are various, not solely reserved for her lovers and champions. Let us turn to these now.

THE TESTS OF MORGAN

Despite the wealth of the earlier Arthurian tradition with its deep roots in Celtic antiquity, it is the Morgan of later tradition who is best known. We may be forgiven for not recognizing the earlier figure, lost as she is in the toils of a stock enchantress who might better furnish a Walt Disney cartoon than grace a medieval epic. The shadow of Morgan in Arthurian literature is longer that the figure who casts it. She represents a potentiality that is feared: sexuality, intrigue and enchantment are the features which have given her her power. Her medieval motivation is only as a sorceress, because Malory has demoted her from Goddess to mortal woman.

One of the first transformations of Morgan is into the sister of Arthur. As we have seen, the tradition was firm in the association of Arthur with Morgan, but only in Avalon; it is subsequent romances that have rationalized Morgan into the kinswoman of Arthur.

Morgan has also been confused with Morgause, the daughter of Igraine and Uther. The daughter called either Anna or Gwyar (pronounced 'Gwire') becomes Morgause, and as she traditionally marries Lot or Lleu of Lothian she is therefore identifiable with the Morgause of later tradition. Has the old Celtic name Gwyar (meaning 'shed-blood') acquired another Celtic prefix as Mor-Gwyar or Morgause?

The incorporation of a goddess into Arthur's family presents certain problems. Deities adhere to cosmic principles rather than parochial concerns. When she is stripped of her original identity, there is no human rationale or motivation for the deeds of Morgan. She becomes a bitter, hating woman, determined to stop Arthur at all turns. As a result, she has acquired a horrid fascination for her writers. In Malory, the implacable hatred of

Morgan for Arthur and his court is worked up to furious heights. Morgan is the younger daughter of Igraine and Gorlois, put out to a nunnery and then requisitioned for marriage to one of Uther's vassal kings. Her attempt to kill off first Arthur, and then Uriens, her husband, shows that she wishes to assume power herself, and her various bids for power always involve the acquisition of dangerous knights who subsequently become her lovers and champions.

In order to understand the underpinning of her nature, however, it is necessary to go back into Celtic tradition. It is clear that one of Morgan's primary roles is that of challenger, a role which she acquired from the Irish goddess Morrighan.

Morgan first shows animosity towards Arthur in the prose *Tristan*. In this text, Arthur banished her for her great disloyalty and would have killed her, except that she possessed many secret retreats in Logres and was able to make herself invisible.[16] This accords interestingly with the Morrighan. She has a similar implacable hatred of Cuchulainn, the Irish hero, who spurns her love. We have seen how Malory's Morgan desires to be served by strong knights. It is so, too, in the Irish tradition.

Although the Morrighan is usually associated with her sisters Badbh and Macha as the Valkyries of Celtic tradition, the scavengers of the slain, she has other appearances for, like Morgan, she is a shapeshifter. She has many partners, including the Dagda, and is concerned with strife and its resolution, with the combats of love and war equally placed in her sights.

In the *Cattle Raid of Regamna*, Cuchulainn is awoken by a terrible noise coming from the North. He goes to find out what causes it and there finds a red woman standing in a chariot whose shaft goes through the middle of a cow's breast. She is the Badbh aspect of the Morrighan in the form of a prophetic satirist. She refuses to give her name to Cuchulainn, but promises to protect him from death. However, she also says that he will remain living only until the calf in the belly of the cow she leads reaches a year's life. She promises to return and challenge him as a black eel, a grey wolf and a white heifer.

In the *Cattle Raid of Cooley*, Cuchulainn is approached by a

beautiful woman in a garment of many colours. She says she is
King Buan's daughter and that she has brought her treasures and
cattle to him because she loves him. He refuses her, being in
the middle of the struggle for the Ulster, so she promises to
hinder him in the shape of a black eel, a grey wolf and a red
heifer. He successfully evades her attack and wounds her three
times. Later he is tricked into healing her, for she appears in the
guise of an old blind woman with a squint and a bad leg. He
blesses her three times in the names of the gods and the non-
gods (i.e. the people) and she is healed.

As the Morrighan seeks the love of Cuchulainn and he will
not accord her this, she is forever his aggressor. This pattern is
established in the myth of many goddesses, notably the Sumerian
Innana who has a similar relationship with the hero Gilgamesh
who refuses her love and has to undergo her tests instead. The
lovers of Morgan, too, are clearly important to her tradition.
While in Avalon, she must always have a partner, it seems.

As Arthur, according to later tradition, is related to Morgan as
half-brother and so cannot be her lover, his only alternative is that
of challenger. Modern fictional tradition, however, has not been
slow to accord a physical relationship between Arthur and
Morgan, so that the Morgan myth is in yet another process of
transformation. If we place this in the context of Celtic tradition,
it makes sense and is in fact true to the early Arthurian tradition
which makes Arthur the partner of Morgan in the Otherworld
paradise of Avalon where they rule as king and queen.

Morgan's antagonism to Guinevere is not surprising. There is
an essential tension between them even in the earlier texts
which is explicable by means of their mythic roles: if Guinevere
is the May Queen, mortal representative of the Otherworld, then
Morgan is the Faery Queen in person. Because they are brought
into antagonistic polarization in the later texts, Guinevere takes
the role of Flower Bride in May to Morgan's Lady of the Wheel
at Samhain. The Morrighan appears first to Cuchulainn in the
form of a Flower Bride, offering him magical cattle and treasure,
but when he rejects her she reverts to the role of Lady of the
Wheel.

Within the later texts, Morgan comes to test Guinevere, bringing her a mantle and a horn, as we have seen in the last chapter. Both objects have their foundation in the Hallows of Britain: they are the ancient objects of sovereignty, possessing otherworldly qualities. Their modern correlatives are seen in the Coronation regalia with which the sovereign is invested; the objects themselves are not used for mundane purposes, but are highly symbolic of inner powers. The mantle is itself emblematic of the land itself, spread about the sovereign's shoulders, while the cup or horn signifies plenty. In both tests, the Hallows are used to test Guinevere's suitability for queenship. This attempt to oust Guinevere suggests that Morgan is desirous of that place for herself, although Malory and others show her working on behalf of her nephew, Mordred. But this is to put a twentieth-century interpretation upon mythological motivation.

The testing cups and cauldrons of Celtic tradition are too numerous to mention here. The prime example of a testing cup is that of Manannan's which in *Echtra Cormaic* has a remarkable property: when three lies are said over it, it shatters, but when three truths are said over it, it reunites.[17] The Grail itself is a test which has to be accomplished. In both these and other cup or cauldron tests/quests, the winner of the test is always the most worthy knight or lady. Only the best can attain to sovereign status.

Morgan comes to test Arthur, Guinevere, Gawain, Lancelot and others. She must have a man in her power, even if it is one under enchantment, as happens in *Gawain and the Green Knight*. This story revolves around the ancient beheading game of Celtic tradition, and is instigated by Morgan, although she appears seldom in the story. Despite this, her pervasive ubiquity speaks of a plan well laid. The beheading game also happens in the story of Cuchulainn, where he is challenged by a mighty giant. The Green Knight of medieval tradition comes into the hall at the Christmas feasting and challenges any knight to behead him, in return for which, he shall behead the knight a year hence. Gawain accepts the challenge to prevent Arthur venturing his own royal person. He chops off the head, but the Green Knight rises and bids him meet him at the Green Chapel next year.

As the year turns, so Gawain sets out, to great lamentation. He finds his way to the castle of Sir Bertilak, a jovial host, who promises to show him the way to Green Chapel when the time is ripe. He meets the beautiful Lady Bertilak, and wonders at her companion. This mysterious woman is none other than Morgan. She appears as a hag, in the guise of Lady Bertilak's duenna or granddam, and is described as swarthy, bony and as ugly as either Kundry or Ragnell (see Chapters 7 and 9). We are left in no doubt that this unnamed hag is significant in some way, because 'Highest in place of honour, the ancient crone sat.'[18]

During his stay, Gawain is visited thrice by Lady Bertilak in his bedroom, where she persuades him to give her a kiss. On the last occasion, she gives him a green baldric or belt which will magically protect him in his coming encounter. Gawain is at last directed to the Pagan howe of the Green Chapel where he finds the Green Knight whetting his axe. Here he kneels while the Green Knight makes three strokes to cut off his head. Only on the last stroke is Gawain's neck slightly nicked by the blade. The Green Knight forbore the first two strokes because Gawain had accepted only a kiss from Lady Bertilak. The cut was because he had accepted her magical protection. Then the Green Knight proclaims his real identity as Sir Bertilak, Gawain's host:

> I was entirely transformed and made terrible of hue
> Through the might of Morgan the Fay, who remains in my house.
> Through the wiles of her witchcraft, a lore well learned,
> Many of the magical arts of Merlin has she acquired,
> For once she lavished her love delightfully
> On that susceptible sage . . .
> So 'Morgan the goddess'
> She accordingly became.[19]

He tells how Morgan planned this enchantment in order to test the calibre of the Round Table and to frighten Guinevere to death.

This complex and significant story weaves many Pagan elements into its Christian chivalric tapestry. Morgan is called a goddess and appears disguised as a hag. Her myth is also pied with that of Nimuë (see Chapter 5), in that she is said to be the lover of Merlin. The gauntlet thrown down by Morgan's enchantment is taken up by Gawain, who champions Arthur, Guinevere and the Round Table. The green baldric becomes a triumphant device, not a badge of shame, when the whole court takes to 'the wearing of the green' thus singularly upholding the colour of faery in the realms of Middle Earth.

Morgan and Lady Bertilak appear in the roles of the Lady of the Wheel and the Flower Bride: Morgan, the severe and testing magical hag; Lady Bertilak, the beautiful and inviting mistress. The story takes place at midwinter, the period between Samhain and Imbolc which the Cailleach traditionally governs and where Morgan can play by her own rules. We note that the chastity tests of Morgan are also part of this story: Lady Bertilak plays the part of temptress in Morgan's plan, while Gawain single-mindedly holds to his quest, refusing to be sidetracked into bed. He emerges vindicated at the return match of the beheading game, for both he and the Round Table have passed the test of Morgan, Lady of the Wheel.

One of the prime tasks of the ninefold sisters is to arm people for combat, and Gawain already approaches his quest well-armed, for he has the five-pointed star or pentacle on one side of his shield - one of the prime signs of the Goddess - while on the other side is an icon of the Virgin. The pentacle equips Gawain with a fivefold blessing similar to that perhaps received by Urien (see p.69), a blessing that enhances his natural virtues. He is empowered to wear the green baldric with pride as a token of faery protection or a kind of Morganian aegis. Like the aegis of Athene which depicted the Gorgon Medusa's head and which was reproduced on Classical breastplates, the sign of the Cailleach wards off evil and protects the wearer. The Hag can have no further fears for Gawain, who conquers the illusions of Morgan. This ability to see through illusion is very important for everyone, and it is one of Morgan's acid tests. Those who succumb to enchantment are not strengthened by her testing, and Morgan is only interested in graduating master-class pupils. Those whom she graduates, she keeps, as she does Arthur, reserving him for him the accolade of her perpetual presence in the realms of Avalon.

Like the Morrighan who proclaims the victory after the Second Battle of Mag Tuiread, Morgan is one who must seek out and acknowledge that which is best. She patrols the boundaries between the worlds, a Goddess careful of the sacred Hallows of the land, bringing them out of their otherworldly hiding places to test those who purport to administer the sovereignty of the land. In many ways, Morgan is the healer of the land of Britain, a guardian and challenger who will not let anything pass her strict vigilance. As raven-queen, she will scavenge that which would pollute the land. As healer, she knows how to restore and recreate that which is wounded.

Morgan starts life as a shapeshifting goddess and ends by having her shape shifted by the Arthurian romancers. Her blackening takes place gradually and is the result of a series of romancers who reframed the myth to suit their own purposes. Like a major character in a soap opera who cannot be entirely dispensed with, Morgan is given many different treatments which render her less and less sympathetic. Instead of being the healing sister, she becomes the skeleton in Arthur's family cupboard. Like the Gnostic Sophia, she has suffered a mighty fall from goddesshood to enchantress and finally into bitter woman. Surely it is time for her to resume her wings and fly where she wills? Just as Merlin survives in the otherworldly retreat of his Esplumoir, so the real Morgan remains in her secret, inviolate realm of Avalon.

With the Raven's Flight
&

You stand on a pathway which leads to the top of a hill. It
winds above you, climbing ever higher. The day is chill and
blustery with great wheeling clouds overhead. Rags and
tatters of leaves are whipped up the wind. As you come to
the top of hill, you are able to look down on the land
below. On the horizon opposite are other, distant hills, and
below you, in the valley, is the serpentine curve of a river.
The land has a bleak, attenuated look that shows it is
preparing for winter. Beside you on the hill is a stunted
thorn tree, bent against the prevailing wind. As you look
over the land below, a raven suddenly alights upon it with a
whirr of wings. It is a great black bird with predatory beak
and a knowing eye. It utters several intelligent cries and
folds its wings, looking towards you as to a companion in a
way that is unnerving.

Suddenly the raven blurs before your eyes, its shape
changing and lengthening. The process is quickly over and
in the raven's place stands a maiden dressed in black leather
garments. They look like body-armour, and there is a shiny
black cloak about her shoulders, its sheen like the
iridescence of the raven's wing. She has a close-fitting
helmet sewn with feathers over her long red hair. She smiles
a long smile at your bewilderment.

'I give you greeting, walker of the ways. Do you dare fly
with the raven-sisters and help protect this land? Look below
and see the need . . .'

She gestures with one narrow hand to the land before you.
As you look again, you see your own land spread out
beneath you. You see its coastlines, rivers, mountains and
settlements. You are seeing it as it now, today. To your sight,
the areas of pollution appear as dark blotches on the land.
Other problems and blockages are also clear to your vision.
But besides these there are also beacons of light, where
individuals and groups are maintaining the watch on the
land and working as responsible guardians . . .

The raven-woman asks, 'Where is the need greatest in this
land?' You look down and decide which problem can be
addressed at this time . . . You indicate what situation you
would like to remedy to the raven-woman.

'Are you then willing to fly with me to fight in its defence?'

You answer her . . .

If you are indeed willing, she touches your breast and utters
a raven-like cry. Suddenly you are shapeshifting into a raven
yourself. Together you take wing and fly down to the land
below.

As you fly, your very wings can feel the Earth's magnetic
field and sense the imbalances in the land beneath you.
Whatever the need you have come to address, it is now
clearly visible to you in an actual or symbolic way. You may,
for example, see an area of pollution that needs cleansing.
Your winged companion utters a cry that brings many
ravens to the place and together you pluck out the
pollutants and bear them away. It may be that you have
come to address an attitude or social evil. In the same way,
your raven companions will come down and bear away
whatever obstructs the clear passage of healing energy. You
see some ravens hovering protectively over the weak, while
others come to the shoulders of people who are disposed to
act but are disempowered or else despairing, to encourage
them into more skilful ways of living.

It is exhausting work and there is much waste matter and
many outworn ideologies to bear away. Your raven-sister bids
you turn from your task and follow her. Soon you are flying
high and swiftly towards the West. The great sea turns
beneath you and beyond the setting sun you see an island.
The ravens wheel and fly down, and you follow them,
burdened like them, with the work of your scavenging.

Unlike the world you have just come from, the island is
peaceful and fertile. As you fly down, you see a volcanic
mountain, its cone thrust up over the island. Into the
depths of this cone you cast down the waste, the pollution,
the outworn attitudes. As they fall into the deep, fiery
darkness below, you feel a lightening of your wings and a
gladness of heart.

The company of ravens alights upon a mound, and one by
one, they become women once more, attired in the same
black garments as your companion, who touches you once
again to transform you into your own shape once more.
Each of you feels tired and dirty. At the foot of the mound

winds a silver spring of great clarity. You each cast off your
garments and splash into the water with gratitude. These
waters have healing qualities and refresh your tired limbs.

In the mound is an ancient stone doorway and the raven-
women bear you within. Here is a rail of many beautiful
garments, into which they now change. You may chose one
for yourself . . .

Then your companion bids you follow her. You pass out of
the mound and are led into the centre of the island where
orchards of apples grow. Buds, blossom and fruit grow
together on one bough for this is the Summerland where all
seasons become one. Seated in the centre of the orchard is
the queen of this realm. She sits upon a throne and is
dressed like your companions, except that upon her head is
a circlet of crystal. About her shoulders is a cloak of
feathers of all hues and in her hand a wand of power, made
of silver upon which hang many bells.

The raven-sisters incline their heads in reverence towards
her and you are presented by your companion: 'Queen and
sister, behold one from the realms of Middle Earth who has
done great service this day.'

The queen takes your hand in hers. 'Walker of the pathways
of my land, I give you thanks. I am Morgan, the Royal
Virgin of Avalon, Keeper of the Land, Guardian of the Deep
Laws, Render in Pieces. On the wings of the wind, my
sisters and I do fly. We welcome all who maintain the
guardianship of the land.'

The eyes of Morgan are deep and intense, her presence
watchful and intent. Her power is so strong that you are
forced to lower your eyes. Yet you know that her purpose is
faithful to the laws of nature and you wonder what will
become of the fruits of your scavenging.

She speaks again: 'All that you have gathered and disposed
of within the depths of the mountain will be reprocessed. In
the cauldron of the dark, all will be remade and come
again. See . . .'

She shows you the basket at her feet which is filled with
clear white crystals. 'Each of these crystals comes from the
dark matter which is cast into the cauldron of remaking. My

sisters and I bear these to the sea and cast them onto the waters that they may once more become part of the living Earth. Take one now in token of your help. Let it be to you a reminder that all things may change and be renewed.' You take a crystal.

She looks within you, searching your heart. 'To strengthen you in your guardianship of the land, you may pluck one of my apples. They have the special property that they will never decay or be lessened. Whoever eats of this will not die but change from shape to shape.' You take one of the apples of Avalon for your own.

Morgan speaks again: 'The work of healing is challenging and needs resolve.' She plucks a raven's feather from her mantle and gives it to you. 'Know that I and my sisters fight by your side in the battle of life. With this feather you may fly in raven-shape and be companioned. As long as there is one being to fight for the laws of nature, then we will be there. When the ravens leave this shore, then you may know that the protection of Morgan no longer covers the land. Now I bid you return to your own time and place, in your own place.'

She taps you with her wand, and you fade from Avalon and return to the place where you now sit. But you have the three gifts to help you maintain the guardianship of the land. The black raven's feather will aid you in the battle, the red apple will give you strength and the power to shapeshift, the white crystal will be your talisman and touchstone when all around you seems hopeless. For even the darkest danger may be transformed by the skilful walker of the path.

REFERENCES

1. Jean Markale, *Women of the Celts*.
2. Geoffrey of Monmouth, *Vita Merlini*, ed. and trans. J.J. Parry.
3. John Rhys, *Celtic Folklore*.
4. D. Parry-Jones, *Welsh Legends and Fairy Lore*.

5. Caitlín Matthews, *Arthur and the Sovereignty of Britain*.
6. *Trioedd Ynys Prydein*, trans. Rachel Bromwich.
7. Ibid.
8. Caitlín Matthews, 'Mabon, the Celtic Divine Child', in *Merlin and Woman*, ed. R.J. Stewart.
9. R.S. Loomis, 'Morgue la Fée in Oral Tradition', *Romania*.
10. R.S. Loomis, *Celtic Myth and Arthurian Romance*.
11. Caitlín Matthews, *Arthur and the Sovereignty of Britain*, op. cit.
12. D. Skeels, *Romance of Perceval in Prose (Didot Perceval)*.
13. Ibid.
14. Alexander H. Krappe, 'Arturus Cosmocrator', *Speculum*.
15. Caitlín Matthews, *Mabon and the Mysteries of Britain: An Exploration of 'The Mabinogion'*.
16. Fanni Bogdanow, 'Morgain's Role in the Thirteenth-Century French Prose Romances of the Arthurian Cycle', *Medium Aevum*.
17. T.P. Cross and C.H. Slover, *Ancient Irish Tales*.
18. *Sir Gawain and the Green Knight*, trans. Brian Stone.
19. Ibid.

TWO

&

The Otherworld

THE SOVEREIGN SISTERHOOD

We pass now into the heartland of the Lake itself. These realms lie contiguous to the court and to the Lands Adventurous, sometimes overlapping them. We know little about the Otherworld from our personal experience, for we visit it only in dreams and visions. Nevertheless, it is the magical analogue of the everyday world which we inhabit.

The Otherworld is a dangerous place to remain because here mortals become convinced of 'their' powers, mistaking otherworldly and divine attributes and forgetting their own essentially human mortality and vulnerability. The call of the Otherworld is strong for many at present, but we must learn the ways of skilful travelling and retain the balance of humility. The Lake and the deer-haunted forests are places where the spirit is refreshed and renewed. The ones who have been there have eyes which turn inwards to remembered scenes of bliss which feed and nourish.

The women who enter the Otherworld do so purposefully, with the intention of becoming empowered. It is a not a place to remain in seclusion from the world for those of mortal stock, but a place which is visited in due season. Those who learn its wisdom must necessarily come forth again to teach others. This is why the Otherworld is the place of the Sovereign Sisterhood - the Lady of the Lake, Nimuë and Enid.

4

Argante

And near him stood the Lady of the Lake,
Who knows a subtler magic than his own -
Clothed in white samite, mystic, wonderful.
She gave the King his huge cross-hilted sword,
Whereby to drive the heathen out: a mist
Of incense curl'd about her, and her face
Well nigh was hidden in the minster gloom;
But there was heard among the holy hymns
A voice as of the waters, for she dwells
Down in a deep; calm, whatsoever storms
May shake the world, and when the surface rolls,
Hath power to walk the waters like our Lord.

Alfred Lord Tennyson, *The Coming of Arthur*,
II, 282 - 93

THE MYTH OF THE LADY OF THE LAKE

This extraordinary quotation from Tennyson puts the Lady of
the Lake on a par with Christ and makes her an agent of Arthur's
Christianizing process. This Victorian viewpoint is not, however,
borne out in Arthurian tradition, although Tennyson's confusion
stems from a native reverence for the spiritual influence of the
Lady of Waters. In the medieval texts, as in earlier, Celtic
tradition, the Lady of the Lake stands on the other side of the
door of the Otherworld, and rarely, if ever, penetrates into
Middle Earth. However, the fact that she operates from the
inside of things, from the Otherworld, does not mean to say that
she is ineffective or disempowered, just that hers is another kind
of influence, one which strikes deeper into the consciousness
of the mortal world because it derives from the world of Faery.

Thus, one of the Lady of the Lake's primary roles is that of foster-mother, as we discover in Layamon's *Brut*, which chronicles the kings of Britain from Constantine to Arthur. Layamon was an Englishman, of Saxon descent, writing about 1190. He draws from an existent faery tradition when he relates:

> There Uther the king took Ygaerne for queen; Ygaerne was with child by Uther the king, all through Merlin's craft, before she was wedded. The time came that was chosen, then was Arthur born. So soon as he came on earth, elves took him; they enchanted the child with magic most strong, they gave him might to be the best of all knights; they gave him another thing, that he should be a rich king; they gave him the third, that he should live long; they gave to him the princely virtues most good, so that he was most generous of all men alive. This the elves gave him, and thus the child thrived.[1]

The place where the elves fostered Arthur was in Brittany, according to Layamon. He speaks of a lake, dug by elves, wherein four kinds of fish swim apart from each other. Arthur speaks intimately of this lake, so that we may wonder whether it is not the place of his fostering.[2]

When Arthur eventually lies mortally wounded, he wills the kingdom to Constantine ap Cador and says: 'And I will fare to Avalun, to the fairest of all maidens, to Argante the queen, an elf most fair, and she shall make my wounds all sound; make me all whole with healing draughts.'[3] So it is that two faery women come to bear Arthur away. Nowhere but here, in this single text, does the name Argante appear. Layamon may have been thinking of the French *argent*, 'silver', when he wrote this, or it may even derive from a more distant Celtic name. If one places an 'M' before the name one arrives at Margante – not a world away from Morgan, who is sometimes called Margan or Morcant! We have already seen how Margot and Morgan are aliases for the faery midwives of Breton tradition. Here we have chosen to adopt Argante (pronounced Ar-gant'ay) to distinguish the chief Lady of the Lake from the other women under discussion.

As it is, the closest association with the character of Argante described by Layamon is with the Celtic Morgan or Morgen, who in various texts takes Arthur to Avalon to heal his wounds with her own hands. But though the Lady of the Lake seems to be associated with Arthur in Layamon, it is primarily with the heroic Lancelot that she is concerned in the Arthurian tradition.

Chrétien de Troyes' *Knight of the Cart*, written *c.*1172, first mentions the Lady of the Lake as Lancelot's protector and fosterer in an episode where Lancelot gets caught between the postern-gate and the portcullis while trying to escape from a castle. He raises to his eyes the ring which the Lady of the Lake has given him:

> 'Lady, lady, so help me God, I'm now in great need of you to come to my help.'
> That lady was a fairy who had given him the ring and brought him up as a child; and he had every confidence that, wherever he might be, she would help and rescue him.[4]

This magically empowering ring crops up again in one of the Arthurian stories of *The Mabinogion* where Owain is given a magical ring which confers invisibility and remembrance by Luned, the servant of the Lady of the Fountain, who may be taken as yet another resonance of the Lady of the Lake.

But the major text to speak extensively of the Lady is *Lanzelet* by Ulrich von Zatzikhoven, which was written in German in about 1200, but which clearly draws upon much earlier and existent traditions about the Otherworld and the Arthurian world.

The story tells how King Pant of Genewis was besieged by enemies and driven from his home, wounded, with his wife Clarine and their year-old son. Clarine watches her husband die and then hides in a tree. 'There came a fay of the sea, with a mist like a wind, and took the child from the queen and carried it with her into her land.'[5] The sea-fay, who is described as a *merfeine* or mermaid, appears in the nick of time, for the enemies return to capture Clarine.

The mermaid proves to be none other than the Queen of Maidenland – a clear parallel of the Irish *Tir na mBan* (Land of Women). The prevailing season in Maidenland is May-time. The mountain stronghold on which the queen's castle stands is built of crystal, and lies upon an impregnable island reached only by a diamond bridge. There the child, Lanzelet, is brought up, instructed in all the courtly arts, in music and in singing. The queen also sends for mermen to teach the boy sword-play, wrestling, hurling, jumping, archery, hawking and hunting. He grows to be 15 years old but has never ridden a horse. In order to acquire this skill he asks to leave Maidenland.

The boy begs the queen to tell him his name and lineage, which have been hidden from him, but she refuses until he has promised to overcome Iweret of Beforet (the Beautiful Forest). If he accomplishes this, she will give him his name. To this end, she gives him white armour, a sword, and a shield with a golden eagle upon it.

After many encounters and adventures, he finds the Castle of Death wherein lives Mabuz the Cowardly. Mabuz turns out to be the son of the Queen of Maidenland. It was prophesied to her before his birth that he would always be cowardly, and the queen accordingly had built for him the castle now called Schâtel le Mort (Castle of Death), which magically sustains his courage, but which saps the strength and hope of all else who enter therein. Lanzelet enters this castle and is thrown into the dungeon. But Mabuz's lands have been taken by Iweret, and reports of further incursions are brought. So Mabuz promises to keep his hostages unharmed for a year if Lanzelet will ride out against Iweret and overcome him.

Lanzelet overcomes Iweret and marries his only daughter, Yblis (an acronym of 'sibyl'). No sooner has he fulfilled the queen's command, than one of her ladies appears and gives him his name and lineage. He gives the lady of Maidenland a ring which has the property that no-one can refuse anything of its wearer. Such a magical ring seems to have originated in any case in Maidenland.

Lanzelet proves to be Arthur's nephew and takes Yblis to

court. Thence comes the Queen of Maidenland's mermaid messenger with a magic mantle with the instruction that whomever it fits shall be its possessor. The mantle is tried on by various ladies, including Guinevere, but it magically shortens on most of them, due, says the mermaid-messenger, to some fault in that lady's affections. Yblis at length tries it on and it fits her perfectly. So it is that the Queen of Maidenland acclaims the worthiness of her fosterling's wife. (This magic mantle test is later attributed to Morgan in the *Morte d'Arthur*, where it takes on a more malign intention, as we saw in Chapter 2.)

Lanzelet wins back his lands and honours his mother, after which he is brought the arms of Iweret by a messenger – the wondrous sword and magical providing net – a suitable gift for a knight raised in the watery queendom of Maidenland. He and Yblis have four children.

In this version of the story we see that, like Arianrhod's son Lleu Llaw Gyffes in *The Mabinogion* story of 'Math, Son of Mathonwy', Lanzelet has no name and no arms until given them by the Queen of Maidenland, though he does gain a wife.

The inhuman character of the faery-abduction is stressed throughout *Lanzelet*, where the hero is taken into otherworldly custody in order to compensate for the Queen of Maidenland's own son, Mabuz, who is, to all intents and purposes a changeling. The changeling theme tells of an ugly faery-child left in a mortal cradle in exchange for a beautiful mortal baby. The Queen of Maidenland has no compunction in stealing Lanzelet for her own ends.

This feature is shared by the story of Ceridwen and Taliesin found in the seventeenth-century text *Hanes Taliesin*. Ceridwen has a beautiful daughter, Creirwy, but an ugly son, Afagddu (Utter Darkness), sometimes also called Morfran (Great Crow). In order to compensate Afagddu for his ugliness, she intends to make him wise by brewing a cauldron of inspiration which will endow him with all knowledge. In order to prepare this brew, she sets a young boy, Gwion, to stir it and an old man to fuel the fire. Drops of the brew intended for Afagddu splash out on Gwion's finger and he becomes omniscient. He is chased through many shape-shiftings and eventually consumed by Ceridwen who, in the form of a red hen, swallows him as a grain of wheat. She then incubates him in her womb, from which he is reborn as Taliesin, the great poet. *Hanes Taliesin* is a many levelled story which depicts poetic initiation as a mystery-drama.

Lanzelet deviates slightly from Celtic tradition, however, in that the Queen of Maidenland's own son is Mabuz - not the wise and innocent youth of Celtic tradition, Mabon, but a dark and sinister medieval devolution of that archetype. Sheltering within the walls of his castle, Mabuz is an archetypal coward. It is interesting that this shift in the story should have taken place, since the Celtic Mabon is famous for being imprisoned for aeons and then liberated, whereafter he helps liberate others. Mabuz is himself both imprisoned by his cowardice, which can only be shielded by the robbed courage of others, but is also an imprisoner.

Apart from faery-abductions, another common Celtic theme is a hero's fosterage by an otherworldly woman who teaches him arms: Fionn mac Cumail is brought up by the druidess Bodhmall and the huntress Liath Luachra; Cuchulainn is trained by Scathach, the eponymous Goddess of the Isle of Skye. In *Lanzelet*, the Queen of Maidenland is a resourceful and providing figure, responsible for giving Lanzelet the best possible education in arms, though she neglects riding - that mainstay of chivalry - because she does not wish her fosterling to leave Maidenland until he is old enough to accomplish her ends.

In this text, Lancelot is not Guinevere's lover. Neither does the Lady of the Lake become his mistress, for Lancelot retains the relationship of son to mother with her. It is in Chrétien's *Knight of the Cart* and afterwards in the *Vulgate Lancelot* that his role as lover is developed. This is because the Lady of the Lake is the mistress of true love: there can be no guilt in the Otherworld, only true love, for here lovers conjoin without sorrow or shame, as in many Celtic texts. In a related text, *Lancelot do Lac*, the Lady of the Lake gives the following advice to Guinevere:

Look after him, keep him close to you, love him above all others, he who loves you above all others, quell all jealousy of him because he desires not, he counts as nothing any woman but you . . . If you judge your love as madness, this madness is to be honoured above all things, because you love the master of the flower of this world.[6]

These are more than just the proud words of a mother concerning her son. The Lady is aware of the crucial role her fosterling is to play in the world, and of the effect his love for Guinevere will have in bringing about the downfall of the Arthurian kingdom, yet she chooses, for whatever reason of her own, to keep silent, allowing Lancelot to go his own way and to experience his own feelings to the full. In this she takes a very different role from that of Perceval's real mother, whose warnings and advice bring nothing but trouble in their wake.

THE CHILD OF THE LAKE

The major text which deals with the fostering and later life of Lancelot is the *Vulgate Lancelot*, written about 1225. It draws upon *Lanzelet* and other related French traditions and tells a similar *enfance* story to them all. We learn how King Ban of Benoic and Queen Elaine fled from their besieged castle and how, when Elaine was tending her dying husband, the Lady of the Lake unswaddled the child from his cradle and bore him into the lake, pressing him to her breast. Elaine pleaded to have him back, but the Lady of the Lake said nothing.

The Lady that nourished him abided only in woods and forests that were vast and dense, and the lake whereinto she sprang with the child was naught but enchantment, and it was in the plain at the foot of a hill . . .in the part where the lake seemed widest and deepest the Lady had many fair and noble dwellings . . .and her abode was so hidden that none might find it, for the semblance of the lake covered it so that it might not be seen.[7]

The Lady sets a master to teach the child archery, games and riding. She also sends one of her women to rescue Lancelot's cousins, Lionel and Bors, from imprisonment, which she does by shapeshifting them into hounds. Together the children grow up, until at the age of 18 Lancelot desires to go away. At this, the Lady instructs him in the duties of a knight, itemizing the qualities of the shield, horse, helmet, sword, etc. She bids him have a heart as hard as diamond against enemies, and a heart as soft as wax for the oppressed.

Then it is the Lady of the Lake who presents Lancelot at court, providing him with white robes. They meet Arthur first of all in the forest outside Camelot, where we read the only description of the Lady: 'She wore a marvellous tunic of white samite and a mantle lined with ermine ... The lady lowered her wimple from before her face, when she came before the king.'[8] This suggests that she kept her face veiled when riding abroad from her realm. The Lady bids Arthur knight Lancelot on the morrow, to which the king agrees, then she gives her fosterling a ring which undoes all enchantment. She tells him that he will gain knowledge of his lineage in due course.

Among Lancelot's adventures is his attempt to overthrow the evil custom of the castle of Dolorous Gard, whereat each passing knight is forced to fight with 10 successive champions until he falls from fatigue. A veiled damsel comes to him, bringing him three shields of silver, one with one red bend across it, the next with two and the last with three. She invites him to use these shields in his coming combat, for the shield with one bend will give him the added strength of another knight and the second will give him the power of two, and so on. She also says he will then learn his own name and lineage.

Lancelot overcomes his assailants and is triumphantly led into the castle, where there is a cemetery containing a stone slab which reads: 'This slab will ne'er be raised by hand or strength of man, save only by him that will conquer this dolorous castle, and his name is written beneath.' Lancelot lifts the slab and reads: 'Here will lie Lancelot of the Lake, the son of King Ban of Benoic.'[9] It is thus that he learns his name, his lineage and his certain mortality (being brought up in the Otherworld, he may well have assumed himself not subject to death).

In the *Morte d'Arthur*, Sir Thomas Malory's fifteenth-century re-working of the *Vulgate Cycle*, the confusion between the Lady of the Lake, Morgan and Nimuë becomes profound. The Lady of the Lake and Morgan, whose functions are so similar in early tradition, become mutually antagonistic. The Lady of the Lake and Nimuë are frequently taken to be one and the same person – though, as we shall see in the next chapter, they are in reality very different characters. In fact Malory refers to the Lady of the Lake by that name on only two occasions – both of them significant.

In the first of these we read how Arthur received his famous sword. Journeying with Merlin to a lakeside he saw 'an arm clothed in white samite, that held a fair sword in that hand . . . With that they saw a damosel going upon the lake. What damosel is that? said Arthur. That is the Lady of the Lake, said Merlin; and within that lake is a rock, and therein is as fair a place as any on earth, and richly beseen; and this damosel will come to, you anon, and then speak ye fair to her that she will give you that sword.'[10]

Arthur does as he is bidden and gets the sword in return for a promise to grant the Lady anything she asks.

This rather rash promise is claimed under curious circumstances soon after, when another lady named, interestingly, Lile of Avalon, comes to Camelot bearing another sword, which is a great burden to her but which only a knight of outstanding prowess can draw. He who does so is the ill-fated Balin le Sauvage, who draws forth the sword, but then refuses to return it. At this moment the Lady of the Lake enters and demands her payment for the gift of Excalibur – the heads either of the Lady Lile or of Balin himself, the one having been the death of her father and the other of her brother. Arthur, naturally enough, is none too keen on this idea, but before any further discussion can take place Balin, recognizing the Lady of the Lake as having been the cause of his mother's death, takes the sword and cuts off her head. For this crime he is banished from the court, but takes the head with him, leaving Arthur to bury the Lady with great sorrow, despite the fact that Balin had defended himself by describing her as a sorceress who has destroyed many good knights.

This curious and conflicting image of the Lady of the Lake is unique. In all the rest of the texts under discussion she is seen as beneficent and, since she is clearly an otherworldly personage, presumably deathless. Yet, here we find her not only meeting her death at the hands of a mortal, but presented as a sorceress who takes advantage of Arthur's rash promise to demand an unreasonable act. Malory's immediate source for this story, the thirteenth-century *Roman du Graal* tells the same story, omitting the names of both ladies, though the implication is still, clearly enough, that the second lady is the same one who gave Arthur the sword.

In all probability this confusion arose from a conflation of stories, in one of which a human tale of strife and vengeance was told. What is interesting is that both women are sword-bearers whose weapons can only be acquired by the best of knights. Arthur earns his, in part, via Merlin; Balin, seemingly, through his own merits. The fact that the first lady is described as coming from Avalon seems almost to suggest a rivalry within the otherworldly realm; while Balin's taking of the Lady's head points to an earlier, Celtic tale.

Throughout the remainder of Malory's long book, although we find frequent references to either 'a lady' or 'a damosel' of 'the lake', and although Nimuë is often referred to by this title, there is no further information to add to what we have already learned from the French texts. The improbability of the episode in 'The Tale of Balin' remains unresolved, and we must look elsewhere for a deeper understanding of the Lady's role and function.

THE FOSTER-SON AND THE GODDESS

It must be evident to all by this time that it is almost impossible to discuss the Lady of the Lake without reference to Lancelot.

Though he is totally absent from the earliest British sources, occurring only in French and German texts of the early period, his antecedents seem to derive from Irish and early Celtic tradition. In character he is closely associated with both the Romano-Celtic deity, Maponus (British, Mabon), who has correlations with the Classical Apollo, and with the Irish deity, Lugh Lamfada (the long-armed), also called Lugh Samildanach (the many-gifted). In studying these antecedents we discover the otherworldly traditions which underlie the figure of the Lady of the Lake.

R.S. Loomis has presented exhaustive evidence to show the derivation of Lancelot from the god Lugh,[11] while his otherworldly nature is paralleled in many ways. The earliest Arthurian poem which we possess, the *Preiddeu Annwn*, speaks of Llwch Llenlleawc flourishing the sword Caledfwlch (Excalibur) before the cauldron of the Lord of Annwn (the Underworld). This same Llwch is a British version of the Irish Lugh Loinnbheimionach (of the Mighty Blows). He is called Llwch the Irishman in *Culhwch and Olwen*, where he vanquishes the giant Diwrnach and his men in a mighty feat with Arthur's sword Caledfwlch. In British tradition, Ireland is often considered to be an otherworldly place. The object of Arthur's raid on Annwn is to obtain the cauldron which brings inspiration. Llwch gains the cauldron, presumably by wielding Caledfwlch, thus impressing the cauldron's guardians, the nine sisters whose breath inspirits the brew. In both texts Llwch wields Arthur's sword (as Gawain was later to do), signalling his importance as a hero.

The theme of the otherworldly knight or champion who fulfils a task which even the most mighty cannot achieve is a feature not only of Llwch, but also of both Lugh and Mabon. Lugh arrives on the eve of the Tuatha de Danaan's possible defeat at the hands of the Fomorians, substitutes for the king, Nuadu, and wins the battle; Mabon is sprung from his long imprisonment in order to fulfil the hunting of the Twrch Trwyth, the otherworldly boar which even Arthur cannot overcome.

Lugh Lamfada is the archetypal god-hero who, among other

deeds of note, overthrows his restrictive grandfather, Balor, and rescues his imprisoned mother from her father's sea-girt tower.[12] The Celtic festival of Lughnasadh (Lammas) was inaugurated by Lugh to commemorate, significantly, his foster-mother Tailtiu. Lugh himself has no wife, though he comes at night to sleep with women. By one such union, with Dectire, the greatest of all Irish heroes, Cuchulainn, is engendered. We may parallel this action with Lancelot's sleeping with Elaine, the union of which produces Galahad who, like Cuchulainn, becomes a prodigious hero who dies young.

If we compare the early history of Lancelot and of Lugh we find many points of similarity:

Lancelot	Lugh
born of King Ban and Queen Helen	born of Cian of Tuatha and Ethniu the Fomorian
fostered by Lady of Lake	fostered by Tailtiu or Goibhniu
learns skill at arms	is possessed of all skills
becomes the Lady of the Lake's champion	institutes feast in honour of foster-mother
kills family enemy Iweret	kills grandfather Balor
rescues his mother and her lands	rescues his mother
sleeps with Elaine	sleeps with Dectire
sires Galahad	sires Cuchulainn
is armed with Caledfwlch (in *Prieddeu Annwn*)	is armed with the spear of Finias
does not marry (except in *Lanzelet*)	does not marry
wins his name by arms	wins his nickname by arms

These traditions seemed to have remained locked within ancient British myth and were not transmitted in any coherent fashion to the Matter of Britain. The major source of transmission seems to have been via a circuitous route: a mixture of Irish tales of the Tuatha de Danaan's many-gifted Lugh, of Mabon the liberator, and of the resourceful but withdrawn (foster) mother of them both, whose deeds and forgotten mythos form the basis of the Lady of the Lake.

The story of Lugh becomes the story of Lancelot in subtle ways, taken into Europe by travelling story-tellers. The inadvertent agents of this transmission may have been the Norman conquerors of both Britain and Ireland. Britain had been Norman since 1066, and Ireland suffered a similar fate when it was 'given' to Henry II by Pope Adrian IV in 1154. By 1171 the country was under Norman rule. Since the ruling Plantagenet family owned a considerable part of Europe, it is from about this time that the rapid spread of Arthurian and Celtic stories started circulating in a freer way.

It is ironic that we must take this circuitous route to come at the textual evidence for the Lady of the Lake, but the mythic parallels are difficult to draw without this means, since the story-tellers were primarily concerned with the deeds of their favourite heroes and rarely mention their wives, mothers or sisters.

The women specifically associated with Lugh and Mabon give us a lineal precedent for the Lady of the Lake. Lugh's mother Ethniu (sometimes also Ethliu) is a woman of the Fomorians – a race preceding the Tuatha de Danaan. The Fomorians are considered to be a subversive people, in much the same way that the faery-folk were once seen by mortals. Ethniu's father is none other than the monstrous giant Balor, who has one baleful eye; one glance from this eye kills all viewers, and he thus keeps a shield over it. Because of a prophecy that his grandson will kill him, he locks Ethniu in a tower on Tory Island, to prevent her taking a mate. However, Cian of the Tuatha de Danaan hears of her beauty and finds a way to lie with her. Balor has the child thrown into the water but he is saved. He is fostered by Goibhniu the smith-god (or by Manannan in other versions). But most ancient traditions give him Tailtiu as a foster-mother. An Irish folk-story tells of how Lugh received his naming from his grandfather: he is picking up apples in Balor's garden, disguised as a gardener's boy, when Balor cries to him, 'Pick them up, little long hand!' It is thus he receives the name Lamfada.

It will be seen from this tradition that Lugh's mother is an otherworldly woman, living apart on a magically-guarded island. His foster-mother, Tailtiu, wife of Eochaidh Mac Erc, is sparsely documented, but responsible for having single-handedly cleared the forest of Brega in order to make a plain. This formidable feat causes her early death, and Lugh honours her by inaugurating a festival and funeral games in her honour. This feast, Lughnasadh (literally 'the spousals of Lugh') is the remembrance of the ancient custom of the marriage of the ruler to the Goddess of the Land, of whom Tailtiu is clearly an archetype.

In Welsh tradition the mother of the liberator, Mabon, is called Modron. Like Argante, this mysterious figure remains stubbornly recessive. Her son, Mabon seems to be an archetypal deity whose symbolic attributes are applicable to many British heroes. Similarly, the title Modron may be equally applied to many women. Early Welsh tradition calls Morgan by the name Modron, making her the mother of Owain and calling her father *Rex Avallonis* or 'King of Avalon'. Taking this tack, Mabon's otherworldly origins give him astounding skills, but the deeds of the ancient archetype of Modron are lost to us, for they have not remained in any myth or story. We must look to the character of Igraine to find anything approaching their power.

The namelessness of the Lady of the Lake is a feature of Celtic faery lore. The *beansidhe* (Woman of the Sidhe) who comes to the hero of the Celtic story of the *Voyage of Bran* with the ever-living silver branch of the Otherworld – his passport upon his immram – to help him discover the Land of Women, is never named. This anonymity has troubled more than one story-teller in the Arthurian tradition, and has led to her conflation with both Morgan and Nimuë at different times. In fact, as noted above, the only text in which she is given a name is Layamon's *Brut*, where she is depicted as a powerful Queen of Faery. It is reasonable to assume therefore that the appellation 'Lady of the Lake' was a title borne by more than one person. So Malory at least seems to have understood it, and his killing the Lady, and subsequent confusion over the various 'ladies' and 'damosels' of the Lake has caused many interpreters to subsume otherworldly women of different kinds under this single figure.

That the Lady is indeed a doublet of Morgan has been surmised more than once. It would seem that the two characters have split a single role into two: Argante retains the nurturing, foster-mother symbolism, while Morgan has taken on the role of faery mistress and adversary. Both women have a tendency to retain their lovers/offspring in the Otherworld, making it very difficult to get back into mortality again. In this, Argante is more generous than Morgan, equipping both Arthur and Lancelot for their earthly tasks.

Arthur is one with the magical motherland of the Lake. His fosterage and secret begetting put him in the same position as that of a new Dalai Lama, the leader whose incarnation must be rediscovered and authenticated. Merlin sets up the sword in the stone, which only Arthur can pull forth. But it is Argante who gives him the sword by which he is empowered: Excalibur. However, the sword alone is as nothing; it is the scabbard that preserves its bearer from loss of blood and thus guards Arthur's life. King Arthur's sovereignty is precisely about the interdependence between the worlds: he defends the land by the sword, and the Goddess of Sovereignty defends him from loss of vigour. The sword given by Argante is thus the contract of Arthur and the Goddess: the theft of the scabbard by Morgan itself points to a breaking of faith in this mystical marriage between land and king (see Chapter 3).

The Lady of the Lake is thus revealed to be a prime-mover of events, one who takes a wider and sometimes prophetic view of the Arthurian world. Like Merlin, she remains the motivation behind some of the major events, giving magical gifts and advice, but seldom appearing in person. She is the foster-mother of heroes, dwelling in the withdrawn and hidden home of the West. While her textual references are meagre, she remains a Faery

Queen in medieval dress, no less mysterious than the Queen of the Isle of Women in Irish tradition who invites male visitors after the fashion of the priestesses spoken about by Pomponius Mela (see p.xxxvi). As Queen of Maidenland, Argante seems to share common features with Igraine in her role as Queen of the Castle of Maidens, and also with the goddess Arianrhod in her solitary tower of Caer Sidi. Each woman is a mother or foster-mother who trains a son or foster-son before she reverts to her otherworldly seclusion once more. Argante is an important initiator and teacher whose wisdom is kept bright within the temenos of her lake. The few who journey there find that her service requires the commitment and application of many years; the rewards of that service are the ability to mediate the sweet waters of the mystical heartland to the dry riverbeds of the world.

The Island of Shimmering Water

You are about to embark on a journey to the place where
the waters of the heart arise. Close your eyes and see before
you in vision a shoreline of silver sand and small stones,
lapped by a sea that seems now green, now blue. Waves
rush in upon this shore, advancing and withdrawing with a
soft roar as the stones turn over. And there, on the back of
the ninth wave, is a ship, long and low in the water, its
sides draped with rose samite, a single sail at its mast-head,
on which is a symbol of nine overlapping circles, etched in
silver on a ground of deepest blue. Gently, the craft touches
the shore and you step aboard. At once you are under way,
the sail billowing out above you, the waters creaming back
from the bow in bright curves . . .

The sea is calm and you make good progress, flying before
the breeze. Ahead, you see the dark blot of an island,
coming swiftly nearer, and soon your craft touches the
shore. You step down from the ship and find yourself
walking on soft golden sand. The way leads inland, through

grass-grown dunes which become softly rounded hills,
cloaked in green. The island is not large, and soon you find
yourself approaching what must be the centre. There, you
see an inland lake of pure, crystalline water, at the centre of
which lies a low knoll of land, crowned by a grove of silver
birches – an island within an island. On it stands the figure
of a woman, dressed in a gown of deepest blue, the colour
of her ship's sail. Her golden hair floats unbound to her
waist and even at this distance there is a kind of
otherworldly sparkle about her. She raises one hand to
beckon you to her, and calls out across the water words you
cannot quite hear . . .

The water seems shallow and without hesitation you begin
to wade out to the knoll. The water is cold, but
extraordinarily exhilarating. You find yourself swimming
through it, even though you may never have swum in your
life before . . . In a moment – all too briefly it seems – you
feel land beneath your feet and walk to where the Lady
awaits you. Surprisingly, your clothes are dry. Then, you are
face to face with Argante, the Lady of the Lake, she who,
long since or only yesterday, gave to Arthur his great sword
Excalibur. Her eyes are the colour of mist, now seeming
silver, now catching the tints of sky or sea. Her manner is
gentle and welcoming, yet there is about her a sense of
powerful strength which few, in any world, would deny. She
welcomes you and bids you walk with her to the birch
grove . . .

The trees are truly beautiful in a way that you have never
seen except in dream or otherworldly state. Tall and
graceful, their leaves seem to dance perpetually as though
stirred by a breeze . . . At the centre of the grove is a well-
head, the stones intricately carved with spiralling patterns.
From it spill out three streams of pure water, so clear that
they are scarcely discernible with mortal sight. You feel,
rather than see them, as they flow out from the fountain
through the trees and out of sight. The thought comes,
unbidden, to your mind, that these are the waters which
give sustenance to the world, perhaps even to all worlds,
above, below and beyond . . .

Gently, the Lady indicates that you should approach the
well-head and look within . . . You do so, and at first see

nothing. It is like looking into a lake of pure sunlight, so clear that, as your eyes grow accustomed, you seem to see, fathoms below you, the bottom of the well, with sands and crystal stones that catch the light and throw it back in a thousand sparkling shards ... Then, slowly, your sight clears, and you see that the water itself is made up of myriads of infinitely tiny droplets, moving and changing so swiftly and in such intricate, endlessly varied patterns that your senses cannot grasp more than a fraction of their reality ...

Amid the rainbow links of light you see a great fish swimming, which you know to be the Salmon of Knowledge. And, somewhere far below - or above, such terms have no meaning now - you see something else ... a sword, sunk deep in the water, glinting as though lights danced along its blade, striking points of fire in the great purple stone of its hilt ... Wondering, knowing that you look upon the great Sword of the Pendragons, you draw back from the brink of the well, unable to see for a moment anything but the endlessly sparking chains of droplets which seem to surround you ...

At your side the Lady Argante lays a hand upon your arm and guides you to a grassy bank beneath one of the graceful birch trees. There, slowly, your sight clears, and when you are able to see clearly again, you realize that you do so with enhanced sight. Where before you saw nought but a circle of graceful trees, now you see nine women dancing an endless dance of joy upon the greensward. And there, beneath another tree, lies a figure whose strong limbs and mighty head are laid in sleep so profound that it seems nothing could wake him ...

You know who the sleeper is without being told - Arthur, the Great King, sleeping on the Island named Avalon until he is woken by a great and terrible need. So profound is his sleep that he seems almost to be at one with the earth, and as you look indeed it seems that all you can see is a low green mound, which has something of the shape of a sleeping figure ...

For the first time, the Lady speaks aloud, though you hear her words in your mind and understand them there, even though she speaks in a tongue long since forgotten in your

world. 'You have swum in the Lake of Life. And have looked
into the Well of Wisdom. And you have seen the Sleeper
and the Sword of which I am guardian. Have you any words
to say to me, any question to ask that I may answer?'

Her words invoke an ancient longing within you - not
unmixed with fear. Here, you stand at the centre of
knowledge and understanding, where all the wisdom of the
Otherworld and of the Nine Sisters finds its source.
Whatever question you ask will be answered with absolute
truth, nor may you turn away from the answer, should it be
different from what you expect to hear. There is no onus
upon you to ask anything, but if you do so you must abide
by what you are told . . .

When you have finished your speech with the Lady it is
time to depart. Make your farewells and begin to return to
normal consciousness. From this place there is no need to
go back by the way you came. Though the way is difficult
to find, the door between the worlds is opened instantly at
the Lady's word. You find yourself returned to the place
from which you began this journey, but you may well be
changed by what you have seen and heard. Take time to
write down anything you wish to remember, and to re-
establish contact with the physical world around you, for
this has been a deep journey, to the centre of the
otherworldly realm of Faery, and you have walked where few
mortals have walked before, and seen what few have heard.
Remember these things.

REFERENCES

1. Wace and Layamon, *Arthurian Chronicles*, ed. E. Mason.
2. Ibid.
3. Ibid.
4. Chrétien de Troyes, *Arthurian Romances*, trans. D.D.R. Owen,
   11.2345-7.
5. Ulrich von Zatzikhoven, *Lanzelet*, ed. and trans. K.T.G. Webster.
6. Jean Markale, *Women of the Celts*, our trans.

7. L.A. Paton, *Lancelot of the Lake*.
8. Ibid.
9. Ibid.
10. Sir Thomas Malory, *Morte d'Arthur*, Book 1, Chapter 21.
11. R.S. Loomis, *Celtic Myth and Arthurian Romance*.
12. Caitlín Matthews, *Mabon and the Mysteries of Britain: An Exploration of 'The Mabinogion'*.

Nimuë

From thy retreat arise, and unfold
The books of Awen without fear;
And the discourse of a maid, and the repose of a dream.
'Dialogue of Myrddin and his Sister Gwenddydd'
from *The Red Book of Hergest*

Variant Names:
Vivienne, Ninian, Neneve.

THE MYTH OF NIMUË

The single act for which Nimuë is most often remembered is her imprisonment of Merlin, variously beneath a stone, in a sarcophagus where his body perishes but his spirit lingers on, in a hawthorn bush, or in a prison of glass. Although she acts thus in response to his continued sexual advances, Nimuë has been repeatedly portrayed as a kind of *femme fatale*, with the resultant diminishing of her character, until we end up with the unwholesome portrayal by Tennyson in his *Idylls of the King*.

There is a great deal more to Nimuë than this, as can be easily shown by putting together something like a unified picture from the various texts in which she makes an appearance. This done, we may then begin to look *behind* the Nimuë of medieval literature to an earlier figure, whose role explains many of the characterizations of her later self.

First, however, let us look at the name Nimuë itself. The spelling Nimuë, which has become one of the most familiar to modern day readers, in fact only appears in William Caxton's edition of Thomas Malory's *Morte d'Arthur*, where it is also spelt Nyneue and Nynyue. Numerous other variants occur in other texts, such as Nymue, Nenyve, Nimiane, Nimiama, Nimyane and so on. The French romances are similarly confused giving, Niniane, Nievienne, Ninienue, Nivienne, Nymenche and Viviane, as well as other, minor, variations. Out of this rich variety of nomenclature the most usually adopted versions are either Nimuë or Vivienne, which can be seen to be closely related. Which of these is actually the earliest has been debated at length by A. Nitze, E. Hamp and A.H.O. Jarman, who vary between seeking a Celtic or French origin for the name. Our own thoughts on this question will be set forth when we return to the matter of Nimuë's original role and personality. In the meantime, we need to put together a more accurate version of her story, as it appears in the various texts in which she makes an appearance.

According to 'The English Merlin', which is itself a translation of the *Vulgate* text, Nimuë's father was 'a vavasour [huntsman] of right high lineage' who had a particular devotion to the Goddess Diana. This in itself may be taken to mean no more than that, as a hunter, the Vavasour shares the attributes of the Huntress herself. But, we learn, the relationship is closer than this. Nimuë's father is named Dionas, which clearly derives from Diana, and he is said to be the Goddess's 'godson', whom she visits often and with whom she remains for 'many days'. On one occasion, as she is leaving, she gives him a gift which pleases him greatly:

> 'Dionas', quoth Diane, 'I grant thee, and so does the god of the sea and of the stars . . . that the first female child you shall have shall be so much coveted by the wisest man that ever lived . . . that he will teach her the most part of his wit and cunning by way of nigromancy, and . . . will be so desirous after he has seen her, that he shall have no power to do anything against her wish, and all things she asks for he shall teach her.'[1]

Thus at once Nimuë – for of course the prophecy of Diana refers to her – is given a remarkable future. The same text continues to relate how Dionas, who had long served the Duke of Burgoyne (Burgundy) is given the latter's daughter for a wife, along with half the forest of Brioke (Broceliande?) When, in due course, the couple have a daughter, she is called Nimiane, a name which, according to the author of the text, is of Hebrew origin, and means, in French, 'I shall not lie.' The author adds, cryptically, 'And this turned upon Merlin.'

The story then turns at once to the meeting of Merlin and Nimuë, whom the former seeks out, disguised as a young squire, at a fountain where Nimuë used often to go, and for whom he demonstrates his miraculous powers by calling up an enchanted orchard and summoning knights and ladies to dance and sing for her. He is clearly already in love with her, and in this version demands surety of her own feelings. Nimuë promises to return his love on condition that he teaches her all his wisdom. To this he agrees, though he must leave her then for other work, but before he goes he teaches her a spell which enables her to conjure up a great river, beyond which lies a magical place into which she may go at will.

There are many points of interest here. It is possible, initially, to see that Diana, the Goddess, who spends many days with Dionas, may at one time have been the actual mother of Nimuë. In 'The Huth Merlin' she is repeatedly referred to as 'the Huntress', a hint of her true nature, while the mage himself relates a further tale of Diana (Diane), which he ironically tells to Nimuë, apparently in ignorance of her connection with the Goddess.[2]

The story concerns the Lake of Diana in the Forêt en Val, so called because it was here that Diana murdered her first lover Faunus. She had fallen in love with Felix and wished to dispose of her former love. In the forest there was a grave-like fountain filled with healing water, which Diana cast out, so that when Faunus returned from a hunting trip with a serious wound, he lay in the basin and was unhealed. Diana bade him lie down, without clothes, while she covered the tomb with a stone, promising to fill it with healing herbs. She returned instead with molten lead which she poured through the hole. Instead of being pleased by this action and falling in love with the Goddess, Felix was revolted and cut off her head, casting it into the lake, whereby it gained its name.

This sinister story, so like to Osiris' fate as well as to the trick played by Blodeuwedd on Lleu, causes us to feel that Merlin should have been forewarned. The old Merlin even tells a story not dissimilar from that which will befall him. But he still builds Nimuë a house near the lake and casts a spell so that no-one shall find it, and later he shows her the cave of a famous pair of lovers which cannot be penetrated save by enchantment. Here, Nimuë enchants Merlin and leaves him under the very slab where the faithful lovers were entombed. From here his cries issue forth, to be heard by Bagdemagu and Tristan as outlined in *The Tale of the Cry* (a text no longer existent).[3]

We note that the Diane of the story, like Morgan herself, is associated with a lake and with healing, though she abuses this skill. There may thus be a shadowy influence from the Celtic story of Blodeuwedd which provides bare parallels with this story in the bath by which Blodeuwedd arranged the death of her husband Llew Llaw Gyffes and in her treacherous love of Gronw. But the most interesting fact is the possible presence of the Flower Maiden in whatever form the story was first transmitted.

The Flower Maiden, or the Maiden of Spring, is she over whose hand the champions of summer and winter fight every year. To possess her is to win an important victory and to acquire great power. Thus if Merlin can be seen as himself seeking her in this way, we may begin to glimpse another strand of the underlying myth. Certainly, the figure of the Flower Maiden is found within so much early Celtic and later Arthurian story that it is more than possible that we are seeing yet another aspect of this complex character in Nimuë herself (see also Chapter 2).

The episode in which Merlin seeks out Nimuë, just as the Goddess had foretold, interestingly takes place at a fountain, which later romances were to identify as Baranton, a magical place hidden in the secret depths of the ancient otherworldly forest of Broceliande. Though disguised as a young squire,

Merlin yet shows his customary abilities to produce strange and wondrous things - in this instance creating an entire scenario, with dancing and singing knights and ladies, and a magical orchard. Nimuë is clearly impressed by this - as she was doubtless meant to be - and when Merlin proffers love for her, 'after some thought' she makes a promise to him, that she will return his love, on condition that her teaches her everything he knows. He begins right away with what reads almost like a description of the modern magical technique of visualization, teaching her to call forth a river, which, when she crosses it, delivers her into a world where anything she desires may happen. This is itself interesting, because it exactly parallels Nimuë's own entrapment of Merlin later on - though he is unable to return from the world she has created for him.

If we accept the dubious interpretation of Nimuë's name as meaning 'I will not lie', we may find another reading of her character: not simply as the 'evil temptress' into which the later authors endeavoured to make her, but as a prophetess incapable of falsehood. Indeed, the overall character of Nimuë, as she appears in 'The Huth Merlin' and related texts, shows her to have been taken advantage of by Merlin, and to have actually hated him sufficiently to justify her eventual entrapment of him - seen here as very much a way of escaping his unwelcome advances. There are deeper reasons for their animosity, as we will see.

Whether the episode of Merlin's first encounter with Nimuë occurs before her first appearance at the Arthurian court is a matter for speculation. 'The English Merlin' does not contain the episode in which Arthur and his fellows are first introduced to her. For that we must turn to Malory's *Morte d'Arthur*, and specifically to the first great adventure of the Round Table, then but lately founded, which is generally known as 'The Quest for the White Hart'. This story is told in full on pp.48-50, but will be briefly summarized here.

As the knights gather for the feast celebrating Arthur's wedding to Guinevere and the establishing of the Round Table, a white hart bounds into the hall pursued by a white brachet (a small ladies' hunting dog) followed in turn by Nimuë herself (then still unnamed). At this one of the knights jumps up and departs with the dog under his arm and, as Nimuë protests loudly, another knight abducts her in turn. Arthur then dispatches King Pellinore, one of his strongest knights, to rescue her and either bring back or kill the knight who stole her away. (He sends others to bring back the dog and the white hart).

Pellinore's journey is marked by ominous events from the start. First he encounters a woman cradling the wounded body of her knight, but when she begs help he refuses to turn aside from his appointed task and after he has ridden away - with the woman's curse in his ears - the wounded knight dies and the maiden kills herself with his sword. Pellinore continues on his way and overtakes the object of his quest, who is being fought over by two knights, the one who carried her off and another, her cousin, who seems to think he should have the ruling of her. Pellinore defeats the knight who had abducted the girl from Arthur's hall and makes friends with the other, who is more than glad to give over the protection of his errant cousin into the hands of the older man. It is then that we learn her name for the first time - Nimuë.

Here she is presented as a purely human character, who behaves in a somewhat noisy and helpless way, allowing herself to be pushed from man to man without much protest. On the return journey she and Pellinore come to the place where the distressed maiden had asked for help, finding only the pitiful remains for her body, consumed save for the head by wild animals. Pellinore now shows shame and regret at his hasty behaviour, and at Nimuë's suggestion carries the head, hung about his neck, back to Camelot.

There is no suggestion of otherworldliness here, nor is Nimuë referred to as a Lady of the Lake. Yet the very next chapter begins with the account of how Merlin 'fell in a dotage on the damosel that King Pellinore brought to court, and she was one of the damosels of the lake . . .'⁴ This is probably due to Malory's clumsy conflation of his various sources, but does suggest that there were two separate traditions, in one the damosel being of mortal stock, and in the other possessed of otherworldly blood.

Certainly Malory's characterization of Nimuë is not always consistent – though she is unfailingly represented as a helpful character. Indeed, once Merlin has been imprisoned, she virtually takes his place, saving Arthur from various attacks by Morgan le Fay. Malory's blunt retelling of the whole episode of Merlin and Nimuë puts her in a much more favourable light than the earlier French or English texts. Merlin follows her everywhere, constantly trying to get her alone in some secluded spot where he may 'have her maidenhead'. She, in turn, is afraid of him, referring to him as a 'devil's son', and finally doing all she can to learn his secrets so that she may use them against him.

Malory characteristically tones down the supernatural element throughout all of this. His vision of Nimuë is of a mortal woman beset by an older, more skilful man who also happens to possess great magical power. In the end, she turns that power against him, imprisoning him for all time. The last we hear of the old wizard is his voice issuing from beneath the rock under which Nimuë has pinned him. The inference is that the only one who can let him out is she who put him there. Her tacit refusal to do so speaks for itself.

By far the most interesting of Nimuë's other appearances in the *Morte d'Arthur* is in the episode of Gawain, Ettard and Pelleas. This tells how Pelleas loved Ettard so much that he allowed himself to be overcome every day by her knights so that he would be taken prisoner to her castle and thus have at least a chance of seeing her. Ettard, on the other hand, hated Pelleas. Gawain, coming on the scene of one of Pelleas' deliberate defeats, learns of the story and promises to do all in his power to persuade the lady to look with favour on the knight. In fact, he is himself attracted to Ettard – an attraction that proves mutual – so that he ends up in bed with her, having told her that he has slain Pelleas. But by chance the love-lorn knight finds them and, though heart-smitten, refrains from killing them, laying the blade of his sword across their necks as they sleep in token of his knowledge of their betrayal. When the pair wake Ettard is dismayed at Gawain's duplicity and sends him away, and it is at this point that Nimuë enters the story. Hearing of Pelleas' intention to starve himself to death, she intervenes, casting a powerful spell over both the knight and Ettard. The latter she causes to love Pelleas without stint, while the knight himself she causes to love herself. Thus the roles are reversed and Ettard now loves Pelleas so much that she is likely to die of it, being left to suffer as she would once have left the knight. He, meanwhile, is carried away by Nimuë, becoming her lover from that moment on. (Indeed, later in the book, in a reference apparently created by Malory himself, Pelleas is referred to as being 'wedded' to Nimuë, who saved him from meeting death at the hands of any knight he fought with thereafter.)

Now this is a very Merlin-like intervention, even though the outcome is very different. In this, her first real act as the mages's successor, Nimuë shows herself to be not only a powerful sorceress, but also clear-sighted and decisive in her resolution of the tangle of relationships.

Her subsequent appearances confirm this. The next episode in which she takes part is that in which Accolon of Gaul, the lover of Morgan le Fay, attempts to kill Arthur with his own sword, which Morgan has stolen. Nimuë comes 'for love of King Arthur, for she knew how Morgan le Fay had ordained that King Arthur should be slain that day, and therefore she came to save his life'.[5] By enchantment she causes Excalibur to fall from Accolon's hand, and Arthur retrieves it and wins the battle forthwith. Merlin had, on a previous occasion, warned Arthur of this very event, so that it is wholly in keeping with the portrayal of Nimuë as the mage's successor that she should participate in this episode.

Soon after this we see Nimuë again aiding Arthur against the plotting of his half-sister. When Morgan sends a beautiful mantle as a gift and peace-offering to Arthur, it is Nimuë who appears and insists that the maiden sent with the cloak should try it on first. When she does so she is wholly consumed by fire.

Of the other mentions of Nimuë in Malory the other most important one occurs towards the end of the book when, in the dark days preceding the final collapse of the Arthurian realm, Guinevere is accused of murdering Sir Patrise. In fact, Lancelot defends the queen, in a mirror image of the story in which he rescues her from the castle of Meleagraunce (see Chapter 2), but the significance of Nimuë's appearance is that here she confirms the innocence of the queen and proves that Lancelot fought in a just cause, whereas later on there is more than a small element of ambiguity about Guinevere's innocence.

In each of these incidents we are shown Nimuë acting in a wholly consistent manner as Merlin's successor. But what are we to make of her imprisonment of Merlin? We have seen that the episode is variously interpreted as tragedy or comedy, as an inevitable consequence of Merlin's besottedness, or as the fate he predicted for himself; while Nimuë's role ranges from that of abused woman to scheming fay. But perhaps there are other reasons which the romancers, not understanding the subtext, have glossed over or ignored?

The Esplumoir

In order to understand the real nature of Merlin's sequestration and to discover Nimuë's true role and identity, we have to look elsewhere, specifically to two texts: *The Didot Perceval*[6] and the long and prolix tale of *Meraugis de la Portlesguez*. In both these texts Merlin's end is described in very different terms from that of a foolish old man overcome by the wiles of a girl. Here there is no mention of Nimuë at all; rather Merlin withdraws from the world by his own desire. The passage from the *Didot Perceval* is as follows:

> And then Merlin came to Perceval and to Blayse his master, and he took leave of them and told them that Our Lord did not wish that he should show himself to people, yet that he would not be able to die before the end of the world; ' . . . and I wish to make a lodging outside your palace and to dwell there and I will prophesy whatever Our Lord commands me. And all those who will see my lodging will name it the *esplumoir* (or moulting cage) of Merlin.'[7]

There has been much speculation about the precise meaning of this word *esplumoir*. No exact equivalent has been found anywhere else, and the interpretation 'moulting cage' has lead to a number of speculations. It may be that the author of the *Didot Perceval* intended nothing more than an elaborate pun on Merlin's name, and that the *esplumoir* is indeed no more than a kind of cage in which hunting birds were kept during moult.

Several commentators have pointed out that the moulting cage is itself a kind of image of the Otherworld, into which mortals often went but seldom returned. If this is the case, and if Merlin either retires voluntarily or is shut up in the cage, or otherworldly place, by Nimuë, then she must, by inference, be seen as an otherworldly figure herself – as, indeed, a faery woman whose role is often to test and to entrap a mortal. To be sure, Merlin is scarcely a mortal himself, but he has enough human blood in him to feel passion for Nimuë.

The whole question of the relationships between human and faery races, and the number of inter-species matings which occur in the literature, make it clear enough that mortal men and women were considered desirable to the otherworldly people, and faery men and women were equally attractive to mortals. This exchange is based upon the interpenetration of the mortal and immortal worlds. The doom of mortals is that they must die, hence the provision, in so many stories, that the mortal half of the couple must actually live in the Otherworld, where time was stretched thin and where they were able to live virtually forever by the simple fact of being there. Mortals who stray from faery revert to their mortal age and infirmities once again, to die almost immediately.

But Merlin's entry into the Otherworld seems more of a carefully planned event than the result of a casual liaison with Nimuë, fay or not. He seems to belong there from the start, and it may be that here we have the clue we need to follow him.

Several commentators have drawn attention to Merlin's shamanistic nature; in particular the accounts of him to be found in the *Historia Regum Brittaniae* and the *Vita Merlini*, of Geoffrey of Monmouth, have a strong flavour of shamanism.

Here he is an inspired prophet and poet who suffers from spells of 'madness' from which he is only cured by the intervention of a hermit, and by the ministrations of his sister Ganieda. Geoffrey's tales, through written in the twelfth century, have been shown to embody material from a much earlier time, and from the evidence they present it is possible to see in the figure of Merlin a kind of inspired, half-mad poet and prophet known to the Celts as a 'geilt'. Some early poems attributed to Merlin describe him as addressing prophecies to a pig and to an apple-tree, clear enough indication of his status as a shaman who possessed animal spirit helpers and understood deeply the connection of humanity and the natural world.

The Irish figure, Suibhne Geilt, to whom Merlin has been often compared, also had a passion for trees, and spent a great deal of time on their branches, dressed in a cloak of feathers which apparently enabled him to fly. Is it possible that Merlin once possessed this ability also, and that when we read of him entering his 'moulting cage' he is in reality simply putting off the feathered cloak of the shaman? In the *Didot Perceval*, where the prime mention of the *esplumoir* appears, Perceval at one time hears the voice of Merlin issuing from a cloud, while in *Meraugis de la Portlesguez*, the only other text to mention the *esplumoir*, the term is applied to the *Roche du Pucelles* (Rock of Women) which is described as a place with no path to the summit, implying that the only way to get there was by flying. If the numerous references to faery women taking the form of birds is acknowledged (see Chapter 3), then once again we have evidence for the *esplumoir* as an otherworldly place to which only someone with birds' wings can reach. Such a place, indeed, as Merlin's 'moulting cage', where the hawk retires to renew itself.

A.C.L. Brown, in investigating the meaning of the *esplumoir*, provides evidence for its ultimate origin within Irish myth. For him *esplumoir* refers to the Otherworld which is represented in numerous stories as a house of glass, or a place with many windows such as that which, in the *Vita Merlini*, is constructed for Merlin by Ganieda. In the Irish myth of Etain, Etain is at one point turned into a fly and kept in a *grianan* (the Irish 'sun-house' where women gathered to weave or embroider) by the god Aengus mac ind Oic, where she is also visited by her lover in the form of a bird; he leaves his bird-dress, or *enchendaich*, on the floor. This *grianan* is transportable and so becomes a kind of glass enclosure for the preservation of Etain.

To this we may add that the god Aengus, who kept Etain in a glass enclosure, has a number of similarities to Merlin, sufficient indeed to suggest that, at one point in the development of the story, Merlin's house of glass was an otherworldly *sid* (a dwelling place of the *sidhe*) over which he ruled, and where dwelt faery women. The *grianan* may be seen as essentially a microcosm of the Land of Women, a place of safety and transformation, inviolately dedicated to faery women.

From this we begin to see a wholly different picture in which Ganieda (Gwenddydd), Merlin's sister, dwells with him in an otherworldly house of glass from which they both observed the passing of events outside, possibly venturing forth at intervals to help those in need or to change the course of larger events. Ganieda is referred to in the *Vita Merlini* as returning frequently to Merlin's house with food – a detail which suggests that Merlin could not himself leave there even if he wished, rather as Maelduin in the Irish *immrama* story cannot leave his faery mistress.[8]

When one views the Merlin-Nimuë story in the light of this, one sees a story with a very different emphasis and motivation. Merlin, tired of the world and of the need constantly to intervene in its concerns, retires to his *esplumoir*, accompanied by his faery lover or sister (who was perhaps both!), where he remains. Nimuë, prepared by him for the role, takes Merlin's place as helper and adviser to Arthur, whom she continues to protect until his passing to Avalon.

In the light of this evidence we may begin to see Nimuë in a different light, no longer as a scheming fay, but as an otherworldly woman whose gift was to enable the passage of mortals from one world to the other. There is only one character associated with Merlin who is both able and willing to do this –

his twin sister. In early Welsh tradition she is called Gwenddydd, or 'White Day', but in the *Vita Merlini* she is called Ganieda, a Latinization of the earlier name. The *Vita* confusingly gives the name of Merlin's wife as Guendolena, a name much closer in sound to that of Gwenddydd: this confusion becomes more significant the further we explore.

THE SIBYLLINE SISTER

Let us begin by examining the evidence of the *Vita Merlini*, looking specifically at the appearances of Ganieda, Merlin's sister. Here she is the wife of King Rodarch of Cumbria. She hears that Merlin is living in the woods and that he has gone mad as a result of the recent great battle in which he served. She sends a messenger to him, who sings of the lamentations of Guendolena, Merlin's wife, and Merlin accompanies him to the court of Rodarch, where Ganieda greets him. Merlin has to be chained to remain at court, for the sight of so many people deranges his senses. No one can persuade him to smile.

Then Merlin sees how Rodarch kisses Ganieda, taking a leaf out of her hair, and this prompts him to immoderate laughter. He explains this by telling the king that Ganieda has just come from lying with her lover in the undergrowth, but Ganieda distracts Rodarch from a cuckold's rage by decrying Merlin's words as insane lies. To further prove her point, she sets up a challenge to Merlin: she calls a boy into the hall and asks her brother how the boy will die. Merlin replies that the boy will die from a fall. Ganieda then dresses the same boy as a girl and asks how she will die; Merlin replies that the girl will be hanged. Ganieda then dresses the boy as a woman and asks Merlin about her manner of death; Merlin replies that she will drown. It transpires that Merlin is later vindicated: the boy falls from his horse from a high place, catches himself in a tree during his fall, and his head is submerged in a river - thus he dies a triple death by falling, hanging and drowning simultaneously.

Ganieda supports the cause of the deserted Guendolena, and

asks Merlin to take her to the forest. 'She will go with you to the forest and will be happy to live in the green forest clearings.' But Merlin peremptorily says, 'Sister, I do not want a cow that pours water in as broad a stream as the Virgin's Urn in flood.'⁹ He gives Guendolena permission to remarry as long as her husband never crosses his path. Later, in his observations, Merlin perceives changes in the kingdom and sees that Guendolena is about to be married. He arrives at court riding on a stag and calls to his ex-wife. Both Guendolena and her prospective husband look out. The bridegroom laughs and Merlin furiously wrenches off the stag's antlers and slays him with them.

Ganieda builds for him an observatory with 70 doors and windows from which Merlin may watch the circling of the stars and planets, and in which he lives and makes prophecies. He begs her to visit him often, prophesies the doom of Britain and bids her send Taliesin to him. On her return, Ganieda finds Rodarch dead. She makes a noble lamentation for him and prepares to take herself off to the woods with Merlin.

After Merlin and Taliesin's long discussion of cosmology and natural history and their reminiscence of ferrying Arthur to Avalon with Barinthus (see Chapter 3), Ganieda appears to fulfil her promise. She acquires the gift of prophecy in such measure that Merlin is moved to say: *'Sister, is it you the spirit has willed to foretell the future? He has curbed my tongue and closed my book. Then this task is given to you. Be glad of it, and under my authority declare everything faithfully.'*¹⁰

It speedily becomes clear that Ganieda is the most important woman in Merlin's life. She is a queen of some power and is never subservient or confused. She manages Merlin's affairs promptly and with ease and is his match in all but prophecy, until the end when he commissions her to continue his work.

It is not too hard to see, in the observatory which she builds for him, a further image of the Otherworld (all places or buildings made all or in part from glass had this dimension); while Gwenddydd/Ganieda, who is herself a prophetess and magician, fits easily into the shape of an otherworldly woman of power.

The correlations between Gwenddydd/Ganieda and Nimuë are plainly visible in the *Vita*:

Ganieda	Nimuë
encourages Merlin	is Merlin's helper
tests Merlin	tempts him to perform magic
meets Merlin in the forest	meets Merlin in the forest
laments the death of Rodarch	accompanies Arthur to Avalon
makes a secluded observatory	conjures a hawthorn/glass tower
continues Merlin's prophetic task	continues Merlin's work

while in the group of Welsh poems from the thirteenth-century *Black Book of Carmarthen* (Four Ancient Books) which relate to a lost Merlin saga,[11] there are several references which extend this idea further. In the *Afallanau* (Appletrees), attributed to Merlin himself, we find:

> Sweet appletree of luxuriant growth!
> I used to find food at its foot,
> When, because of a maid,
> I slept alone in the woods of Celyddon,
> Shield on shoulder, sword on thigh . . .
> Sweet appletree, growing by the river,
> Who will thrive on its wondrous fruit?
> When my reason was intact
> I used to lie at its foot
> With a fair wanton maid, of slender form.[12]

Who is this woman? Can we descry the identity of the lover with whom Ganieda sneaks away to the undergrowth? Later in the same poem there is a reference to the *chwyfleian*, who 'foretells a tale that will come to pass'. There has been some debate over the exact meaning of this word and its variation, *hwimleian*.

A.O.H. Jarman translates it as 'a wanderer of pallid countenance', while the eighteenth-century scholar Lewis Morris believed that it meant 'sibyl'. In his influential study *Celtic Remains* he wrote: 'Myrddin Wyllt . . . quotes the British Sybil by the title of Chwibleian and Chwimbleian, as if the word were formed from *lleian*, a nun, vestal virgin, or priestess.' Although the word is still used to refer to a nun today, the derivation 'priestess' is less likely, though interesting in the context of the poem.

Of crucial import is the association of Merlin with 'a wanton maid, of fair form', with whom he used to sport beneath a tree, and with a character who possessed the ability of prophecy. Could they be one and the same? In the context of the story hinted at here and elsewhere in the old poems it seems more than likely. Even if, as Jarman suggests, the word *chwibleian* once referred to a male prophet or wild man, this need not deter us from making the association of the prophet and the maiden, as indeed subsequent romance writers seem to have done.

The most interesting point, for our current argument, is the obvious similarity between *chwibleian*, *hwimleian* and the name of Merlin's mistress Niniane or Vivien. Either could have derived from the old Welsh word, and carried with it the idea of a prophetess or woman of power, erotically associated with Merlin. It seems clear that Geoffrey of Monmouth was thinking of this in the *Vita Merlini* when he wrote the following passage.

Arriving at a fountain, Merlin and his companions find some fragrant apples which, when eaten, cause the companions to go temporarily mad. Merlin explains that they were in all probability meant for him, for there was, in that district,

> . . . a woman who had formerly been infatuated with me, and had satisfied her love for me during many years. After I had spurned her and had refused to cohabit with her she was suddenly seized with an evil desire to do me harm, and when with all her plotting she could not find any other means of approach, she placed the gifts smeared with poison by the fountain to which I was going to return, planning by this device to injure me if I could chance to find the apples in the grass and eat them.[13]

Is this the origin of Nimuë? A woman who loved Merlin and, on being spurned by him, turned against him and attempted to destroy him by poisoned apples? If so, it completely reverses the story as we know it from the medieval sources.

The answer lies in the nature of the apples themselves. Apples were well known to the Celts as otherworldly fruit, and there are numerous stories in which heroes are found sleeping beneath apple trees and are carried off by otherworldly women, or again are offered apples which have the effect of bespelling them so that they waken in faeryland. If we see Nimuë-Gwenddydd as the guardian of such apples, then we are nearer to the idea of her as an otherworldly or faery woman who has the power *in her own right* to convey people into the Otherworld. And if, as in the Welsh Merlin poems, she was the mage's sister, then what more natural that she possess magical skills of her own? Is Ganieda's lover Merlin? He who spends his life in the woods might indeed laugh to see a leaf in Ganieda's hair when she embraces her husband Rodarch. Is Merlin's mistress his own sister, and does this lie at the foundation of the Nimuë-Merlin relationship?

THE KEEPER OF THE WAYS

Merlin is the perfect counterpart of Nimuë. She is the huntress and he is the wild man, the hunter who becomes her prey. In the *Vita Merlini* he becomes a man of the woods, like an outlaw or recluse. There are parallels between both Robin Hood and Merlin: both have their careers treacherously ended by the woman they dearly loved. Maid Marian becomes the Abbess of Kirklees and is said to have been responsible for poisoning Robin; Nimuë ceases to be the innocent woodland girl and becomes an enchantress of great magical ability. The nature of Merlin's character actually dictates this change, in some respects.

Mythically, Merlin in his madness reverts to an earlier archetype – that of wild man. In the *Vita Merlini* he can command the deer to do his bidding, even riding upon one. In Malory Merlin comes from his master, Blaise, to Arthur at the castle of Bedegraine in Sherwood Forest.[14] Merlin disguises himself with black sheepskins, boots, a russet gown and a bow and arrow – the attire of a huntsman – and brings Arthur a wild goose. He comes to reveal to Arthur the whereabouts of a treasure, but he does it in a jesting, tricksterish way, which amuses the court when Arthur fails to recognize his own magician in disguise. This episode is borrowed from the *Vita Merlini*.

The presence of the Goddess Diana in the myth of Nimuë may point to a more native understanding. The figure of the white hart or white doe frequently appears in Celtic tradition as a messenger of the Otherworld. It is the shape in which faery beings sometimes chose to appear to mortal eyes. The Irish hero Ossian's mother, Sadb, was enchanted by the Dark Druid into doe shape. As a woman she became Fionn Mac Cumhail's mistress, but she bore Ossian while in doe shape. One of Sadb's other names is Blaí – Flower.

Another mistress of stags was the Irish goddess Flidais. Little is known of her, but she was the protector of wild animals, and possessed supernatural cattle. She also had a chariot which was drawn by deer. Whether it is she who is depicted in the bronze horned Goddess statue in the British Museum is not known for certain. Flidais is mentioned as the mate of Fergus mac Roich – a man allegedly so virile that he needs seven women to satisfy his desires. The Cailleach of Lochaber in Scotland is similarly credited with a herd of wild deer, rather than cows.[15]

Does this give Nimuë roots in a deeper tradition? We find that the Deer Goddess is associated with the wild woodland, that she keeps a herd of magical cows or deer and sometimes a chariot pulled by deer, that she is sexually active and seeks out suitable men who can satisfy her desires. She has elements of the Flower Bride, in that she possesses magical cattle and does not settle on one mate.

It seems that these qualities revert to an almost pre-Celtic antiquity. The only people who still cultivate deer like cattle today are those peoples who live within sight of the Arctic Circle, like the Lapps who manage herds of reindeer. In our distant past, during the Ice Ages, our ancestors would have had a similar lifestyle. The reverence in which the deer was held is still a feature of shamanic cultures around the North Pole. The deer becomes a magical persona for shamans, a mode by which they may travel and interrelate with the Otherworld – features of which are traceable in *Vita Merlini* when Merlin mounts a stag and rides to the court of his ex-wife Guendolena to prevent her remarriage.

The connection between Nimuë and the Deer Goddess may be further instanced by the story of Liban, who survives the flooding of Loch Neagh half as a salmon, half as a woman, like a mermaid. She emerges to meet to the hero Caoilte out hunting, takes his spear and slays the deer. Finally she appears to St Beoan who baptizes her Muirgen (Sea-Born). Worn out by the weight of years, she dies, but is borne to heaven by stags.[16] We note that Liban lives in a lake, has otherworldly longevity and appears to men of power.

The Deer Goddess is so remote from us that we have little information about her. Traces of her remain in the myths of the Cailleach, the ancient mountain mother of the North, and we can see a few remnants of her power in the medieval figure of Nimuë as well as in the oracular figure of Gwenddydd, the original sister of Merlin. The title of *chwibleian* or sibyl, applied to the companion of Merlin in the *Afallanau* poem may give us a clue to another feature of Nimuë's character, for it is a term that may be translated as 'Votaress of the Vagina'.[17] Nimuë's sibylline abilities are practised side by side with what the Celts called 'the friendship of the thighs'. She is that most Celtic of combinations – a huntress who is also a priestess. But she is no vestal.

It is significant that Venus is said to govern venery, a term which can imply both hunting and sexuality. *Gwener* is the Welsh word for Venus, meaning 'White One'. There are shadowy connections between Gwenddydd/Ganieda/Guendolena and Gwener/Venus which may become clearer when we consider that Ganieda has a lover as well as a husband, and that Merlin is contemplating the planet Venus when he divines that Guendolena is about to remarry. Both Ganieda *and* Guendolena are willing to go to the woods to live with Merlin, though in the end only Ganieda does so. Their companionship in the forest leads to the gradual passing of power from Merlin to his sister.

The emphasis in *Suite du Merlin* and *Mort Artu* on Nimuë's careful preservation of her virginity does suggest the lingering memory of her sacredness as a priestess. Also her age, given sometimes as 12 but more often as 15, is significant (Vestal Virgins entered the temple in Rome at this age); while Robert Graves, in his seminal study of 'poetic myth', *The White Goddess*, classes Vivien as the Muse Cardea-Cerridwen, 'who inspires *cerddeu*, "poems", in Greek *cerdia*'. He also quotes the early Welsh poem 'The Dialogue of Gwenddydd and Merddin' in which Gwenddydd instructs her 'twin' brother to rise from his prison and 'open the Books of Inspiration without fear'. In the same poem she is described as *Gwenddydd wen adlam Cerddeu*, which Graves translates as 'White Lady of Day, refuge of Poems', making her goddessly status plain enough. If we add to this the evidence presented above, which identifies Gwenddydd as the *chwifleian*, or priestess-sybyl, this makes a very strong case for seeing Nimuë in a very different light to that of her usual character. It also gives us a giant key with which to unlock the last mystery of her role.

Cardea is the Roman Goddess of the Door-hinges and in nature is very similar to both Artemis and Diana in that she is also a virgin-goddess of the hunt.[18] She obtained her post as guardian of doorways from Janus, in return for her favours. This fact staggeringly affirms Nimuë as the successor of Gwenddydd/Ganieda, for Nimuë *encloses* Merlin behind a door which will not open save for her, although she is only given this power in return for her embraces.

Geoffrey of Monmouth speaks of how Cordelia buried her father King Lear in a vault under the River Soar at Leicester, ground which had been sacred to Janus. The tomb was already the meeting-place for workmen who would convene here on the first day of the year to begin their year's work.[19] Again we note the connection of Cardea/Cordelia with Janus and with sacred work. This image of Cordelia sealing Lear into a vault resonates strongly with Nimuë and Merlin – the young maiden who comes to emtomb the ancient prophet.

The Goddess of the Door is also instanced importantly in Merlin's prophecies within the *History of the Kings of Britain*. There she appears as the goddess Ariadne who closes the door of the aeon. Varro confirms that Cardea ruled over the Celestial Hinge at the back of the North Wind, around which the millstone of the world revolves.[20] Gwenddydd/Ganieda is the creator of Merlin's otherworldly observatory of 70 *doors and windows*.

Nimuë emerges as the representative of a native Goddess of the Door, one who guards the borderlands of this world with the other. It is her sacred work to accompany Merlin, becoming his lineal successor in the Arthurian world.

As in the case of many other figures from medieval romance, the modern view of Nimuë as a temptress bent upon the destruction of Merlin is not only untrue but also a huge oversimplification. As we have seen, she is a far more complex figure when all the versions are examined. She functions not only as an essential helper to Arthur, but as a prophetess and priestess of tremendous qualities. Her modern image is very largely due to a fundamental misunderstanding of the natures of both Merlin *and* Nimuë. Merlin's withdrawal from the world is just that, and the idea that he was entrapped by a faery woman reads like a piece of medieval rationalization of a much older theme, one which is better preserved in the *Vita Merlini* than elsewhere.

Even in Malory Nimuë's role is one of continuing Merlin's work. Far from being the evil enchantress or *femme fatale* figure that most people seem to see, she is described as someone who 'did great good to King Arthur and all his knights'. She helps Arthur against the plots of Morgan, and later, towards the end of Malory's book, appears in the story of the poisoning of Sir

Patrise, explaining that it was all a plot to kill Gawain. Her final appearance in the *Morte d'Arthur* is as one of the queenly women in the barge which ambiguously carries Arthur either to his death or to Avalon. Other commentators have suggested that she is there specifically to counter-balance Morgan.[21] Thus the two women who are Arthur's helper and his chief opponent are brought together at the end to cancel each other out, as well as adding to the ambiguity of Arthur's fate. In fact the apparent turn in Morgan's allegiance is not what it seems (see Chapter 3), but the way in which Malory understood it upholds the theory of the two women as magical opponents, balanced in polarity at the end of the Arthurian dream.

Nimuë is thus seen clearly at last, in the shape of Gwenddydd, the empowering priestess and prophet every bit as important and powerful as her twin, Merlin. She changes from Gwenddydd, the sister and helper of Merlin, into the temptress and betrayer, whose only defence against Merlin's wiles is to flatter him and smile at him until she has gained enough of his knowledge to turn it against him. Thus the empowerer becomes the betrayer, and as so often in the world of Arthurian romance, the role of the woman is subverted and changed from positive to negative. The power of Nimuë could not be wholly crushed however, and in texts such as Malory's *Morte d'Arthur* she continues to fulfil her role as a Lady of the Lake, while in the *Vita Merlini* her true function as the holder of the ways between this world and the Otherworld is clearly revealed.

The Tower of Glass

Close your eyes and enter a quiet place within you from which you may journey forth into the realms of the Otherworld. See before you the rough, gnarled trunks of two great trees, between which you see the tangled ways of a mighty forest, a mixture of shadowed rides and sun-illuminated clearings. Step between the trees and walk

ahead, letting your steps lead you where they will until you
hear, distantly at first, but growing gradually stronger, the
calling of birds. High and silvery their voices penetrate deep
within you, drawing you deeper and deeper into the
forest . . .

Gradually, the land on which you walk rises, until you are
climbing through the great bastions of the trees, clinging to
root and branch to pull yourself up. Panting, you arrive at a
level place and see before you a tall tower sparkling in the
sunlight. But this is no ordinary tower of stone and mortar;
the sun reflects back from it in dazzling rays, for its walls
are of gleaming glass . . .

For a moment you stand, bemused by the sight, then you go
forward towards an arched entrance leading within . . .
Surprisingly, the interior of the tower is dim, the walls
opaque. Sunlight strikes through, but is somehow caught,
filtered and turned back again. Outside, all is brilliance and
glittering light; within, there is a cool, diffuse glow . . . A
stairway leads upwards, curving to the right around the
softly glowing wall . . . you follow it, upward, for a long
time . . .

At length you find yourself in a circular room the walls of
which shimmer and seem at times translucent, at others,
opaque. In the centre sits a figure weaving at an ancient
loom. Her hair is long and black, her face pale; she wears a
dress of many colours which shift like a rainbow, showing
now blue, now yellow, now red, now violet, with many
subtle shifts between. The pattern of her weaving is beyond
description, being of light and colour, endlessly shifting and
changing. You see shapes there as you look, but they are
gone before you are able to grasp their significance . . .

Without pausing in the swift movement of shuttle and weft
the woman looks up at you, scanning you with such
penetration that you feel naked before her. Then, abruptly,
she stands up, and though her hands are removed from the
warp and web, yet the shuttle continues to move, even
faster now it seems. The lady beckons you to follow her to
the side of the room, from where you look out through a
window of clear glass in the fabric of the tower. Below is
the forest, spreading far into the distance. Yet now its mood
is autumnal; the leaves have turned to deepest bronze and

strong winds snatch them and drive them into mounds on
the forest floor . . .

Then Nimuë, for she it is, raises a hand and opens a door
in the tower before her. She walks through and you follow
in her wake, trusting yourself to her guidance. She moves
more swiftly than you could have imagined, and caught in
her train you are drawn after her into the sky itself . . . and
there before you you see a second tower, like the first,
radiating light, but this time set amid points of starlight . . .

Within the tower all is bright, as though the darkness
without were compressed and turned about to form a
border of light. Again the stair leads you upward, until you
enter a room identical to the one in the earthly tower. Yet
there are two differences. Here the loom is still, and a
woven cloth, almost completed, is stretched in its frame.
And beside it, on a great bed, lies the figure of a man,
whose age is beyond calculation and whose sleeping face
possesses such beauty that you are breathless at the
sight . . . A suspicion as to the identity of the sleeper enters
your mind, and you seem to hear Nimuë's voice in your
ears. 'Yes, this is indeed Merlin, who sleeps here until the
time for his waking dawns. It was not I who placed him
here, nor is it I who keep him so. I am the guardian only,
and when the time is right I shall wake him again . . .'

Now Nimuë moves to stand before the loom and bids you
look upon her work. You hear her words: 'I am she who
weaves all threads into a pattern that none may read save
one, and that my brother Merlin. Yet the weaving is almost
finished, and because you have come here with me you may
look upon the pattern and see one thing that you desire to
see. Look well, for only once is this offer made . . .'

You look at the woven cloth and there amid the pattern, so
complex that your eyes cannot read it, is a single, glowing
picture, a scene perhaps, or words that mean something to
you alone. Look with care, and remember what you see, for
this opportunity will not come again . . .

When you have looked, and understood, what is there for
you to see, you follow the Lady of the Web once again to
the door of the tower, only somehow it is no longer set
amid the starry sky, but opens again onto the greenwood

where you began your journey. A few last words she speaks to you: 'I am the Keeper of Wisdom, the Bespeller of Night and Day, the Queen who rules over Space and Time in the Wood of Wonders. Remember well your journey, and all that you have learned. It is only part of the mystery of the Nine, which you will come to know better . . .'

As her words ring in your ears you walk forward and pass almost at once between the gnarled trunks of two great trees. Your consciousness shifts, and you are again in the room from which you began this journey to the realms of the Otherworld. Take time to recover, and write down anything you wish of your time in the Tower of Glass.

REFERENCES

1. H.B. Wheatley (ed.), *Merlin*.
2. Ibid.
3. Samuel N. Rosenberg, 'The Prose Merlin and the Suite Merlin', *The Romance of Arthur*.
4. Sir Thomas Malory, *The Morte d'Arthur*.
5. Ibid.
6. D. Skeels, *Romance of Perceval in Prose (Didot Perceval)*.
7. Ibid.
8. Caitlín Matthews, *The Celtic Book of the Dead*.
9. Geoffrey of Monmouth, *Vita Merlini*, trans. Basil Clarke.
10. Ibid.
11. A.O.H. Jarman, 'A Note on the Possible Welsh Derivation of Viviane', *Gallicia: Essays Presented to J.H. Thomas*.
12. Our translation.
13. Geoffrey of Monmouth, *Vita Merlini*, ed. and trans. J.J. Parry.
14. Malory, op. cit, Book 1, xviii.
15. Anne Ross, *Pagan Celtic Britain*.
16. Lady Gregory, *Voyages of Brendan the Navigator and Tales of the Irish Saints*.
17. John Matthews, *Taliesin: Shamanism and the Bardic Mysteries in Britain and Ireland*.
18. Adrian Room, *Room's Classical Dictionary*.
19. Geoffrey of Monmouth, *History of the Kings of Britain*.

20. Robert Graves, *The White Goddess*.
21. S.E. Holbrook, 'Nymue, the Chief Lady of the Lake in Malory's *Morte Darthur*', *Speculum*, and R.M. Lumiansky, 'Arthur's Final Companions in Malory's *Le Morte Darthur*', *Tulane Studies in English*.

6
Enid

'Alas, Enid,' said Arthur, 'what expedition is this?'
'I know not, lord,' said she, 'save that it behoves me to journey by the same road that he journeys.'

Gereint and Enid from *The Mabinogion*

THE MYTH OF ENID

Many characters within Arthurian legend are rendered unbelievable because their original otherworldly nature is denied. Many romancers took the characters straight from Celtic oral tradition and attempted to kit them out as ready-made medieval knights and ladies. Enid suffers from this treatment. Her otherworldly origins are not immediately apparent, nor are her apparent attributes those which many would seek to emulate. Yet she is basically an otherworldly Deliverer: one who tastes the bitterness of mortality to the dregs, but who retains her vivacity and love.

The story of Enid appears in the cross-related texts *Erec and Enide* by Chrétien de Troyes and the British Arthurian romance, bound with *The Mabinogion*, *Gereint and Enid*. In terms of oral transmission, it is virtually impossible to say which text predated the other. They each present different facets, while retaining the main story-line. We will be comparing and referring to both of them here, but *Gereint and Enid* has been treated fully in *Arthur and the Sovereignty of Britain*, so the main emphasis will be upon the French text.

Erec and Enide begins with Arthur announcing that he wishes to revive the tradition of hunting for the white hart. Gawain counsels against this, for whoever wins the stag may kiss the most beautiful woman at court, which will cause contention. But the hunt sets off, though without Guinevere and Erec, who accompanies her. They meet a knight accompanied by a damsel and a dwarf. Guinevere sends her maid to enquire who this is. The dwarf uncourteously strikes the maid. Erec wishes to avenge this insult to the queen and rides after the party, although he is unarmed. Meanwhile Arthur wins the white hart himself, though on hearing of Guinevere's adventures, he agrees to postpone the awarding of the kiss until Erec has returned.

Erec follows the party into a town where an old Vavasour (vassal of a nobleman) greets him and offers hospitality. He calls his wife and daughter from their workshop and bids them tend to Erec. The daughter, Enid, is dressed in old worn clothes. She acts as the horse's groom. Erec learns that Enid is dowerless, because her father the Vavasour has lost his lands during the wars. He also finds out that the town is full of people come to play the Sparrowhawk contest. This hawk is awarded to the knight whose lady surpasses others in beauty. This year's test seems to be a mere formality, since the knight who has previously won it twice will take it unchallenged. This knight is the very one who insulted Guinevere.

For the contest, the Vavasour offers Erec his own armour and a mount. Erec then asks for Enid to be his lady, which her father agrees to readily. Enid arms Erec, and they ride together to the field of the Sparrowhawk where he claims the bird. Erec and the knight fight, and the insult to Guinevere is avenged when the knight is overcome. Erec discovers his name is Yder, son of Nut. He sends Yder and his lady back to Guinevere, there to be judged by her. It is thus that the court learns that Erec is about to return.

Erec asks for Enid's hand in marriage, and promises to make good the Vavasour's landless condition with castles of his own. He asks that Enid retain her poor dress so that Guinevere can reclothe her appropriately. When this has been done and Enid has been presented at court, Arthur accords the custom of the white hart to her, kissing her. Many guests come to the wedding of Enid and Erec, the queen prepares the wedding chamber herself and the young couple rejoice in their love. They return to the castle of Erec's father, King Lac.

During their honeymoon, Erec avoids all deeds of arms and attends to his wife, but Enid becomes unhappy at hearing how the knights and men at arms blame her for this change in their master. In bed, she falls weeping because of it, lamenting her husband's fall from chivalry. Erec awakens and overhears her. He arises speedily, bidding her dress in her finest dress, and rides forth to vindicate himself. He bids Enid not speak unless he first speaks to her. Riding out unescorted, they encounter many ambushes and adventures in which Enid ventures to warn Erec of his danger, contrary to his command that she keep silence. Erec overcomes many knights and cut-throats who would kill him and rape Enid. At one castle, a count begs Enid to become his lady and stop following the reckless Erec, but she declines.

Erec fights and overcomes a small knight called Guivret, who offers him medical assistance, for he is sorely wounded. Relentlessly, though, Erec rides on with Enid until they come to a part of the forest where Arthur and his court are encamped. Kay comes across them and, not recognizing them, threatens to bring them before Arthur, but Erec fights and overcomes him. Gawain then attempts to bring them to Arthur and finally recognizes them both. Erec's wounds are treated with Morgan's ointment, but he refuses to rest and recover.

Then in an encounter with some giants, Erec is again sorely wounded and falls unconscious from his horse. Enid laments his death and is about to kill herself when a count rides by and begs her to become his wife. With Erec's body laid out in the castle, the count hales Enid to the chapel and there attempts to get her to marry him by force. Her protestations are so loud that Erec awakes from his stupor and kills the count. Everyone assumes that the dead man has returned to life and flees.

Erec assures Enid of his love, and that his ill-advised actions have been solely to test her love for him. They struggle onwards until met again by Guivret, who gives them shelter. Much restored by Guivret's healing sisters, Erec continues his journey with Guivret and Enid. They approach Castle Brandigan, which Guivret informs them is ruled by King Evrain. There is an evil custom there from which no brave knight has ever returned. This custom is called the Joy of the Court. Erec is much fired by this challenge and makes to go there, to his companions' dismay.

King Evrain welcomes them hospitably and Erec asks for the Joy of the Court, though Evrain tries to dissuade him. Amid widespread lamentation, he enters an enchanted garden and there finds a row of stakes with a severed head upon each, save for one, whereon a horn hangs. Whoever overcomes the customs and blows the horn shall be honoured among the best. Then Erec finds a maiden seated upon a silver bed. He is challenged by a gigantic red knight and overcomes him. The red knight is called Mabonograin. He tells how when he was a squire at King Lac's court he made a promise to the maiden that he would do her will. She redeemed this promise by asking him never to leave the enchanted garden unless another knight overcame him in combat. Faithful to his vow, Mabonograin defeated and killed many. He instructs Erec to blow the horn to signal the Joy of the Court, since he is now released from his vow and the evil custom is broken.

The inhabitants of Castle Brandigan rejoice in song, with the only dejected person being the maiden of the garden. Enid speaks with her and discovers that she is none other than her cousin. The two women exchange the story of their adventures in love, which consoles the maiden. After three days of rejoicing Erec and Enid return to Arthur's court where they are welcomed gladly. At Christmas the news of King Lac's death reaches them and, with the majority of the court, they sail to Nantes to celebrate their coronation as king and queen.

Gereint and Enid follows the course of this tale, with some significant variations. Yder son of Nut is called Edern ap Nudd, while King Evrain is Owain ap Urien. The white hart's head is awarded to the fairest maiden, but no kiss is given. Most striking is the difference between Erec and Gereint. Gereint misunderstands Enid's tears, thinking that she mourns for an illicit lover. He is much rougher in his treatment of Enid: he not only forbids her to speak to him, but makes her dress in her oldest dress. The Joy of the Court is here called the Enchanted Games, and the horn of liberation hangs upon an apple tree. Neither the gigantic knight nor his lady are named. *Gereint and Enid* also omits the triumphal conclusion of Chrétien's version.

Enid is also referred to in Ulrich von Zatzikhoven's *Lanzelet*, when, as we have seen in Chapter 4, a magical mantle is brought to the court by a mermaid from Maidenland. This mantle tests the chastity of the wearer; if the woman is unfaithful in love, it contracts. The author says that it might have fitted Enid, had she been present, thus affirming her reputed virtue.

Enid does not appear in Malory or in the later texts, but there is reason to suggest that she fused with the independent tradition of Luned or Lynette, who became a popular figure of later story.[1] She became a character much beloved of the Victorian public, however, through Tennyson's rendition of the medieval tale in his *Idylls of the King*.

THE WHITE HART

The otherworldly deer – whether doe or stag – frequently appears in Celtic tradition as a messenger or the herald of a great quest. In *Gereint* we hear that the stag is pure white and 'does not herd with any other animal through stateliness and pride, so royal is his bearing'. The awe and mystery surrounding this beast was paralleled by the medieval passion for the unicorn, the legendary beast of the chase, representing both earthly and heavenly love. This imagery was so rooted in European consciousness that the unicorn or chained white hart also became one of the mystical emblems of Christ. We have seen already how the Quest for the White Hart is the object of the first quest in the *Morte d'Arthur*, and that this adventure is tied up with Arthur's sovereignty (pp.48-50).

In *Erec*, Arthur's sudden announcement that he wants to

hunt the white hart in order to restore the ancient custom is met with disquiet by Gawain, as we have seen. Arthur nevertheless sticks to his decision in a way which implies that this is his kingly *geas* or obligation, 'for the word of a king must not be contravened'.

There is further evidence of the antiquity and sovereignty-implication of Quest for the White Hart in *Lanzelet*. Here we learn that the hunt was established by Arthur's father, Uther Pendragon, who 'instituted this custom; and his son has maintained it ever since . . . The king was to take by right, and as it became him, a kiss from the most beautiful woman.'

Underlying this quest is the Celtic myth of the Goddess of Sovereignty, the Goddess of the Land, who alone of all has the right to appoint a ruler for her land. She can take whatever form pleases her to test the candidates for this role, and there are two major tests in which she manifests either as a white doe or a hideous woman. We will be considering this last appearance in Chapter 9.

In the ancient Irish stories, the Goddess of the Land appears as a white or golden doe. In the story of *The Adventures of the Sons of King Daire* from the medieval compilation known as *The Book of Ballymote*, she is pursued by Daire's five sons and slain by the one destined to become king. In this story the Goddess appears as the hideous woman: the same son sleeps with her willingly and to him sovereignty is given (see Chapter 9).

So we begin to see the significance of the winner of the white hart either kissing or awarding the head to the fairest woman at court. That woman represents the Goddess of Sovereignty in her role of priestess who confers royal status. And in *Erec* it is not Guinevere but Enid, a maiden who has already had one such award accorded to her at the Sparrowhawk contest, who fulfils this role.

This means that Enid is none other than the representative of Sovereignty, and is herself a kind of white doe in that her attainment is proof of royal prowess. Erec/Gereint wins her as his wife, but he does not truly deserve her until he has undergone the most harrowing of challenges within the enchanted garden where the Joy of the Court is to be achieved.

The white hart quest in Malory is not only about the mystical sovereignty quest, but is full of curious symbolism concerning maidens and their heads. It does not take a Freudian approach to see the immediate significance of this. The quest concerns Arthur's newly established sovereignty, his 'virgin quest', in effect. Gawain, who acts as Arthur's champion on the quest, accidentally beheads the maiden who owned the white hart, and so has to return to court not only with the white hart's head, but also with the maiden's head around his neck as a token of shame. The loss of virginity, or the giving of the land by the Goddess to her chosen king, Arthur, is thus symbolically portrayed by this quest. It is significant that Guinevere's judgement upon Gawain's beheading of the land's priestessly representative is for him to be forever afterwards a servant of all women. It may also be that we have lost an earlier tale in which Enid slept with Arthur, rather than just giving him a kiss. The fully fledged Celtic sovereignty stories invariably are so bowdlerized in later tradition.

Enid's role as priestess of Sovereignty is not immediately apparent, however, until we examine the shape of her story. When she is given to Erec in marriage, she 'was well aware that he would be king and she herself would be honoured and crowned queen'.[2] This royal destiny is also prefigured by the fact that she is proved, in every way, to be the best of women. Myths of Sovereignty have protagonists who are worthy of representing both the Goddess of the Land and her champion, and Enid is proved to be so no less than three times. First she is awarded the prize in the Sparrowhawk contest, ousting the favourites, because, as Erec says, 'No one can compare with you, any more than the moon compares with the sun, neither in beauty, nor in worth, nor in nobility, nor in honour.'[3] Then she is awarded the white hart's head in *Gereint*, and a kiss from Arthur in *Erec*. The whole court acclaims her 'the most beautiful; in her there is far more beauty than there is brightness in the sun'.[4] Her third award is one more dear to her than any – the free and unimpeded love of Erec. The crown which she achieves at the end of the story is as nothing to being loved for herself alone.

Two games bracket the story of Erec and Enid, one considered a good custom (the Hunting of the White Hart), the other an evil custom (the Enchanted Games). Both have the same effect, for Enid is given the honour which is due to her.

The Enchanted Games echo the beheading game which Morgan enforces upon both the Green Knight and Gawain in *Gawain and the Green Knight*. They are sited at the castle of Morgan's son, Evrain (Owain ap Urien), where Erec finds a stake waiting to receive his own head. He overcomes the evil custom of the Castle of Ravens (Brandigan), just as Gawain overcomes the custom of the Green Chapel. Evrain presides over the Enchanted Games, just as his mother, Morgan, presides over the Beheading Game. These are clearly the games of the Goddess which test the worthiness of her champions. In both tests, the temptation is to give in to lust or hubris, but only by doing what honour demands, at the cost of personal satisfaction, can either test be overcome.

While Enid does not present the Goddess of Sovereignty's *cailleach* aspect, remaining young and beautiful throughout, she nevertheless comes to Erec as a poor, dowerless maiden, dressed in a shabby dress. Her beauty, too, is noticeably dimmed by her trials, following Erec roughshod round the country in fear of her life. The cry that she utters when the count forcibly attempts to marry her is the very shrieking of the Earth itself, one of the cries of Sovereignty herself. These cries are a feature of Celtic tradition from its early to its medieval appearances: the Lia Fail which only shrieks under a rightful king; the cry of the dragons, indicative of a wasted land; the scream of the Perilous Seat when an unworthy knight attempts to sit in the chair of the Grail-winner.[5] Enid's cry is so loud that it wakes the almost-dead, penetrating Erec's coma sufficiently for him to rise and champion her.

This is evidence of an antique tradition of Sovereignty which is subtly hidden in the courtly retelling of Chrétien, who cannot conceal that Enid has a greater stature than he consciously accords her. From the first, she is destined to be a queen. When Erec forbids her to be dressed in anything other than the shabby white dress in which he first meets her, even after he has liberated her family from poverty, he does not intend to humiliate her by this action, but to bring her, poor as she is, to court, so that Guinevere can clothe her in one of her own dresses of sovereign red silk. And when Gereint's own sovereignty is called into question by his peers, and he goes upon his headlong course of challenge and ambush, he commands Enid to dress in her worst dress, for she must share his exile. So she wears dusty black for the road. Enid's progression in this way through the sacred colours is remarkable. The appearance of white, red and black in any story indicate the strong presence of the Goddess of the Land, whose sacred colours these are. They permeate Indo-European tradition, in folk-story and myth, lodging in the subtle processes of alchemy. The Goddess assumes white in her maiden aspect, red in her queenly aspect, and black in her *cailleach* aspect. (Sometimes she also has a fourth appearance, a messenger or warrior aspect, represented by the pied colours of black and white combined.) Enid appears clothed in all three colours. Significantly, her coronation mantle is described as follows:

> The fur lining that was sewn into it was from strange beasts that have completely blond heads and necks as black as mulberries and backs that are bright red on top, with black bellies and indigo tails.[6]

These composite colours of Sovereignty only appear at the story's conclusion, when Enid has undergone all stages of the Goddess's alchemical transformations.

THE CALUMNIATED WIFE

Many have seen the story of Enid as one that merely reinforces
the medieval image of woman - a being to be alternatively
abused or pedestalled. Certainly, Enid receives both the
approbation of the court and distrust of her husband. Her
portrayal shows the least acceptable modern image of woman:
the quiet, unassuming yet all-fulfilling woman,'just a housewife',
who bears all brunts and hardships, remaining faithful under
fire, is not the self-image desired by many women. Enid becomes
the woman who bears the brunt of medieval misogyny. She has
barely any character of her own and we must look to a layer
beneath the courtly romance to supply us with confirmation
that there is something more here, that Enid is worthy to be one
of our Ladies of the Lake.

One of the over-riding themes of Enid's myth is that of
patience and unjust calumny. This is a common theme in
medieval tradition, as instanced in 'The Clerk's Tale' in
Chaucer's *Canterbury Tales*, where Patient Griselda must bear all
vicissitudes stoically in order to become vindicated. This
situation is also one of the major themes of many folk-stories
where, for example, the heroine cannot speak even to justify
herself because she has taken a prior vow of silence, as in
Grimm's tale, *The Twelve Brothers*, where the sister must keep
silence for seven years in order to turn her brothers from ravens
back into men. At the end of that tale, she is barely rescued in
time from the stake because she cannot justify herself against
false report.[7]

British tradition's major myth on this theme is the story of
Rhiannon. She comes from the Underworld to marry Pwyll as
a woman of power. He goes to court her in the Underworld
and finds acceptance, but at the wedding feast a petitioner
comes in asking for a boon. Pwyll foolishly agrees to anything
in his power to grant, without defining the limits of the boon.
The petitioner is none other than Gwawl, a former suitor of
Rhiannon's, who asks for Pwyll's wife and the feast. Rhiannon
is exasperated at Pwyll's lack of wit, but she arranges a year's

delay and instructs Pwyll very carefully. She gives him her magical bag and bids him come to marriage feast of herself and Gwawl and demand a boon. Pwyll enters the hall disguised and begs his boon, but Gwawl is more circumspect in granting it. Pwyll modestly requests that his bag be filled with food. Gwawl grants this, but Rhiannon's bag is bottomless and Gwawl grows angry. Pwyll explains that it will only be full when a nobleman puts both feet into the bag and declares that enough has been put into it. Cross beyond caution, Gwawl finds himself trapped in the bag and belaboured by sharp blows as Pwyll blows his horn to signal the entry of his men.

Rhiannon is not popular with Pwyll's people, since she is of otherworldly stock, and they berate her for barrenness. But she eventually has a child. However, as already related in Chapter 1, the baby is mysteriously stolen away, and Rhiannon is accused of cannibalism and forced to stand for seven years at the mounting block to tell all comers about her 'crime' and to offer to carry them into the hall on her back. Pwyll does not move to help her, for he is bound by the laws of his country; though he loves her, he must let her suffer this ignominy.[8]

There are a few significant parallels between the story of Rhiannon and that of Enid. We note that Enid, uncharacteristically for a medieval woman, acts as a groom to Erec's horse. We also note that when Erec asks the Vavasour for a boon, he does not specify it before mentioning it and that the Vavasour agrees. As Rhiannon is threatened by Gwawl so Enid is challenged by Edern/Yder. Both men are from the Underworld. Gwawl is Rhiannon's first Underworld suitor, while Chrétien's Yder fitz Nut is none other than Edern ap Nudd. Edern's kinsman, Gwyn ap Nudd, is the leader of the Wild Hunt and Master of the Underworld in the legends of South Wales. Chrétien tells us that Yder is Enid's uncle. Like Rhiannon, Enid is forbidden to speak in her own defence and must allow events to unfold trusting to ultimate vindication. She is isolated from Erec's love, even as Rhiannon is seemingly abandoned by Pwyll.

Rhiannon is one of the major goddesses of Britain. Her myth

is complex and movingly apposite for our time. She is the 'horse's mouth', a woman who cannot be false. Associated with the European Celtic goddess, Epona, she is also one who unlocks doors. She brings true dreams, sometimes appearing as the nightmare if her message is not heeded. The horse or mare so central to her myth is the regnal beast of Indo-European sovereignty stories. While Enid's Celtic antecedents are difficult to establish, we see remarkable parallels between the two women, for both are archetypally calumniated wives, both originate in another world, come into mortal realms briefly and unhappily and are vindicated after much suffering. The same is true of Ragnell, as we shall see in Chapter 9.

One of the major underlying themes in the myth of Enid is easily overlooked, for it is none other than the freedom of love. Here we can again draw parallels with the story of Rhiannon. Rhiannon wants Pwyll as her mate, but she gives him freedom to do as he wishes, and submits to mortal rules. Enid also allows Gereint to go his own way; a method of training which puts her to some pain. She rejects the role expected of medieval society of the doting, adoring wife whose every whim must be satisfied. In every respect Enid is the very opposite of the emasculating Woman of the Enchanted Garden in *Erec*, who refuses to allow Mabonograin out of her domain.

Another of the themes shared by Rhiannon and Enid is that both are accused of taking their husbands away from their mortal, manly business. Rhiannon is disliked because she is initially barren and likely to upset the ruling of Dyfed; Enid is accused of stopping Gereint from exercising his chivalric duty, and for turning him soft.

In effect, Enid gives Erec the freedom of his own sovereignty. She does not dictate terms or even insist on the rights and privileges of her class, but remains silent, allowing him to run to the furthest extent of his own limits. She might have resisted him and so brought her misery to a close much earlier, but she choses instead to let Erec learn from his own experience. She enables him to explore the extent and limitations of a loving relationship. We shall see how Ragnell explores this freedom from the other side of the question in Chapter 9.

Many women today, when asked why they stay in untenable and abusive relationships, often report that it is *because* they love their partner and would not want to leave him alone. They realize that the abuse itself has become a kind of dependency, and that to withdraw it is to kill the relationship. They live in the hope that the relationship itself will change; most times hoping in vain.

Enid also has the patience and forbearance of Rhiannon, that bearer of burdens who accepts the inequities of mortality in order that her child might become the representative of the Mabon, the liberating god of Celtic tradition. Although Enid does not bear a child herself, her myth does include a similar overlay. As Rhiannon is liberated from her Underworld suitor by the blowing of Pwyll's horn, so too, in the story of Enid, Erec blows the horn to sound the Joy of the Court, which liberates all lovers.

RESTORER OF THE JOY

One of the features of the Celtic Otherworld, as already noted, is the innocence and lack of guilt surrounding love-making. In *Immram Bran*, the God of the Otherworld, Manannan Mac Lir, tells how his people conjoin without guilt. Pleasure may have no strings in the Otherworld, but the primal love-relationship is the one from which we are all exiled in the mundane realm. It is the initiatory trial through which both Gereint and Enid pass, in order to restore the Courts of Joy. When the Joy of the Court is announced by the horn in this story, the ladies composed a Lay of Joy which, says Chrétien, is little known. It is a song which our own society badly needs to sing right now, but it cannot be based on the abuse of one partner by another. Only in free and frank exchange can true love flourish.

The Joy of the Court custom is about this very thing. The Woman of the Garden who keeps Mabonograin captive as her champion, destined to combat all challengers and to fight them to the death, is the very reverse of Enid, who gives Erec his head.

Neither extreme is a correct mode of living, but through the meeting and combat of Erec and Mabonograin, freedom to love can be achieved.

Mabonograin is like many other champions of faery women in medieval tradition: captive for all time until released by death at the hands of a worthier champion. He has chosen to serve his mistress's desires at the cost of his own freedom; he is thus forever imprisoned. His release comes at the hands of Erec, a man who embarks on a course of equitable love but who has second thoughts and has to live with those doubts by testing his wife. Erec is also in prison because he ignores the evidence of his senses which tell him of Enid's faithful love, and attends instead to what people think about him. When two such polarized combatants come together, they are both released from their self-imposed prisons.

In her partnership of Erec/Gereint, Enid shows how interrelated is the action of the ninefold sisterhood. Like Ragnell and other ladies, her destiny is twined with another's. This mutual dependency is based on love and service. It is often stated that the Arthurian women do not go forth as do the knights, but Enid is the exception. Like the women of the Lands Adventurous, she puts herself to the hazard of quest. She acts as a companion to the knight's travels and adventures in a way which is not commonly paralleled in other stories save those relating to Luned, or Lynette, as she is later called. Enid is the companion of Gereint's mortality, sticking to her chosen course and seeing it through with love and patience. They travel together towards their destiny. For them, the laws which normally govern Logres seem in abeyance. 'In King Arthur's land the safety of maidens is guaranteed, the king having assured them of safe conduct and thus protection in his charge,' reports Chrétien in his *Perceval*. But Enid is certainly at risk during her journey, despite the haphazard protection of Erec.

The test of reciprocal love is shown in Gereint's initiatory struggle to find true manhood: Enid's gift is to aid him by standing back and letting him discover it. Erec thinks that he is on the track of the vindication of his manliness and chivalry, but he is mistaken. Enid is the only one who has the patience to temper the fierceness and independence of men. Her association with the white hart demonstrates that she is a woman who merits the rewards of love, for she has ever been in its service. This service can be viewed at many levels: service to the land, to the communication of men and women, to love itself.

The priestessly role of Enid may indeed lie at the root of Erec/Gereint's misunderstanding. Like Rhiannon, Enid cannot do other than be true to her nature. Like the white hart, the symbol of the Goddess of the Land, she must allow her husband space to find his own sovereignty. In return, he mistakes her tears as the evidence of guilty love. As priestess of Sovereignty, Enid has kissed Arthur - if one, why not all men? But Enid's eyes are fixed on the messenger of the Goddess, the white hart, that emblem of eternal love. Gereint's eyes are turned towards Enid in unthinking adoration at first, but when he has had time to assimilate her presence properly in his life, he has time for reconsideration. When Enid becomes an object of hatred and abuse, she is sustained by the image and power of real love and remains faithful to the heart of love.

There is a famous picture by Dante Gabriel Rossetti entitled 'How They Met Themselves'. It depicts a pair of lovers travelling along a road encountering a pair of lovers who are their mirror image. They look shocked and distressed by this revelation. Erec and Enid similarly travel on a journey - the quest for love. They are not only on the same track that both Arthur and Guinevere have travelled in the past, but also on parallel tracks to those of Mabonograin and the Woman of the Enchanted Garden. Their series of adventures can be seen as a set of trials which test their love and endurance. But their meeting with the couple of the Joy of the Court is a liberation, not a shock. The enchanted lovers are the Erec and Enid bound by chains of coercion, the Erec and Enid who might have been, had they stayed at court and lived conventional lives. By striking out into the lands adventurous, the couple overcome that fate; in a short space, they learn all that life can throw at them.

The otherworldly nature of Enid is affirmed by the fact that she is the subject of each of the sovereignty contests within the story: she is fairest woman worthy of receiving the head of the white hart, she is also the cause of Gereint's winning the Sparrowhawk contest, and she is truly the reward of the Enchanted Games, becoming Gereint's own joy.

The Joy of the Court cannot be enjoyed by anyone while the restrictive custom of the Enchanted Games continues: no partnership is safe. Enid sacrifices her own pleasure in order to enable Erec to free the land of its stasis, in which love is compelled, not freely exchanged. Her task is parallel to Ragnell's, which is to determine what women most desire. Enid must determine how love is served. The answer, like the answer to the Grail Question, is unequivocable: by love alone.

That Chrétien's text ends with the coronation of Erec and Enid is both significant and appropriate: the games of sovereignty have been truly won by Erec and the rigorous trials mean that Enid and Erec can exchange their love in equal measure.

The Path of the White Hart
❧

Before you is an ancient woodland, one of the primal forests of the foretime. Leading towards it is a pathway which enters the tangled trees, but you are not encouraged by this. Here is no tame wood, with neatly forested trees at serried intervals, but a thick forest in which you will have no map. Discouraged, fearful of becoming lost, you begin to turn away when an extraordinary sight greets your eyes. It is a white hart.

Astounded by its sudden brilliance, flashing towards the trees, you are upon the path before your mind has even assented. The hart enters the trees and you follow, moving fast to keep it in sight, for it is your only guide in this uncharted wildness. The path twists and turns, and is frequently overgrown. You cannot leap over such obstructions like the fleet-footed deer ahead of you, so you go slower. Brambles catch your sleeve, causing you annoyance. No sooner has one obstacle been overcome then there seem to be more and more.

The white hart is distant now and the path less clear. You strain to see how far ahead it has gone, and can only just glimpse the golden scut of its tail bounding away in the distance. Without the hart, the path is difficult to find, and you strive to find the way ahead. You have clearly wandered from your way and you berate yourself for being so foolish as to have entered the forest in the first place. The trees which seemed just obstacles to your pursuit now seem to draw in around you. You cannot hear the bird song that ought to flood these branches above you. Lost in a lonely wood, you stumble onwards, looking for any sign of life.

You see a hopeful clearing and strike towards it. Something shines from the branches and you make for it. In the clearing you find a perfect crystal mirror hanging. You walk around it to view this strange object. Who has set it here? For what purpose? It is a beautiful thing, catching the sun's rays, but there is no-one to appreciate it here. Would anyone miss it? As you go to detach it from its hanging, the crystal mirror seems to come to life, uttering sounds from deep within it.

Disquieted, you drop your hands quickly. The reverberations are quite clear - the mirror has just spoken to you. It swings and turns to face you so that you have a good view of its face. This is even more disquieting, because it does not return your reflection. Look closely and you will see the face of one you once knew well and professed to love. Reflected in the crystal mirror is the face of a past friend or lover whose love you refused or betrayed. Their image comes before you now and, despite the painful memories which are invoked, you are enabled to speak and answer the reflection in a way which heals all hurts.

Let that face come before you now and, without recrimination or guilt, speak and make answer to the questions asked by the mirror: 'What did I give you? What did you give me?'

Consider the nature of the exchange that you experienced at that time, and make your peace with the image reflected. You notice that beside you in the clearing is a little stream which runs throughout the forest. Cleanse the crystal mirror - which you now have no desire to take with you - with some of the water, uttering words of blessing and farewell to the image that lies within.

Shaken by this encounter, you turn to your path and begin to see it clearly. After walking a little further, you are confirmed of your way by a tip of shed antler upon the path, which you pick up. With great determination, you hurry onwards, confident of finding the magical beast. Then you hear the crying of a little girl. She runs out of the dense undergrowth and begs you to find her plaything which is lost. You would rather go onwards and do not welcome the squalling of a child, but you turn aside to help her.

She leads you into what seems the thickest of the undergrowth, full of nettles, thorns and thistles. 'Why was she playing in this place anyway?' you think. Scrabbling around under bushes in the densest scrub with the antler as a pick, you find a golden ball, which has rolled in here. The girl claps her hands with glee when you return it to her. She tosses it up and bids you catch it. You have no time for a game, but you oblige her. As the golden ball enters your hands, it splits in two and out flies not one, but a flight of birds. They rise singing into the forest until it is filled with bird song. Of the girl, there is no sign.

You travel further along the path, walking more slowly now to listen to the new-found song of the woods. The trees seem more friendly and you look about you with appreciation. The path is easier to follow and your haste less urgent. Almost unawares, you arrive in a clearing where the meandering stream curves. Here is the white hart, drinking unperturbed. Now that it is still, you can observe it better. It hide is brilliantly white, its antlers and hooves touched with gold. It raises its head and regards you with lambent intelligent eyes. It is no shock when it addresses you.

'Many have sought me. Hunters for my hide, kings for my golden horn. But only lovers find me. I am the guardian of these woods and none can come further in without answering to me. What is your sole, unchanging desire? What lies at the heart of your life? Answer me that and I will let you ride upon my back.'

The deep and beautiful voice urges you to answer in your own words. You look into your own heart and find the words . . .

A tear rolls down the cheek of the white hart as you speak. 'Come now, mount upon my back and I will take you to your sole desire.'

With awe and trembling, you stand upon a stone and mount, letting the white hart bear you across the stream into the depths of the forest. You hold tightly to the antlers and close your eyes, so fast is your flight.

You find yourself in the inmost depths of the forest, in a clearing which is shrouded by mist. The white hart sets you down and nudges you to enter. Fearful of the unknown, you pass the magical boundary of this place and find yourself within an apple orchard. Within it sits a woman in a red dress. Her lack of ornament seems to enhance her strange beauty, for she is white of skin and black of hair. There is a silver bed beside her, which is empty. The place is so peaceful and restful that you wish you could lie down, but that is not why you have come. You notice that a horn hangs from a nearby tree.

The woman speaks. 'Desire is a bridge to another country. Many have striven to enforce their desire in this place, but all have faded away. What is your wish? To lie upon this bed and dream the fulfilment of your sole desire? Or to blow the horn yonder? If you would be free of selfish desire, if you would know how love is served, then take the horn and blow it. But, before you do, know that nothing in your life will remain as it was afterwards. If you are fearful of change, weigh well these words before setting the horn to your lips. It would be better for you to lie upon the bed and dream than to blow the horn unworthily.'

You weigh the decision. To blow the horn you must relinquish your own desire. To achieve it you must lie upon the bed. Is this a trick? You think back to the white hart and know that it is not, for how could a beast of such purity and wisdom lead you astray?

You think upon your avowed desire and test it . . . Lie upon
the bed, if that is what you have chosen, and watch the
images that form in dream. Take the horn, if that is what
you have chosen, and blow with all your might, paying close
attention to what is happening . . . Take time to experience
this now . . .

It is time to attend once more. The woman rises and takes
your hand. 'Friend and loved one, may the desire of your
heart be fulfilled in every place. I am she whom you
rejected in the crystal mirror, I am she whose toy you
retrieved in the forest, I am she who led you here in the
shape of the white hart. Know that I am Enid, the Lady of
the Enclosed Garden. Keep such a place as this within your
heart for the healing of the world, and let those into it as
need delivering from their own hatefulness.'

She anoints your brow with a pungent bitter-smelling oil.
'By the balm of love's pain, may all desires be purified.'

She garlands your neck with apple-blossom. 'By the grace of
love's gladness, may all be brought to joy.'

She salutes you and lets you go. You pass through the
magical mist and into the forest where the white hart takes
you up once again, and delivers you to the forest's edge.
The hart speaks once more.

'Go gladly and be at peace. May the love of the Lady Enid
live forever in your heart.'

In your own words, bid farewell to love's messenger and
return to your own time and place.

REFERENCES

1. R.S. Loomis, *Arthurian Tradition and Chrétien de Troyes.*
2. Chrétien de Troyes, *Erec and Enide* in *Arthurian Romances*, trans.
   W.W. Kibler and C.W. Carroll.
3. Ibid.

4. Ibid.
5. Caitlín Matthews, *Arthur and the Sovereignty of Britain*.
6. Chrétien, op. cit.
7. *Grimm's Tales for Young and Old: the Complete Stories*, trans. R. Mannheim.
8. *The Mabinogion*, ed. Lady Charlotte Guest.

THREE

*The Lands
Adventurous*

The Grail Maidens

We pass finally into the Lands Adventurous, wherein many wondrous quests and adventures abound. This is a dangerous and uncertain world where lurk many terrors. It is a place of thick forest, cross-tracked by springs and rivers. This is the world wherein many women find themselves today, sometimes without map and compass, and usually without a thought of a knight in shining armour to come and liberate them.

This is a world where women fend for themselves, where personal quests are pursued with courage and individual verve. The Grail Maidens are those who pursue their course with single-minded determination and aplomb. These are the women who most nearly resemble knights in their own right, although they are not living on men's terms. Motivated from the heart of the Lake itself, they uphold the individual quest with daring.

The Grail that they guard has many aspects: it can be a cauldron, an oracular head, a stone, a food-bestowing dish, a cup or a chalice. The Grail is one of the highest Hallows in that it appears in every generation, in one form or another. It is not the sole possession of Pagans or of Christians: it is an otherworldly gift which is bestowed and mediated by those true in heart. The Grail is an alchemical hallow, for whoever encounters it is changed. Those who know how to wield it worthily are able to create great changes in the world, so that the Grail's benefits can be experienced by all. Most mysteriously of all, the Grail can appear as a woman.

The Grail Maidens are Kundry, Dindraine and Ragnell.

7

Kundry

Merciful,
Vessel of mercy . . .
Mother of Time
Thou art brilliant as the fires
of the final dissolution . . .
Night of darkness,
Yet liberator from the bonds of desire . . .
Destroyer of fear,
Who assumeth all forms at will . . .
To Thee I make obeisance.
'Adyakali' (Hymn to Kali) from the *Mahanirvana Tantra*

Variant Names:
Cundrie, the Proud Damsel, la Demoisele Maldisant,
le Demoisele Sauvage, the Black Maiden, the Loathly
Lady.

The Myth of Kundry

If any of the ninefold Ladies of the Lake has best claim to act as the sisterhood's summoner, then it is Kundry. She represents an archetype which is usually entitled the Black Maiden in Celtic tradition, where she is often nameless. Such a want of name usually points to the archetype in question stemming from great antiquity. Certainly, she is such a compelling figure that few romancers left her out of their narratives, but we must look far to gather relevant information about her in one place.

She appears in Wolfram von Eschenbach's *Parzival* for the first time as a named individual, as Kundry the Sorceress, and we shall tell her story first. Wolfram's story of the Grail quest and its winner, Perceval, or Parzival as he is in this story, has many features which are not shared by any other British or French stories, Wolfram's tendency being to evolve each character and incident in complex and sometimes fanciful ways.

We first meet Kundry just after the inauguration of Parzival as a knight. The foolish young man had fled from court before he could be dubbed, pursuing his headlong adventures, and has just returned from the Grail castle where he failed to ask the all important Grail Question by which the Wounded King would have been healed. Arthur has gone in search of his errant knight and found him. In a clearing, the Round Table is convened by dint of a mantle spread out upon the ground. As all the court gather around it, Kundry rides into the clearing upon a mule. She is a beautifully dressed woman, attired in the latest style with great elegance; however, the clothes do not hide the fact that she is hideous: 'Her nose was like a dog's, and the length of several spans, a pair of tusks jutted from her jaws.'[1] She has dark-coloured skin, and claw-like hands, which hold a whip.

Kundry speaks all languages, and is familiar with dialectic; geometry and astronomy. She greets Arthur by lamenting his fall from greatness, due to Parzival being allowed to sit at the Round Table. Next she castigates Parzival himself for failing to ask the Grail Question. She names him and his lineage before the court, which has hitherto known him only as 'the Red Knight'. As she rides away, Parzival determines to seek the Grail.

On his quest, Parzival encounters his cousin, Sigune, who has become an anchoress, an enclosed female hermit, after the death of her lover. On asking how she is able to sustain herself in the wilderness, so enclosed, he learns that Kundry visits her every Saturday night with food from the Grail. Parzival already knows that the Grail dispenses the food each most desires. Sigune counsels him to follow Kundry, but she travels too fast for him and he becomes lost.

Parzival comes to the cell of his hermit uncle, Trevirizent, who teaches him the secrets of the Grail. He learns that the virtue of the Grail ensures that the Wounded King, Anfortas, cannot die and that he will continue suffering until the Grail Question is asked. He is also told that the Grail family gathered at Munsalvach are sent there as children, their names having miraculously appeared upon the stone of the Grail. A group of knights, called Templeisen, guard the castle, sworn to the service of the Grail family.

When Gawain also goes upon his adventures, he arrives at the Castle of Maidens and meets Arnive (Igraine) who tells him that Kundry is a frequent visitor, bringing medicines and some of the salve that helps sustain Anfortas. He learns from her about the evil magician Klingsor, who keeps the lands about the Castle of Maidens in thrall. Arnive tells him that Klingsor once loved Iblis, the King of Sicily's wife. Finding them together, the King of Sicily castrated Klingsor. Since then Klingsor has taken pleasure only in putting the will of all people under his enchantment. Gawain is able to disenchant them by his exploits at the Castle of Maidens.

After many adventures and much seeking, Parzival returns to court, where the Round Table again convenes. Kundry appears, dressed in a hood which is embroidered with turtle-doves – the device of the Grail. She kneels before Parzival and asks to be reconciled with him, which he grants. She then tosses off her hood and wimple so that everyone recognizes her. Ugly as before, she proclaims the message of the Grail. A new inscription has appeared, commanding Parzival to be the new Grail king. He is to accompany her to ask the Grail Question once more. She speaks learnedly of the movement of the seven planets and their beneficent augury for Parzival's career. Parzival proclaims her publicly as the true messenger of the Grail, since her clothes are covered with the Grail insignia of the turtle dove. Everyone rejoices, and Kundry asks to see Arnive, now released from Klingsor's captivity.

Parzival and Kundry ride to the Grail castle. The Templeisen would have challenged Parzival's progress had not Kundry been with him, but seeing Kundry's riding habit covered in turtle-doves, they cry with joy at this sign of deliverance from sorrow.

Parzival asks the question and Anfortas is restored. Of Kundry, we hear no more.

This is not the only appearance of the archetype whom Kundry represents, however. The earliest reference to her is found in *Peredur*, the Welsh Perceval story from *The Mabinogion*. (For a full breakdown of this story, see *Arthur and the Sovereignty of Britain*.) *Peredur* follows a similar course to the other versions, but has more ancient and noticeably Celtic features within it. There is no Grail, as such, within the story, and the quest is not one for a transcendent object, but is a vengeance quest. In his uncle's castle Peredur sees a spear that drips blood continually and a dish that holds the head of a youth, borne in procession. His adventures include the defence of a castle which is besieged by the Nine Witches of Gloucester. He strikes one of the witches, who acclaims him by name and speaks of a prophecy that she will train him in arms. He stays with her for three weeks for this training.

Like Parzival, Peredur returns to Arthur's court where he is reproached by a Hideous Damsel for not having asked about the spear and dish. These objects are from the early British tradition of the Thirteen Treasures and parallel the healing and transformative qualities of the Grail. The Hideous Damsel tells of the besieged castle Syberw: whoever relieves it will gain the greatest honour in the world. There is a maiden to be rescued within. Gwalchmai (Gawain) goes on this quest, while Peredur goes to find the significance of the spear and dish.

Peredur finds the Castle of Wonders and there plays a game of *gwyddbwyll* on a magical board which plays itself. When his side loses, he tips the board in the lake. The Hideous Damsel reappears and berates him for losing one of the Empress's treasures. To restore it, he must go to Castle Ysbidinongyl where a black man is ravaging the Empress's lands. In his combat with his black adversary, Peredur negotiates the gaming board back while granting the black man mercy. The Hideous Damsel reappears to berate him for not killing the black man.

Peredur then discovers a single-horned stag which has dried up the waters of that land. He kills it and is again berated by a horsewoman. He eventually finds his way to the Grail castle where a golden-haired youth greets him. The youth is none other than the Hideous Damsel, who tells him that s/he has also been the black man and the horsewoman, as well as the one who carried the spear and dish. She reveals that the head in the dish was none other than that of Peredur's cousin and it was destined that he should avenge his kinsman. She also tells how the Nine Witches were responsible for laming Peredur's uncle with the spear. Peredur and Gwalchmai then go to fight the witches. As Peredur strikes the first one, she proclaims that their destroyer is at hand, as prophesied.

Chrétien's *Conte du Graal* is held by scholars to be the earliest Grail text – certainly it may have been the first to be transcribed – but *Peredur* betrays earlier features. The Black Maiden is of surpassing ugliness in this text and she berates Perceval's neglect in failing to ask why the Fisher King suffers and what is the meaning of the Grail procession. 'Ladies will lose their husbands, lands will be laid waste, and maidens will remain helpless as orphans; many a knight will die. All these troubles will occur because of you,' she says accusingly.[2]

The wealth of the Grail texts present many other appearances of the Black Maiden or Hideous Damsel. In the *Didot Perceval*, the Hideous Damsel is called Rosete li Bloie, or 'the Blonde Red-One', in contradistinction to her black appearance. We may note that the three sacred colours, black, red and white, appear together in her person as clear indication of her Sovereignty associations. Although she is fearfully ugly, the text mysteriously tells us that she was fair thereafter.

Perlesvaus presents a different kind of Black Maiden, in the shape of the Maiden of the Cart. She, with her two female companions, travels about the countryside bringing messages concerning the Grail and acting as courier and adviser for the Grail-seekers. The Maiden of the Cart is beautiful but bald – her hair is restored only when the Grail is achieved.

To this venerable tradition we must add the simplifications of Richard Wagner, who has presented a totally different picture of Kundry, and one which is now generally accepted, for his

opera of *Parsival* is better known than Wolfram's text. Here
Kundry appears as the enchantress who, at the instigation of
Klingsor, tempts Anfortas into the sin which causes his wound.
She is doomed to eternal laughter when she laughs at the
crucified Christ, and it is Parsifal who breaks this curse. This
reading of Kundry sets the archetype of the Black Maiden on
its head, making of her a temptress who disempowers men
rather than as a prime empowerer of great knowledge.

THE BLACK MAIDEN

Significantly, the few 'active' women of the medieval Arthurian
stories appear as ugly, black or misshapen. This may initially
appear to be in line with the universal convention of beauty.
Arthurian story reveals a series of incidents in which the golden-
haired princess in her tower must be fought for, whereas her
dark-haired sister who comes with the message of her
imprisonment is discounted as an object of romance. This
happens in the story of Gareth, who answers the call of Lynette
to rescue her sister, Lionors – whom he marries.[3] Similarly,
Owain marries the Lady of the Fountain, ignoring the love of
her servant-companion, Luned, who has brought him thither.[4]
The parallels between the stories are quite marked.
Luned/Lynette acts as the active messenger in the same way that
Kundry and the Black Maiden do; Lionors marries Gareth; the
Lady of the Fountain marries Owain; Repanse de Schoy,
Kundry's beautiful counterpart, marries Parzival's brother,
Feirfitz.

The preference for the golden or blonde woman over the dark
may also seem the result of the same kind of ingrained cultural
obsession, as still exists in India where advertisements for wives
stress a preference for 'light-skinned' candidates. But the
darkness of the Black Maiden has nothing to do with racial
derivation or skin pigmentation, and everything to do with the
nature of her archetype. The beauty of blackness is known by
those who know the true worth of the soul, those who have ever

sought the dark, not the light, mistress. The impassioned lover and the yearning mystic have not written about the pretty blonde girl, but about the Nut-Brown Maid and the Dark Lady. Women similarly perceive the empowering inner masculine not as a blond knight in shining armour, but as a dark, mysterious lover whose gift is to change the soul. This ability is reflected in his own changeable nature and appearance, which may be daemonic, angelic or bestial – the very reverse of the conventional handsome and sought-after Adonis.

Despite this, the Black Maiden seldom has a mate of her own. She is wedded to her task. Kundry is like a maiden-aunt, her care always for others, never for herself. She does not mate and has no children. She is a warrior who battles on alone and remains available to all.

Kundry is a guardian of tradition like the Celtic Dark Woman of Knowledge or the Gnostic Sophia. Because she is an active principle of wisdom, she appears in a black or wrathful manifestation, since practical or skilful wisdom involves the practitioner getting her hands dirty with hard work and maintaining a determined attitude. Kundry is not black because she has been purposely down-graded by theologians: her blackness is an essential part of her archetype. We could no more countenance a wholly white Kundry than we could a Kali without power. Unfortunately, Western tradition has turned its back on the wrathful appearances of Deity, thus cutting itself off from the source of much esoteric teaching. The challenge of Kundry's reproach gives more incentive to the flagging Grail aspirant than the pointless advice of well-wishers. Likewise, her acclamation is worth more to the successful Grail-winner, because it is truly earned and freely given. This takes us on to one of the major aspects of the Black Maiden, for she is the voice of the Earth.

Kundry represents the voice of the Goddess of Sovereignty. This archetype goes back into the Celtic tradition as far as the Morrighan, the Great Queen, who formally announces the victory of the Tuatha de Danaans to the land itself:

Then, after the battle of Mag Tuiread had been won and the
bodies of the dead cleared away, the Morrighan, daughter of
Ernmas, announced the battle and the great victory which had
taken place to the royal hills of Ireland, to the armies of the *sidhe*,
to the principle rivers and their estuaries. It is thus that the
Badbh announces high deeds. 'What is the news,' say the hills
and rivers to her, and she replies:

> 'Peace up to heaven;
> Heaven down to earth,
> Earth under heaven,
> Strength in everyone.'[5]

While this may be very gratifying for the victorious Danaans,
the Morrighan then goes on to prophesy the end of the world.
Her voice is at the service of the Goddess of the Land, and she
speaks its joy or sorrow without fear or favour.

The Morrighan's cry of victory is also Kundry's. Her voice is
most important in bringing about the Grail quest. Her public
and shaming denouncement of Perceval for failing to ask the
Grail Question spurs him to seek harder, and her cry of shame
is changed to one of joy at the end of the story, when she
announces the Grail to all.

As we saw in the last chapter, the voice of the land has many
manifestations. Significantly, many versions of the Grail legend
depict a pair of dwarfs at Arthur's court who laugh or speak
when Perceval first appears. Kay is angry with them for not
talking sooner, since they clearly have the ability to do so, and
he strikes them. Perceval later gets the opportunity to avenge
the dwarfs by striking Kay. Dwarfs are nearly always associated
with the Earth and may be seen as voices of the Earth. Their
spontaneous greeting and naming of Perceval is likewise part of
Goddess of the Land's response to the one who comes to
champion the land. Wolfram drew upon this tradition, for he
makes Kundry's brother, Malcriature, a dwarf. We also note that
in *Peredur*, the Nine Witches of Gloucester similarly proclaim
Peredur by name, give him arms-training and later announce his
coming to destroy them. Kundry is the Grail-messenger, the one
who announces the quest, keeps knights faithful to it, and who
has the duty of announcing the great joy which the Grail's

achievement brings. Her function of guardian and messenger is borne by the Hideous Damsel or the Black Maiden in the other Grail legends.

In *Perlesvaus*, the same character appears as the Bald Maiden, or the Maiden of the Cart. She is analogous to both Kundry and the Hideous Damsel, and is more obviously associated with the medieval concept of Fortuna, who is bald behind and well-tressed at the front. The cyclic nature of mutable fortune is a clear indication of the nature of the native Celtic Fortuna figure who is more usually known as Sovereignty.

The medieval appearance of Fortuna is enshrined within the Tarot card of The Wheel of Fortune, which depicts the many stages of life: a king atop the wheel and a beggar clinging to its lower edge, while others scramble to reach the top or struggle to avoid the bottom. Arthur dreams of Fortuna before his death, seeing himself cast down.[6] Gawain also has a significant encounter with Lady Fortune in *Diu Cröne*.[7] Fortuna represents the mutable face of the Goddess, who does not believe in unbreakable institutions. The Goddess, like the seasonal year over which she presides, moves and changes.

The remarkable consistency of the Goddess of Sovereignty as Fortuna is borne out in Wolfram's *Parzival* in the character of Sigune, Perceval's cousin, whose character is harmonious with both those of Kundry and Dindraine (see Chapter 8). Parzival discovers her shortly after having failed to ask the Grail Question.

Malory calls Sigune the Queen of the Waste Land: 'For some called me sometime the Queen of the Waste Lands and I was called the queen of most riches in the world; and it pleased me never my riches so much as doth my poverty.'[8] These words may strike us as orthodoxly Christian, however, she reminds us that knowledge is sometimes a filling and at other times an emptying experience, as it waxes and wanes in us. Knowledge, like wealth, is not finite. She informs Perceval of his mother's death, and also gives us the interior knowledge of the Round Table, about its construction and meaning. She is a Lady of the Wheel as complete as Fortuna, prognosticating like a sibyl.

Fortuna, like Kundry, rolls along like the ancient Goddess of the Cart, once worshipped by the Germanic and Celtic peoples. The Goddess of the Cart had power of life and death over her people and was propitiated by the sacrifice of human victims who were buried in bogs and drowned in lakes. Kundry and the many Black Maidens always appear with a riding whip as part of their regalia, but they never ride a horse, always a mule.

A similar maiden comes to summon knights to adventure in the French text, *La Mule Sans Freins*, which tells of a maiden coming to Arthur's court. She laments that she will never again know joy until her mule's lost bridle is returned to her, and requires a champion to seek it, promising herself to the victor. Her mule leads the knight on the path to the quest's achievement, requiring no other guidance. Kay undertakes the quest but is deterred by the otherworldly dangers that he meets and it is Gawain who succeeds, passing through the borderlands into the Otherworld and there finding the bridle.

The bridle is an important symbol in Celtic folk-tradition. It can become a magical device which calls the fastest horse from the stable. The horse is held in highest esteem in Britain and Ireland. Alone of Europe, these countries hold the horse taboo, for no person will knowingly eat its flesh. The horse is a prime symbol of Sovereignty, Goddess of the Land. If we understand this, we see that the horse or mule without a bridle is symbolic of the land itself, without responsible leadership. The kiss that the maiden of the mule grants to the one who regains the bridle is the kiss that bestows sovereignty.

This Maiden without a Bridle, as we can term her, is, like the archetype of the Black Maiden, a nag; she tests, torments and teaches by her unbounded tongue. This female method of goading men into action has been universally remarked upon and in medieval times particularly vicious nags would have been punished by being made to wear the scold's bridle, a nasty piece of ironmongery that fitted the face like a muzzle. However, we are not looking at the social history of nagging here; rather we wish to understand the nature of the Black Maiden. She can certainly cause the ear to ache, as we have seen with Nimuë and the Quest for the White Hart: 'When she was gone the king was glad, for she made such a noise!'[9]

It is not insignificant that the Black Maiden is associated with the mule, one of the beasts of Rhiannon/Epona. Rhiannon's horse cannot be overtaken by anyone; Kundry moves faster than any of the Grail knights. Rhiannon is reduced to the status of a pack-mare and made to tell the story against herself; Kundry becomes the ever-busy Grail messenger and speaks reproachfully and with sorrow.

Sovereignty is the Goddess of the Land whose appearance reflects the nature of the land. When waste land reigns, Sovereignty appears as an ugly woman, a grieving widow, a raped virgin or as native virago whose words sting passive knights into resourceful action. When the true quest is achieved, only then can she turn back into her beautiful self. The evidence for Sovereignty has been examined in *Arthur and the Sovereignty of Britain*, where a full range of examples may be studied. It is clear that she is the prime Goddess figure underlying the Arthurian corpus. The ninefold women of Arthurian legend whom we are examining here are her garments and appearances.

THE DARK WOMAN OF KNOWLEDGE

Celtic tradition has a figure who is concerned with the teaching and training of initiates. She has been identified as the Dark Woman of Knowledge.[10] She may be old or young, but she is invariably ugly or terrifying to behold. Each Celtic country has its own version of her: in Breton, she is the *Hroeck*, in Gaelic, the *Cailleach*, in Welsh the *Gwrach*. She is touchy, unchancy, wise, prophetic and, if approached in the right way, has much to teach. The British goddess Ceridwen is one such figure, she who chases Gwion through many transformations until he has undergone many levels of experience, to emerge as the master-poet, Taliesin. The Dark Woman of Knowledge is essentially the Celtic Goddess of Wisdom and her representative in Arthurian legend is invariably the Black Maiden.

The Dark Woman of Knowledge has two faces and they both concern the ways in which we approach experience. Similarly, knowledge is a word that can have two distinct meanings in the English language: the knowledge of the intellect and the knowledge of the body. This latter meaning is intended in the Biblical use of the word: 'Then Adam *knew* Eve, his wife.' The Dark Woman of Knowledge comprehends both of these meanings, for she can appear as the teacher or as the mistress of the candidate for initiation. She may sometimes manifest as both. In this she is the mistress of Western tantra. The West has a limited definition of the word 'tantra', understanding it solely as a form of Eastern sex-magic and little else. The full definition is 'a practice involving identification of oneself with a fully Enlightened deity'.[11] A tantric practitioner therefore studies the esoteric practices of his tradition, the unwritten script which the Goddess writes upon the elements, scraps of which can be gleaned from the living of his life. The West has largely mislaid or forgotten its own tantric tradition, which many practitioners are striving to recover, following in the steps of Isis, whose task is to reassemble the scattered fragments of sacred knowledge.[12] Its greatest initiator in Celtic tradition is the Dark Woman of Knowledge, or the Black Maiden.

There are manifest clues to this tradition in the Grail stories, which revolve around the acquisition of esoteric knowledge. The later Grail legends stress the attainment of the symbolic object itself, the Grail, but the earlier ones are true to the tantric tradition, for the Grail-seekers find their enlightenment in the person of the Grail Maiden, rather than in the object which she carries. Such dualism is an ever-gaping trap for those travelling the spiritual path - to confuse the moon with the finger pointing at the moon. The Grail is not a piece of treasure trove, valuable solely for its gold or jewels: it is a symbol of inner transcendence which only the highest order of perseverance and virtue will bring about. The knowledge that it brings *can* be attained on a purely intellectual level, but there it merely stagnates in a theoretical vacuum. The knowledge of the body is invariably achieved through the undualistic channel of sexual congress, where again, it can become trapped in a round of selfish desire. Truly integrated knowledge is achieved by the combination of intellectual and physical levels. The most successful tantric initiates are those who do not despise the enlightenment of the woman. Indeed, many traditions – Qabalism, alchemy and the Tibetan 'Crazy Wisdom' sect founded by the master Padmasambhava – stress the impossibility of attaining true enlightenment without the help of an enlightened woman as partner. These traditions are aware that to attempt to espouse Deity without having first espoused the creation of Deity is a fruitless exercise. Asceticism and celibacy may help to discipline spiritual practice, but total dependency on asceticism alone will not reveal the inmost truths.

We have spoken a great deal here of the Eastern tantra in order to illuminate the lost Western tantra. Celtic tradition shows us a model in which the initiate, who most usually appears as a young hero and warrior, is brought under the tutelage of an aged wise woman who not only trains him in arms but also initiates him into sexual knowledge. This can be seen in the story of Cuchulainn, who goes to Alba to be trained by Scathach, the eponymous goddess of the Isle of Skye. She teaches him weapon-craft and gives him her own daughter, Uathach, to sleep with. Uathach means 'terrible', and the girl is truly ugly. Cuchulainn's own quest is not just eminence in the lore of arms, but to return to Ireland, there to win the beautiful Emer. Emer has not accepted his suit because he is not old, learned or experienced enough for her taste. She virtually sends him away from her in order to be educated and initiated. Emer is Cuchulainn's Grail in this story. He returns fully initiated into his manhood and Emer accepts him as her partner.

Peredur is similarly trained by the Nine Witches of Gloucester – our ninefold sisterhood of the Ladies of the Lake in their most ancient form. They take many appearances in his story, but they give him the knowledge by which he may win his quest and even overcome his teachers! Why do the Ninefold desire this seemingly terrible thing? It is because the true inner teacher's ambition is to be overcome, outdone and surpassed by the pupil. This is true of any master or mistress of arts, crafts and skills. For the true mistress of her craft, the craft is more important than the self-image: it is more important to produce a worthy tradition-bearer than it is to turn out endless copies of the teacher, who will parrot the tradition without the anchor of deep knowledge.

The Black Maiden is well aware that she cannot be eradicated from existence. She is one appearance of the Lady of Life, from whose womb all things proceed, to whose womb all things return. Though the West has forgotten its Creating Goddess, it retains the Black Maiden who comes to bring things to their dissolution and change. Western culture is charged with the image of the witch, the destroying woman. While some of this imagery is wrought of the spiritual paranoia which arises when the Divine Feminine is expunged, it is also an integral part of the esoteric tradition, which associates the cyclicity of life with the changing faces of the Goddess.

This is nowhere plainer to be seen than in the Black Maiden's only given name. The word 'kundry' derives from a north-west European root that also gives us 'cunt' and 'cunning'. (Wolfram's *Parzival* gives us Cunneware, a virtuous lady, whose name nevertheless implies 'one who is free with her favours'.) How does such an ugly woman acquire this name? The answer lies in the depths of the ancient spiritual traditions of Europe.

When Deity was officially defined as male in imagery and symbolism, this did not mean that the Goddess ceased to live in the hearts or minds of Her people. Traditions, symbols, stories and images passed down into the folk-custom of many cultures. Those who lived by the work of their hands were in continual communion with the ancient lore, none more so than the masons of the early Christian churches who carved into the enduring fabric of stone the images which had enlivened the hearts of their ancestors for generations. It is so that we find the foliate head of the Green Man, rustling in a stone canopy within the pillared forest of a cathedral. It is here also that we find ancient images of the Goddess enshrined.

There are numerous reliefs and statues of the sheela na gig, the ugly hag who squats akimbo, revealing her cunt for all to see and touch. These statues were often incorporated into the fabric of churches, usually over the western door, where the congregation entered the church. She represents the *fons et origo* of human existence. In Hindu tradition, this same figure appears frequently as Mahadevi, the Great Goddess, as Kali. There are many yoni shrines in India, where the female generative organs of the Goddess are ritually venerated at certain springs, cloven trees or rocks and in the simple symbolized form of the pear-shaped yoni. There, the faithful devoutly touch the Goddess's yoni.[13] From the degree of wear upon the sheela na gig reliefs, we may assume that this practice was also followed in Britain and Ireland, where the images were at shoulder height or below. Many sheelas were destroyed in fits of puritanical iconoclasm, many languish in the basements of museums as 'archaeological pornography'.

The extreme ugliness of many of the sheela na gig statues in Britain and Ireland testify to the resident traditions of Sovereignty. The Goddess of the Land, as we have seen, usually makes her first appearance as a *cailleach* of astounding ugliness: in this she is acting as a threshold deity. Threshold deities appear in every tradition all over the world; they are watch-dogs and guardians set to repel the unwary or the unprepared from making fools of themselves.

It is significant that the Black Maiden appears invariably linked with Perceval, who is the archetypal fool and ignoramus. His failure to penetrate the mysteries of the Grail at the first attempt is immediately followed by the appearance of the Black Maiden to reproach him. She comes to bring him to full awareness of his responsibilities and skilfully provides him with tests that will stretch his abilities until he *is* able to succeed in his quest.

So many people have overlooked the Black Maiden in their headlong search for the Grail. She is ugly and earthy: the Grail is mystically beautiful. All spiritual quests, of which the most venerable and universal is the study of alchemy, warn us at our peril to overlook the blackened *prima materia* lying in the dungheap at our feet in favour of the immortal pearl which lies in another country.

Kundry represents the workaday face of the Goddess in exile, 'She who seeks to be recognized' beneath her veil of obscure ugliness. The Black Maiden represents the true alchemical transformation of the Grail, her harsh voice perpetually at our ear urging us to heed and act.

KUNDRY THE DRAKAINA

The character of both Kundry and the Black Maiden is firmly related to the Earth itself and the wisdom that lies within it. The romancers were subliminally aware of this tradition and sought to distance Kundry and her prototypes from accusations of being fays or witches by giving them the respectability of wise-women. Of course, the tradition of the wise-woman was itself a more literary than actual career for real medieval women. The paths of ministry were closed to all but the nun. Wherever possible, the romancers associated the Kundry archetype with that of the sibyl.

Sibyls had achieved an honorary respectable status within Christian tradition almost solely due to the Roman poet Virgil's *Aeneid*, which was one of the most widely read works in the Middle Ages. In the fourth Eclogue of Aeneas' adventures, we read a prophecy, uttered by the Sibyl of Cumae, which seemed to give Pagan credence to Christianity:

> Now has the last great age begun,
> by Cumae's seer foretold;
> new born the mighty cycles run
> their course, and quit the old.
> Now too, the Virgin reappears,
> and Saturn re-controls the spheres.
>
> Now is a new race on the way
> from heaven; do thou befriend

the Infant, all but born, whose day
the iron brood shall end
and with the golden fill the earth.[14]

The works of the Sibyl of Cumae and others were thus given Christian houseroom in a way which other Pagan sources were not. The sibyl sat alongside King David in the ranks of venerable prophets and Michaelangelo's ceiling of the Sistine Chapel in the Vatican depicts many famous sibyls.

This traditional linking of Pagan prophetesses with Christian tradition is maintained in the Grail stories. The *Quest del San Graal* provides us with another Pagan figure venerated by Christian tradition who literally acts as a bridge-builder between the two. This is the Queen of Sheba, wife of King Solomon. We will read more about her in the next chapter.

Unaware of the venerable tradition of the Black Maiden in native stories, but keen to plug into the sibylline tradition, Wolfram gives Kundry an Oriental origin. He tells how Adam learned from God the secret knowledge of the seven planetary powers. Adam told his daughters never to meddle with medicinal herbs while they were pregnant, so as to deform their offspring, but they did so experiment that their offspring were different from the rest of mortalkind. Queen Secundille of India was of this race, and she, desirous of finding out more about the Grail sent Kundry and her brother, Malcriature, a dwarf, to Anfortas, the Grail king.

The daughters of Adam are most mysterious and it would seem that they are his progeny by Lilith, not by Eve. If this is so then Wolfram has given Kundry descent from Lilith, herself a goddess of great magical power, before Jewish legend turned her into a fearful demon of evil craft. Certainly, Kundry displays a knowledge of Arabic astronomy which confirms this matrilineal descent.

Lilith is primarily a goddess of both earthly and transcendent knowledge. Like Sheba, she sometimes has non-human feet, denoting her earthly side. She also has wings with which to fly, denoting her transcendent nature. Lilith's unique combination of earthly wisdom and heavenly gnosis give her great power. She has not lost sight of her destiny.

Kundry has an ugly appearance, which many find loathsome or bestial. Yet she also has esoteric knowledge and even handles the Grail itself, bringing the anchoress, Sigune, her daily food from its depths. Kundry represents the admixture of the Pagan Earth traditions of prophecy and guardianship with the Christian ministry of a holy woman, acting as a bridge between the traditions.

She is a *drakaina*, or Earth-speaker, which is what the Greeks called their sibylline priestess, the pythoness. The snake which holds to the Earth and is faithful to its commands, giving warning of earth-tremor and other natural disasters, is often despised as a creeping thing of no worth. Yet the snake is the inhabitant of sacred places and many shrines and domestic houses had their resident snake, which was fed with morsels from the table and encouraged to remain as a household guardian. This is likewise the function of Kundry.

Snakes, like dragons, have fallen into disrepute in the West, largely as the result of the myth of Eden. The Adversary, in the form of a serpent, tempts Eve to eat of the Tree of the Knowledge of Good and Evil, with the result that humankind are gifted with the mutually-cancelling gifts of god-like knowledge coupled to inevitable mortality. The snake or dragon once symbolized the knowledge of the Earth. The sibyl or drakaina who spoke for the Earth was like a snake, living often in hollows in the ground, near to the Earth's heartbeat, the better to hear and tell.

One of the many appearances of the Black Maiden, which Kundry, among others, exemplifies is actually as a dragon or monster. This is one of the prime stories of the Goddess of Sovereignty whose ugliness is often given credibility by a rationalization: that a beautiful young woman, through the ill-will of a bent magician, is turned into monstrous shape. She can only be released from her terrible shape by a man who is brave enough to kiss her. This kiss, called in medieval tradition, the *fier baiser* or 'daring kiss', is like the embrace which releases the

Goddess of the Land from her *cailleach* appearance to resume her beautiful face. This story occurs throughout folk and Arthurian tradition, and is an essential part of the transformations of Sovereignty. We will see a further variant of this tradition in Chapter 9.

Kundry's own story lacks a transformative ending for her. It is suggested in the *Didot Perceval* where, as Rosete li Bloie, she somehow turns from being the ugliest to the most beautiful woman in the world. In *Perlesvaus*, the Maiden of the Cart appears at the beginning of the story with a bald head, overtly signifying the waste land and the withdrawal of the Grail's influence; she reappears at the end with a full head of hair after the Grail has restored everything to rights.

What happens to Kundry at the end - does she change her ugly shape? She has no mate or champion to kiss her back to beauty, after all. Can we see any significant changes in her?

The ugly Grail Messenger who has faithfully served as the bridge between the Grail family and the mundane world announces the joy of transformation by assuming a wimple embroidered with golden turtle doves. This may seem a very little thing, an aside in our story, if it were not for the significant fact that the Goddess of Wisdom, Sophia, is symbolized by a dove when she is expressing her transcendent nature. Sophia, like Kundry and Sheba, can assume more homely guises, and her greatness can be revealed by the common snake when she goes in her earthly mode.[15] 'Be cunning as serpents, innocent as doves,' is the instruction which Christ commands his apostles in their dealings with the world.[16]

Kundry enacts this advice. Whatever her physical appearance, it is her voice and welcome presence that brings the joy of the Grail's achievement to the beleaguered occupants of the Grail Castle. Her many years of toil and travelling are over. Her exile is no more. She is able to rejoice that the Grail is available to all and that the waste land of every heart can at last be healed.

The Serpent and the Dove

You stand at the entrance to a wood. It is springtime. The
fresh buds are opening, and the early flowers clothing the
forest floor. The path unfolds clearly before you and, with
glad heart, you enter. Ahead of you, standing at the bend of
the path, are a pair of dwarfs – a man and a woman. They
welcome you to the woods with smiles and gestures, but
they seem unable to speak. They show willingness to be
your guides and you go with them.

The woodland grows less tame the further in you go. You
come to a river over which you must pass. It is deep, swiftly
running and full of rocks. There seems no way to cross
over. The female dwarf unties a mule which crops the grass
beside the river and holds its head for you to mount it. It
seems unlikely that such a small animal will be able to carry
you across such a fiercely-flowing river, but the dwarfs insist
that it is safe with reassuring nods. The mule has no bridle
and you have to cling on to the short mane. The mule
nonchalantly wades into the water and swims you across,
while the dwarfs cling to your either leg and kick with their
own short legs.

On the far side, you shake yourselves and continue on your
way. Now you notice that the landscape is changing rapidly,
becoming wilder still, with fewer trees. In the middle of this
wilderness is a tented pavilion, its door-cloths raised on
either side. Above it flies a pennant of two intertwined
dragons. You look within and see a table and two chairs,
with a board game set ready to play. The board is of black
onyx and white marble. The pieces are of silver and red
gold. There is a faint humming coming from the board and
you feel very drawn to it. As you approach, you see that a
spear hangs vertically from the centre of the pavilion. Its
point drips a spot of blood onto the central white square.
The scene is urgently charged and you are moved to ask:
'Why does this happen? What does it mean?'

The dwarfs immediately burst into tears of joy and begin to
speak. 'Blessed be the hour of our release. We have been
unable to speak until now. Your questions have set us free
of silence. The board which you see is the Earth itself. The
squares represent the joys and sorrows of life, in equal

measure. The pieces are the players of the game, the walkers in the maze, the people of the Earth who can change all things by one false step upon the squares. The spear that drips blood has hung there since the beginning of time. It is a scion of the Tree of Life and its blood is the sap of life. If you are courageous, you may go beyond the veil yonder and learn more of the mystery.'

You see a great tapestry hanging beyond the gaming board. You look upon it and see the patterns of creation woven there. In one corner of the web is your own life and for a moment you contemplate its shaping . . .

The time has come to step beyond the veil. You lift the tapestry and pass beyond. Within is darkness, the darkness of space itself. As your eyes acclimatize, you see the faint pin-prick of stars and the wheeling constellations. In the distance is a whirling symbol which comes at great velocity towards you, stopping short when it fills your vision.

Before you is a mighty tree such as you have never seen before. It is divided into two distinct parts. The left half of the foliage is bright green and the right half is golden with flame which mysteriously does not consume. In the green half perches a dove, in the burning half coils a serpent. The image glows with the intense clarity of starlight and yet is vitally substantial.

The serpent speaks to you. 'I guard the knowledge of the body. I am the heart of matter. Way-shower to the seeker on quest am I. I am the Grail in exile. See me as I am, and do not fear.'

The coiling serpent glides down the tree and becomes a black-skinned woman of great ugliness. She carries a bridle in her hands. 'With this bridle comes the discipline of the seeker. Take it for the wise ruling of the world.' And she gives it into your hands.

The dove then speaks to you. 'I guard the knowledge of the spirit. I am the heart of the unmanifest. I am the journey's end of heart's desire. I am the immanent Grail. See me as I am, and be joyful.'

The dove flies down and becomes a beautiful woman who holds a vessel in her hands. 'With this cup comes the spirit's freedom. Drink from it for the liberation of all prisoned hearts.' And she offers you the cup to drink.

When you next open your eyes, the two women have become as one. As the image of the tree whirls slowly from you into the distance of space, you see the cosmic image of a being larger than the stars. She pours out the grain of the stars like dust from her sheaf of corn. It falls in a spiral, making a starry stairway. But her descent is a mystery which it is not for you to see at this time.

The scene fades from your sight and you are standing in a clearing in the forest. The pavilion and the dwarfs are gone. Only the mule remains cropping the grass. You are strengthened by the Grail, but it is time to return to your own world. You place the bridle about the mule's head and go to mount.

The mule speaks to you. 'Well did you ask the question, kindly did you treat my small messengers. The vision you have seen is not for you alone. Go forth into the world bearing the news that the Grail is abroad, that the Lady returns once more to the Earth. You who have drunk from the cup and borne the bridle, know me now: I am Kundry, she who bears all. Call upon me and I shall come to you on your quest. Question me and you shall hear the true speech from the horse's mouth. Mount now and remember the shape of your life's pattern.'

It is odd, riding back through the forest on the back of a talking mule. She bears you across the river and leaves you on the path homeward. She bids you farewell. 'But I will come to you again. When you are lost, look for me and do not despise my advice on the quest. When you find your heart's desire, rejoice with me. And may the wisdom of the serpent and the innocence of the dove accompany your quest!'

You return to your own time and place and quietly contemplate the mysteries you have witnessed.

REFERENCES

1. Wolfram von Eschenbach, *Parzival*, trans. A.T. Hatto.
2. Chrétien de Troyes, *Arthurian Romances*, trans. W.W. Kibler and C.W. Carroll.
3. Sir Thomas Malory, *The Morte d'Arthur*.
4. *The Mabinogion*, ed. Lady Charlotte Guest.
5. Our translation.
6. Malory, op. cit.
7. John Matthews, *Gawain: Knight of the Goddess*.
8. Malory, op. cit.
9. Ibid.
10. Caitlín Matthews, *Mabon and the Mysteries of Britain: An Exploration of 'The Mabinogion'*.
11. Geshe Rabten, *The Essential Nectar*.
12. Caitlín Matthews, *Sophia: Goddess of Wisdom*.
13. Ajit Mookerjee, *Kali: the Feminine Force*.
14. J. and J.M. Todd, *Voices from the Past*.
15. *Sophia*, op. cit.
16. Matthew 10:20.

Dindraine

Women's flesh lives the quest of the Grail
  in the change from Camelot to Carbonek and from
  Carbonek to Sarras,
puberty to Carbonek, and the stanching, and Carbonek
  to death.
Blessed is she who gives herself to the journey.
                    Charles Williams, *Taliessin in the Rose Garden*

Variant Names:
Dandrane, Dandrenor, Danbrann.

THE MYTH OF DINDRAINE

Dindraine is the last of the Ladies of the Lake to manifest, both
in terms of chronological sequence within the Arthurian story
as a whole, and within the transmission of literary tradition. Just
as Kundry alone gives her name to the Black Maiden archetype,
so too Dindraine is the only named persona to typify the usually
unnamed sister of the Grail-winner. The character of Perceval's
sister or kinswoman can be identified with the archetype of the
Grail-empowerer – she who is the representative of the Grail
itself.

In *Peredur*, Peredur meets a woman lamenting a dead knight.
She tells him that Peredur has killed his mother by his untimely
departure. She herself is his foster-sister and her husband has
been slain by the Knight of the Glade. Peredur overcomes this
knight and commands to make amends to his widowed foster-

sister by marrying her forthwith. Chrétien's *Conte del Graal* has a parallel incident, but the woman is Perceval's first cousin. In Wauchier's *Second Continuation* of the Grail story, the woman has become Perceval's sister.

Wolfram's *Parzival* substitutes a cousin, the anchoress Sigune, for Perceval's sister. Sigune becomes a holy woman after the death of her lover. She is enclosed in a cell in the forest, which is where Parzival finds her. She gives him advice about the Grail quest, counselling him to follow Kundry. At the conclusion of the quest, she is discovered dead in her cell and is interred with her lover. This figure of the recluse or nun has become further interwoven with Dindraine's character. She it is who has first knowledge of the Grail's appearing and the subsequent events in which she will herself be a prime mover.

Dindraine emerges first of all in *Perlesvaus*, where she is called Dandrane. Here the Grail quest begins when three maidens come into Arthur's hall: a bald, ugly damsel who is called the Maiden of the Cart, who travels in a cart drawn by three stags; a maiden attired as a squire on horseback, bearing a brachet or hunting dog and a shield; and a short beautiful maiden on foot. The shield is that of Joseph of Arimathea and is destined to belong to the Grail-winner. The brachet will not greet anyone until that knight's arrival.

Later on, Dandrane comes to court and asks the help of the knight who is destined to carry Joseph's shield. Her mother's lands have been stolen from her and now she has ridden through inhospitable regions to seek Perceval. The brachet immediately greets her, to the astonishment of Guinevere, since it has never greeted anyone before. Later that night, a mysterious ship comes to shore. Its sole passenger is an unnamed knight who enters the court, takes the shield and is greeted effusively by the dog, whom he takes with him. In the morning, Dandrane is peeved with Arthur for not having woken her, for she has missed her brother and has to resume her quest for him.

Later when Perceval is lodging near a hermitage he overhears Dandrane praying for assistance. Her prayer outlines their mother's peril and Dandrane's own dangerous quest for

Perceval. He shows himself and Dandrane acclaims him as the answer to her prayer. She tells him of her determination to make a vigil in the Perilous Cemetery – a place of great dread, wherein is a chapel which has a relic of Christ's shroud. She has been assured by a hermit that her mother's enemy, the Lord of the Fens, cannot be overcome by anyone unless they carry a piece of this relic. Only a maiden can accomplish this quest.

Ghostly knights with flaming lances haunt the cemetery, and the sounds of slaughter continually strike the ear. Dandrane attains the chapel, seizes hold of the shroud and takes part of it. A ghostly voice informs her that the Fisher King is dead, that the Grail and other hallows have ceased to appear and that the King of Castle Mortel (the Grail adversary) has triumphed. Dandrane's only hope now is in Perceval. She rides to her mother's castle where he has just appeared. Outside it is a tomb which only the best knight in the world can open. Perceval opens it in the presence of his mother and sister: it contains the body of Joseph of Arimathea and several relics of Christ's Passion. Dandrane gives Perceval the piece of the shroud from the Perilous Cemetery and he does battle with the Lord of the Fens, defeating him.

Later, Perceval hears that the Lord of the Fens' cousin, Aristor, has carried off Dandrane, intending to submit her to his usual cruel custom. He is famed for marrying, raping and then killing his wives by beheading them after a year's elapse. Perceval rides to his sister's wedding, beheads Aristor and gives the head to Dandrane.

As he is about to restore the Grail, the Maiden of Cart reappears, now complete with a head of hair once more. She accompanies him to the conclusion of his quest and brings his mother and Dandrane to the Grail castle. There they live together until their death, when Perceval sets sail on a ship that bears him away from mortal to heavenly realms.

The *Queste del San Graal* is a major source for the acts of Dindraine. It is part of the *Vulgate Cycle*, from which Malory took his own Grail story, and develops many of the themes outlined above. Within the story are reflections of Dindraine, for example, the Queen of the Waste Land who counsels Perceval, telling him the history of the Round Table. This text is the one which ousts Perceval from his position of sole Grail-winner and substitutes Galahad, the son of Elaine and Lancelot.

Dindraine comes to Galahad towards the end of the Grail quest and leads him to a ship to which Bors and Perceval have also been brought. They sail to another ship, the one on which they will complete their quest. This is the Ship of Solomon. On it is a bed on which is a sword which cannot be drawn from its scabbard save by the best knight. The scabbard will keep its bearer from scathe and cannot be fastened on save by a princess who is destined later to remove the belt and exchange it for the thing she prizes most. This princess is destined to call the sword by its true name. The wood from which the bed is made is of three different colours: white, green and red. Dindraine explains that the wood is of the Tree of the Knowledge of Good and Evil in Eden, of which Eve took a twig when she was a virgin, when the wood was white. After she conjoined with Adam, new cuttings of the tree turned green. After the slaughter of Abel by Cain, all new cuttings became red.

Dindraine further tells how Solomon's wife was wiser than he. Solomon had knowledge that Christ would come and that a certain knight would be the last of his line. The king wished to leave a testimonial to advise the knight that he had known and prepared for his coming, but the destined knight would live 2,000 years hence and he knew not how to frame something that would last so long. Solomon's wife counselled him to make a ship of rot-proof timbers, using wood from the slips which Eve had taken from the Tree of Life. King David's sword was placed in the ship, which Solomon's wife bedecked with hangings. Thus Solomon prepared the ship for his descendant, the Grail-winner.

Dindraine then shows the belt intended for the sword, a belt woven from her own hair. She names the sword 'the Sword of the Strange Belt' and the scabbard 'Memory of Blood,' and then Galahad draws it forth.

When they come to land again, the company is accosted by 10 armed knights who demand that Dindraine be taken to a nearby castle where she must submit to the custom there. Every maiden who passes that way must give enough blood from her right arm to fill a silver basin. The company fight to defend Dindraine and then break off to hear why the custom was instituted. The castle is owned by a leprous maiden who can only be healed if a maiden princess gives of her blood. Dindraine begs to be allowed to give her healing. After mass the next morning, she is bled, but the loss is too great and she begins to die. As she lays dying, she makes Perceval promise to put her body in a boat, set it forth, and then to make for Sarras, the otherworldly Grail city, where they will find and bury her. She prophesies that she will lie next to Galahad.

Dindraine is then embalmed and set in the boat; letters are placed in her hands, telling all travellers about her history. Lancelot encounters the boat and reads the letter, thus learning of his son's progress on the quest. Afterwards, the Grail knights arrive in Sarras where Dindraine's boat also arrives. She is buried there with great honour. After the deaths of Galahad and Perceval, Bors buries them beside her, returning to relate the Grail quest to Arthur.

Dindraine also appears in the Welsh Grail story, *Y Seint Graal*, where she is called Danbrann. This peculiar variant recalls the sacrificial beheading of the Welsh god, Bran the Blessed.[1]

Malory's *Morte d'Arthur* draws upon the tradition of Perceval's sister in the white hart quest, where, as we have seen, King Pellinore finds a maiden lamenting the death of her knight. Because he is occupied with his quest he ignores her, but on his return that way, he finds her dead, gnawed by wild beasts. Merlin then informs him that this maiden is none other than Eleine, his own daughter by the Lady of Rule.[2] King Pellinore is also Perceval's father. Malory, however, gives Perceval another sister who accords in every respect with the figure of Dindraine in the *Queste*. She relates the history of Solomon's ship, where the beams of wood from the Tree of Life are spindles. When Galahad draws forth the Sword of the Strange Girdles from the sheath, here called 'Mover of Blood', she proclaims: 'Now reck I not though I die, for now I hold me one of the blessed maidens of the world, which hath made the worthiest knight of the world.' The virgin knight Galahad declares: 'Damsel, ye have done so much that I shall be your knight all the days of my life.'[3]

The twentieth-century mystical poet, Charles Williams, made Perceval's sister a very Beatrice of the Grail legend. His esoteric insights into her nature are often profound. He calls her Dindrane while she is at court and Blanchfleur after she takes religious vows, thus marking an important distinction between her twin roles.

SACRED BLOOD AND THE SOVEREIGN ADVENTURE

By what right does Dindraine appear here as a Lady of the Lake, you might ask? Her presence is a manifestly late arrival in the Arthurian canon. Does she have a traditional, pre-Christian basis?

The archetype of Dindraine stems partially from the Sorrowful Maiden who mourns the Wounded King in the Grail romances. We note that in nearly every appearance, Dindraine is discovered in a forest mourning her dead lover. In the fifteenth-century *Corpus Christi Carol*, a wounded knight lies on a bed in the middle of a forest:

> And at his bedside, there kneeleth a may,
> And she weepeth night and day.[4]

This 'may' is none other than the Sorrowful Maiden who, like a *bansidhe*, bewails the Wounded King and the waste land. She mourns the dislocation of the primal waters, which are no longer able to flow into this world from the Otherworld.

The reason for her sorrow is not hard to seek, if we explore Celtic tradition. The Sorrowful Maiden was once the Hallows Queen herself, the empowering priestess of Sovereignty. In the earliest versions, Perceval's sister is both a virgin and a widow: her rightful husband lies slain and the Grail king is wounded, so that there is no-one with whom the sacred wedding of the land can take place.

As we have seen, Perceval's aunt, the recluse, tells him, 'For some called me sometime the Queen of the Waste Lands, and I was called the queen of most riches in the world.'[5] Dindraine is her counterpart: once the bountiful Lady of Sovereignty, now despoiled and grieving as the Queen of the Waste Land.

In the prime myths of Sovereignty, the Goddess guards the waters of a well or ford as a hag. The only one who can drink or cross her waters is the worthiest man who will be king by virtue of wisdom. The foolish and unworthy will refuse to embrace her; the worthy one will kiss and transform her, just as the land is transformed by a wise and just ruler.

It is possible that these traditional stories are remembrances of when the clan matriarchs chose the tribal ruler. The candidate might have been confronted by a series of choices: a set of weapons and tools, and the ultimate test in the forest where he would be confronted by a representative of the Ladies of the Lake. If he chose to kiss the ugly hag, he would have been given a wife of the royal blood, a young maiden.

In Celtic tradition, Sovereignty pours out different liquids. In the Irish text *Baile in Scail* (The Phantom's Prophecy), Conn is presented with a dynastic vision by the god Lugh. Sovereignty sits in her chair surrounded by buckets of beer and wine, and asks Lugh for whom she should pour her cup. If we study the Sovereignty tradition deeply, we find that three cups are proffered: the white milk of fostering, the red drink of lordship (kingship) and the dark drink of forgetfulness or healing. Each draught brings its own knowledge and empowerment.[6]

The Grail is a vessel of grace. Its antithesis is the drought of the waste land. Without the saving waters of grace, both soul and land are dry as dust.

Dindraine at first appears as the ultimate sacrifice - she does not attain the Grail, but enables others to do so. Even at this supreme moment, she is allowed, like Moses, only a glimpse of the Holy Land. She is like the circumscribed Maid of Astolat, who floats by on her barge – the only way of striking at the heart of her desired but hard-hearted lover.

But is Dindraine really a victim and martyr or is she the empowering Grail Maiden? She is the first to have sight of the Grail, has prophetic knowledge of what her own role shall be, and is the only female Grail-seeker. She suffers the disadvantages of womanhood upon her quest, however, since she is not trained in arms. Dandrane's remark to Perceval as she goes go fulfil her Perilous Cemetery vigil has the ring of reality: 'Look at *my* path; it is little frequented, for I tell you, no knight dares take it without grave peril to himself and deep fear: may God guard your body, for mine will be in great danger tonight.'[7] Without chivalric skills, she nonetheless goes armed with only her integrity into peril.

The Grail quest, as the *Vulgate* text makes clear, is no place for women. They are deliberately excluded from the Grail vision in the *Queste*, and even their outcry at losing their menfolk to the quest is unsympathetically dealt with:

> For every lady, married or maid, offered to accompany her knight in the Quest . . . had it not it not been for an old and venerable man wearing the religious habit . . . 'None may take maid or lady with him on this Quest without falling into mortal sin . . . for this is no search for earthly things but a seeking out of the mysteries and hidden sweets of Our Lord.'[8]

The women are accordingly left at court. However, this is the very same text in which Dindraine plays a major role!

To resolve this contradiction, we must further explore Dindraine's special qualities. As a woman, she does what none of the Grail knights can do: she menstruates. She also bleeds to death. The collusion of the twin themes of giving blood and the ever-giving powers of the Grail are purposeful, even though the medieval story of Dindraine sometimes lacks the framework of female understanding. Charles Williams wrote:

Well are women warned from serving the altar
who, by the nature of their creature, from Caucasia
    to Carbonek,
share with the Sacrifice the victimization of blood.[9]

The exclusion of women from many activities and functions seems to stem from their magical ability to menstruate. What started as the reverential sequestration of women during their time of power, to dream and envision, rapidly led to their exclusion from all manner of spiritual and everyday activities. That women are indeed already central to the Grail quest, Williams is in no doubt:

Women's flesh lives the quest of the Grail
in the change from Camelot to Carbonek and from
    Carbonek to Sarras,
puberty to Carbonek, and the stanching, and
    Carbonek to death.[10]

In Williams' terminology, Camelot signifies the worldly court to which Princess Dindraine is born, Carbonek is the Grail castle where Dindraine prepares herself for her quest, and Sarras is the heavenly realm whence the Grail's power emanates. His likening of the Grail quest to the female cycle is both challenging and worth deeper investigation.

Menstruation has ceased to be one of the greatest taboo subjects of the civilized world, although it is still poorly understood. Its appearance in a girl at the menarche signifies her nubility, her ability to be fertile. In Hindu tradition, where child-brides were commonplace, there was considerable pressure upon the parents of a nubile girl to marry her off straight away, so that no opportunity for her fertility would be wasted. Menstruation only occurs during the infertile period of the month in human females, normally ceasing only at pregnancy or at the change of life. In this, women differ from female animals, which are only fertile when they are on heat.

The process of the shedding of the ovum each month is thus primarily about sterility. The taboos surrounding this time of the female monthly cycle are significantly about fear of infertility or loss. Butter will not come if churned by a menstruating woman, nor will bread rise. Basic food-stuffs are believed dangerous if touched by a menstruating woman. Menstrual taboos and isolation customs are found even in Eastern Orthodoxy where women are supposed not to receive the sacrament while menstruating. Women are not permitted in the sanctuary of a church for this reason. Orthodox Jewish women must abstain from handling various domestic items and from sleeping with their husbands at this time, and must enter a *mikveh* or ritual bath at the cessation of blood in order to be ritually clean once more. Blood is only safe or beneficial when it is used in a fertile manner, as when a woman is pregnant, or during the sacramental transubstantiation of water into wine, when it becomes the blood of Christ.

Within the Gospels, Christ is touched by a woman with an issue of blood. It is unclear as to whether she is haemorrhaging or whether she suffers irregular periods – whichever the case, such a woman would have been ritually unclean to Judaic society. Yet Christ, who feels the power go out of him as she touches his garment, heals her, an action which would set him apart from any other Jewish man for allowing such a liberty. Why does power leave him at that moment? Because of the free siphoning off of energy during the healing or because the woman has power to draw on that energy?

Dindraine's action is not immediately related to menstruation, however, in that she gives her blood in fulfilment of a magical ritual in order to heal a suffering woman. The letting of blood has many traditional functions in our society. There is no doubt that blood has power. The blood-letting of bull-fights, wherein both beast or matador may suffer, stems from pre-Christian sacrificial cults. Beasts were offered in appeasement to gods of many kinds. Human beings were also offered as a holocaust. The idea of a blood sacrifice also underlies the crucifixion and redemptive action of Christ. By suffering death on the cross, he overcame the necessity for other sacrifices. However, people still like their 'pound of flesh' and whether this manifests as a predilection for crime or horror stories or as a fascination with accidents and disasters, it is an atavistic obsession still very much with us. This gory fascination also animated our more recent ancestors who used to attend public hangings, whippings and tooth-drawings with similar relish.

The notion that 'it is a good thing for a man to die for the people' is still enacted on a regular basis throughout world politics: political assassinations, whether in bloody fact or at the hands of the no-less brutal media, occur daily. The exercise of power itself draws others to demand a blood-letting of some kind.

Another major source of blood satisfaction is the blood-feud, whereby one tribe or family slay members of another. This vengeance motif is the major motivation for the Welsh Grail story of *Peredur*, and is still apparent today in many cultures where civil strife flourishes or where associations like the Mafia or the IRA sustain a terrorist campaign.

These atavistic reminders of our ancestral roots are often unpleasant, especially when children or women become victims of crazed and criminal acts of blood-letting. Youth, innocence and strength are seen as targets for power-release. Significantly, in Western penal tradition, women were usually slain in ways that ensured that their blood was unshed: burning or hanging was the normal capital punishment, with only noblewomen or queens being allowed the 'privilege' of beheading. On the other hand, most methods of execution for men involved the spilling of blood.

So it seems that fascination for blood is inerradicable from the human condition. We measure mortality by the spillage of blood. Can it ever be stopped? Life is a cyclic phenomenon which has no beginning or end of its own. Individual lives begin and end, but collectively life goes on. Different spiritual traditions have sought to find the solution to the death of the body by promoting the immortality of the spirit. The Grail itself is a vessel of this immortality. In every generation it returns in different forms to renew whatever needs new life. Its followers, the hidden Grail family, are mediators of its power. These people are those who are able to act in a non-dual way, to react affirmatively to life's problems. Their innocence is the mirror in which evil is reflected back to the sender; their courage breaks the chain of despair and creates the circumstances for change. Dindraine is herself an example of pure innocence. She does not resist evil, actively stopping her escort of Grail-seekers from overcoming her aggressors, just as Christ forbids his disciples to resist violently when he is captured in the Garden of Gethsemane. By healing the leprous woman, she heals the wasteland face of the Goddess of the Land.

But how and why does waste land come about? What is the cause of such evil? To answer this we must discover the roots of the Grail tradition.

THE WELLS AND THE WASTE LAND

Myths of loss and exile appear in every culture. Christianity, Judaism and Islam share the same myth, that of the primal parents, Adam and Eve. This myth has been accepted by many fundamentalists as historical fact, an abuse of a sacred story which has alienated many, who have disassociated themselves from it entirely. The Christian version of the Edenic myth lays particular stress upon the fault of Eve in such a way that it has enforced the suppression of female independence and spiritual autonomy. But mystical Christians, Sufis and Qabalists have accepted it for what it is – a sacred story which explains the dislocation of creation from the Divine.

The retelling of this story by Dindraine, in the *Queste*, is remarkable in itself. Dindraine is like the Muse of history, for she chronicles the whole of the Arthurian cycle, the history of humanity and the ages of the world. She keeps her distance from the action because she is wholly one with the immensity of this knowledge. It means that she has no partner, no personal life, no thought save this perpetual dwelling upon the cosmic patterns which she holds in her hands. She bears the traditions concerning the Hallows in the Grail ship of her heart, she is in direct succession to the one who precedes her, Sheba, wife of Solomon. As the last link in the chain, she passes her knowledge to those who come to the uttermost Innerworld. It is Dindraine who gives the secret knowledge of the three spindles, telling how the Tree of Life was first white in token of purity, then green in token of Adam and Eve's life-giving union, then red in token of Abel's blood spilt by Cain. These three spindles appearing on the head of the bed in the Ship of Solomon bring us closely back to the work of the Ladies of the Lake as weavers and spinners of life.

The loss of the Grail in our world is symbolized by the drying up of the waters. Water is itself the ambient means of life. Without rain, crops, trees and plants wither. Without rivers, we have no water to drink. Water is also the symbolic element of spiritual fertility. Without spiritual nourishment, our physical lives wither. Imagine an existence without culture, without the dynamic of creativity, without the fulfilment of spiritual service. Such an existence would be a waste land indeed.

The Grail legend has its own Pagan version of how the Grail, representing all that is beneficial, became exiled or disconnected from our world. This is 'The Story of the Well-Maidens' and appears in the little-known text called *The Elucidation*.[11] It starts in a far-off time before King Arthur. Otherworldly maidens offer the hospitality of the wells to all travellers, giving freely to all. Then King Amangons rapes one of their number, stealing her golden cup. His men rape the other maidens. From that time onwards, no maiden will serve. The power of the Grail is withdrawn from the land, which becomes waste. After the Round Table knights hear this old story they determine to kill Amangons' descendants. They find a wandering group of knights and maidens who say they are the descendants of the Well-Maidens and of Amangons and his followers. They are destined to wander thus until the Grail is found, telling their story in the hope that someone will discover it. Many Round Table knights go on quest and the Grail is eventually achieved. The waste land is restored to fertility.

This mythic narrative must be viewed like the Edenic myth – a story which attempts to explain the advent of evil into paradisal innocence. That the Grail is withdrawn when the Well-Maidens are raped is, however, in startling counterpoint to the Edenic myth, where Eve provokes the Fall.

Dindraine points the way to the resacralization of life. She takes up the quest with her whole heart and will. She fulfils the role of priestess, both as a Lady of the Lake and as a Christian woman. This statement may well be disputed by many who disapprove of Christianity as a valid spiritual path, as well as by those Christians who disapprove of female ministry. To overcome both objections, we point out that the ways of love and service pass beyond gendural or spiritual boundaries. Dindraine as a priestess of the new dispensation, nevertheless, brings the potent mysteries of the ancient waters of the Earth. Her indisputable role is exemplified by her blood-giving. Are Lake and cloister so far apart in reality?

Dindraine retains something of the imagery of the Maid of Astolat who died for love of Lancelot: like her, she comes down the water-ways in a boat. But the letters in her hands are not those of painful self-destruction but a record of joyful pilgrimage. Just as the Ship of Solomon floats down the rivers of time to the age of Arthur, so the message of Dindraine is to be found in the hands of all who would, like her, prepare the way of the Grail.

DINDRAINE THE SAVIOUR

Why Dindraine should appear and be given house room in what had become an increasing Christianized narrative is an interesting question. With Galahad, Bors and Perceval, she is one of the Grail questers. But while the knights achieve the Grail, Dindraine is taken out of the story before that event. She strays onto the verges of the paradisal Grail-city of Sarras, entering it only as a dead woman. However a parallel between this and the Assumption of the Blessed Virgin to heaven could be made.

According to mystical theology, Mary is the only human being in heaven: like Dindraine, she drinks from her Grail before any other mortal.

To continue this parallel, although in the later Grail texts the original Grail-winner, Perceval, cedes place to Galahad, each of the knights becomes identifiable with Christ – a young man of devout spirit whose strengths and virtues lead him to approach perfection. This is much more marked in Galahad who, following the logical Christic path, ends his life by entering a kind of Grail *nirvana*, achieving the Grail on behalf of all others. That this religious correlation should occur within the Arthurian legends is reasonable, considering the fact that this native, apocryphal tale is part of the Western spiritual tradition. What is unusual is the unorthodox step of presenting a woman as a co-redemptress. Within Christianity, Christ alone, the offspring of a divine Father and a human mother, is the redeemer of creation. Mary's role is to assent to her child's conception and to prepare him for his mission. The campaign to proclaim Mary as co-redemptress with Christ is still strong within some areas of the Church, but has never been officially defined.

Dindraine's role is not like Mary's, save in the fact that she foresees, prepares and dedicates her life to the achieving of the Grail. In Christianity, it is Christ whose blood is shed for all beings. In the Grail quest, it is Dindraine whose blood is shed. This gives us the amazing revelation of the possibility of redemption through a woman, a revelation of considerable impact in the context of medieval understanding. From the earliest stories in which the Grail is exemplified by a woman, right up to the Christianized legends, this possibility is continually being hinted at.

In *Perlesvaus*, for example, the three maidens who announce the Grail quest – the Maiden of the Cart, the Maiden on Horseback and the Maiden on Foot – represent the three faces of the goddess Fortuna. Later on Gawain encounters three maidens at a golden fountain. They carry bread, wine and meat, and place their offerings at the fountain. When Gawain stares after them, it seems that there is but one maiden. Afterwards he comes to the Castle of Enquiry, where all mysteries are explained, but its helpful hermit refuses to explain the strange single appearance of the triple maidens, saying, 'I will tell you no more than you have heard . . . for no-one should reveal the secrets of the Saviour; they should be kept secret by him to whom they are entrusted.'[12] This Gnostic-sounding phrase, 'the secrets of the Saviour', covers an open mystery, which has been revealed to all who enter the sanctuary of the Grail: that the revealers and guardians of the Grail are indeed priestesses and that the source of the mystery is the Grail-Goddess herself.

Dindraine literally gives her own blood in the same unstinting way that the Grail-Goddess does, paralleling the pelican, the mystic emblem of Christ's sacrifice which, in medieval times, was believed to tear its own breast in order to feed its young with its own blood. The Well-Maidens are her daughters, giving the Grail's bounty to all. It is only when Dindraine consciously and willingly offers herself that the Grail becomes available once more. The giving of Dindraine's blood is the giving of life itself. Like a feminine Christ, she redeems the time and allows all people to go onwards on the quest. In an age where personal empowerment has become the over-riding factor in spiritual exploration, it is rare to find someone who is content to exemplify the spiritual goal in this way. Her words, 'Now reck I not though I die, for now I hold me one of the blessed maidens of the world, which hath made the worthiest knight of the world' are her own recognition that she has *become the Grail* at which others may drink. She does not merely empower the Grail-winner, but all people of that age.

Every age has to solve the problem of evil and find within its people those who are willing to go on quest, putting themselves at the service of the Grail. For the Grail does not just appear in medieval and Celtic story, it is an ongoing cycle. To help us see the current pattern of events and find the Grail-bearer for this age, we can examine the pattern of the Grail's manifestation as follows:

1. The Dolorous Blow afflicts the land – this is usually caused by a publicly responsible person acting in a privately personal or selfish way, e.g. King Amangons raping the Damsel of Wells. It can also happen when one of the Hallows is misused, as when Balin strikes Pelles with the spear by way of self-defence.[13] The ancient analogue of this blow is shown in the incident where Gwenhwyfar has a cup of wine thrown into her lap – an insult to the representative of Sovereignty.

2. The Dolorous Blow afflicts both king and land with infertility and wasting disease. The land becomes overrun with opportunist foes who waste remaining resources and terrorize the weak. The kingdom becomes anarchistic.

3. The Grail becomes active, appearing symbolically or actually to those who have dedicated themselves to restoring the king and the waste land to rights again.

4. The healing grace of the Grail is sought by way of chivalric quest, a journey of personal danger, by prayer and seership, by the formation of network of dedicated followers of seekers. These form the Grail family.

5. Of the many seekers, one has a greater affinity with the Grail than others. He or she is often weaker, less able, ill-educated, young or 'foolish'. This foolishness actually is the result of the non-duality of innocent perception, so that it is this youngest son or maiden who is able to perceive and attain the Grail.

6. The Grail-winner heals the wounds of land and king by being sufficiently open to the Grail's grace. The land becomes fertile again, the old king dies or retires, the Grail-winner and companions become the new guardians of the Grail, which no longer appears in symbolic form but is manifest everywhere.

This mythological template can be used in all times and by all traditions and cultures. If you examine the history of your land and age, you will find this pattern endlessly repeated. It can be an act of real seership to recognize the unfolding patterns and protagonists of the Grail in your own time and place. This is true alchemy, where the Great Work is the perfecting of the times.

Perceval and Dindraine are brother and sister, the alchemical *rebus* of the achieved work. Like Isis and Osiris, or the White Queen of Alchemical Salt and the Red King of Alchemical Sulphur, their effect upon the world is far-reaching. Also, as in the Coronation of the Virgin Mary and her mystical nuptials with Christ in heaven, so Dindraine is partnered by Galahad in Sarras, where he and she remain in Paradise. Malory's Galahad swears to be Dindraine's knight to the end of his days. Their sacred marriage takes place after death rather than in the body. This sacred relationship of the quester and the priestess of the mysteries is one of the most profound mysteries of the Grail.

The old rituals of Sovereignty saw the conjoining of Grail-maiden and Seeker, the representative of the Goddess of the Land and the would-be king. In the myth of Dindraine we find a dedicated virgin who allows her blood to flow in order to heal a leprous lady. Her virginity, like the virtue of the Grail itself, is withheld until it can be given forth where it will have most effect. Her virginal fertility and potential are poured into the healing process in the same way in which the Grail itself is poured out.

Dindraine opens the ways of grace, for the healing powers of the Grail to come into the world. As a Grail-seer, she helps the spiritual waters flow in every soul.

The Way of the Well

You stand on the bank of a swiftly-flowing river. A thin, piercing rain is beginning to fall and it is getting chilly. You are about to turn from the bank when you see a long, narrow boat coming down the river. The boat is made of green wood. Lying in it is a woman, asleep or dead, you cannot tell. As it comes towards you at the bend of the bank you are able to jump on board.

The woman is very pale and has on a long plain dress. There is neither breath nor movement in her. You conclude that she is dead. In her hand is a scroll, addressed: 'To the one who finds this boat.' You check that the boat is safely floating downriver and does not require your care and then break the seal on the scroll. It reads:

'Traveller of the ways between,
Know that the lady who rests in this boat is Dindraine. Though her body sleeps, her guidance is most powerful. You who read this, trust to the quest for the Grail, which is your life's journey. Into your hands this quest now passes. Seek the service of the wells and your quest will begin.
Blessings on your road,
from One who quested with this Lady.'

When you stepped into this boat, you had no idea of going on a quest, rather you meant to satisfy your curiosity. Another bend is up ahead and you could step from the boat if you wished. You look upon the face of Dindraine for guidance. As you gaze, it is borne in upon you that the quest which she followed has now become your quest and that the only way to proceed is to either take it up or find someone else who will. In this spirit you remain in the boat and see what will happen.

The trees on either bank hang low over you and you pass through their green canopy. As you emerge, the boat slows down and halts at a stone jetty. You are clearly intended to leave the boat and proceed on foot. You enter the woods and walk the clearly marked path. It leads to a clearing wherein is an ancient spring. The waters have ceased the flow and a thin, slimy ooze seeps from the stones to congeal into a thick, viscid pool. There is nowhere else to drink and you are thirsty. The sight of the blocked spring is very depressing and it obviously requires much hard work to make the waters flow freely again.

Nevertheless you decide to clean the spring as best you can and see if its waters can be restored. Taking handfuls of fresh green grass you cleanse the stones and look at the source of the problem. The spring is silted up and is beyond your skill to unblock. Something long and sharp is required to scrape the stones. You bring the face of Dindraine to mind and ask her what you can do. As you utter this question, you see a flash of silver through the trees, as of a swift beast passing.

It is a unicorn. Its solitary beauty takes your breath away. It looks willing to help you but will not approach. You remember that only virgins are supposed to be able to catch unicorns. Dindraine's face comes to your mind and her voice speaks. 'The maidenhood of the body matters not if it is maintained with hardness and coldness of heart. The maidenhood of the spirit lies in your integrity. Call upon the deepest source of your own integrity wherein lies your deep virginity.' You bring to mind the place within yourself which is never compromised or sullied by outside influences, the place where innocence of heart still plays unbounded . . .

The unicorn comes towards you and you show it the blocked and muddied spring. It places its horn into the deep cracks of the stone and moves its head to clear the blockage of centuries of disuse. The world seems to shift, the earth shakes and out of the stone the waters spring once more. It arises in a fountain of brilliance and soon the slimy pool is no more and all the stones are cleansed. The unicorn dips its horn into the waters and dances with gladness. You drink, savouring its cool, sweet refreshment. When you open your eyes once more you see three maidens standing before you.

'We are the Maidens of the Wells, we are the Daughters of Life, we are the Keepers of the Waters. Look within the pool and see your own world . . . See its wounds and unhealing places, see where the waters flow not . . .'

You look, and your inner sight is drawn to notice the wounds that you know about. Like the blocked spring, the work seems depressing and overwhelming, too much for one person to shift.

One of the Well-Maidens leans towards you and puts a golden vessel into your hands. 'Fill the cup with water and pour it out upon the wounds that you see. See with deep knowledge how the world is also healed as the waters flow.'

You take the cup and do as she bids. The waters flow into your inner vision of the world and its wounding. You may see many changes; some places may seem overcast with a mist as they slowly change. Be trustful of the waters and their healing . . .

You look once more upon the Well-Maidens before you and have a fleeting vision of them as one single woman whose arms are open to you. She speaks with triple voice: 'Child of the Waters, restore the wells! Guard well this golden cup and let it never fall from your hands. It is the most precious thing that ever was or ever will be.' She anoints your head with water from the well. 'Go signed with the saining of the waters of the deep Earth, whose sweet blood is poured out for the life of all.'

The golden cup is no more within your hands, but is sealed within your heart where all may drink from it.

The Well-Maidens fade from your sight. The unicorn dances back along the path, urging you to return to the boat. You take the path again, treasuring the experience you have had. Dindraine lies quietly within the boat, but the scroll flutters in the breeze. You realize that your part of the quest is concluded in this world and that you must go forth into your own world to manifest what you have seen and known. The letter must be sealed up again and left in her hands for another to find. There is no new or different message. But how shall the letter be sealed?

You see a piece of flint lying on the bank and pick it up. Its sharp edge cuts your hand and the drops fall upon the letter to create a seal. The unicorn once more sets its horn to work and the blood congeals into a solid seal, to be broken by the next traveller between the worlds. You place the scroll in Dindraine's hands and step into the boat. It bears you to a place where you can step out back into your own world.

You bid farewell to Dindraine, the Lady of the Quest, the messenger who passes through time to new ages where the quest awaits new seekers.

REFERENCES

1. *The Mabinogion*, ed. Lady Charlotte Guest.
2. Sir Thomas Malory, *The Morte d'Arthur.*
3. Ibid.
4. John Matthews, *The Grail: Quest for the Eternal.*
5. Malory, op. cit.
6. Caitlín Matthews, *Arthur and the Sovereignty of Britain.*
7. Nigel Bryant, *The High Book of the Grail (Perlesvaus).*
8. *Quest of the Holy Grail*, trans. P. Matarasso.
9. Charles Williams, *Taliessin in the Rose Garden.*
10. Ibid.
11. Caitlín Matthews, op. cit.
12. Bryant, op. cit.
13. Malory, op. cit.

Ragnell

And as he rode upon a moor
He saw a lady where she sat
Betwixt an oak and a green hollen -
She was clad in red scarlet.

The Wedding of Sir Gawaine

THE MYTH OF RAGNELL

Ragnell is another aspect of the Loathly Lady, but one who transforms into the likeness of the Flower Bride. Her gift is sovereignty, which may be taken either in the conventional meaning of rulership of the land, or as the sovereign love of two hearts for each other. Like Enid she must be recognized for the beauty which is inherent within her, though before this can happen she must suffer a long and wearisome period of despite.

The story of Ragnell appears in two fifteenth-century texts: *The Wedding of Sir Gawain and Dame Ragnell* and a fragmentary poem in balled metre called *The Marriage of Sir Gawain*. The same story, with an anonymous hero and heroine, was retold by Geoffrey Chaucer in 'The Wife of Bath's Tale' in *The Canterbury Tales* and by John Gower in his *Confessio Amantis*. Essentially, the story they tell is the same.

Arthur goes hunting in Inglewood forest, pursing a great hart ahead of his fellows. Stalking it alone, he shoots and kills the buck and is butchering it when an extraordinary man appears, fully armed, and threatens to take the king's life. His name is Gromer Somer Jour and his grievance is that Arthur has given his lands to Sir Gawain. He agrees to spare the king's life on one condition, that he return to the same spot a year hence with the answer to a question: What is it that women love best? Arthur agrees and rejoins the hunting party, saying nothing of what has occurred.

Time passes and Arthur is clearly downcast. At length Gawain asks him what troubles him and Arthur relates all that occurred in the forest. Gawain's answer is to suggest that they both set out at once, riding in different directions through the country and into distant lands, asking every woman they meet for their answers to the question. Arthur agrees and they set out at once. They meet many women, of both high and low station, some of whom love to be well dressed, others to be flattered, while others say that they like nothing so much as to be loved by a lusty man.

At the end of several months Arthur and Gawain return to the court with sufficient answers to make large book. But Arthur is still concerned that he has not got the right answer, and sets out again, this time alone, into Inglewood forest itself. There he meets a lady riding a beautiful and richly comparisoned palfrey. She carries a lute across her back, but is herself so hideous that no tongue could possibly describe her. She approaches Arthur and tells him, in no uncertain terms, that the answers he has collected are useless and that he will certainly lose his head unless he places his life in her hands. Suspicious, Arthur asks her what she means. She replies that in return for a favour she will give him the correct answer. The boon she asks is that she be given to Gawain in marriage. Dismayed, Arthur says that he cannot make such a promise without asking Gawain himself, but that if her answer proves correct he will do all that he can to see that such a wedding comes about.

The hideous lady agrees to wait while Arthur returns to Carlisle to speak with Gawain. When he comments on her ugliness, she says that though she is foul, 'even an owl can choose a mate' and that, though ugly, she is full of life. She further tells the king that her name is Dame Ragnell.

On arriving in Carlisle the first person Arthur meets is Gawain, who asks how he has fared. Arthur tells him about the hideous woman and her offer to save him. Without hesitation Gawain replies that he would marry her twice if she were as ugly as Beelzebub and receives Arthur's praise for his chivalry. The king then returns to the forest in due time for his encounter with Gromer Somer Jour. On the way he meets Ragnell, who provides him with the answer: what every woman wants the most is to have sovereignty over men.

Arthur continues on his way and finds Gromer waiting. He shows both books of answers only to have Gromer dismiss them all. Then the king gives Ragnell's answer and in a rage Gromer admits it is correct. He curses his 'sister', who alone of all women could have known the answer.

Arthur departs from Gromer and soon meets Ragnell again. She resolutely refuses to leave the king's side, and rides with him all the way to Carlisle, where she at once demands that Gawain be brought forth to plight his troth. This is done, much to the sorrow of all the court – especially the women, who love Sir Gawain greatly and cannot believe that he will actually marry this foul and hideous hag. Plans for the wedding proceed, with Ragnell insisting on a full-scale affair, at high mass, with as many people invited as possible, and a great banquet to follow, despite Guinevere's request that she get married quietly.

When the day dawns everyone mourns Gawain as though he were going to his death. The bride is dressed in the most lavish and expensive clothes, which cannot hide her loathsome and misshapen appearance. At the banquet afterwards her table manners appall everyone. Afterwards, when the couple have retired to their chamber, Ragnell demands that Gawain approach her as husband should, and he turns to her to find a beautiful woman at his side. Astonished, Gawain asks who or what she is, to which she replies merely that she is his wife and that he may have her fair either by night or by day, but not both. Gawain agonizes over the choice which will condemn him either to miserable nights or shameful days. At last he tells Ragnell that the choice is her own to make, and she, delightedly, tells him that by giving her sovereignty he has broken the spell put upon both her and her brother Gromer by their step-mother. She will be fair always from that time.

Next morning Arthur comes knocking on Gawain's door, fearful lest the demoness may have killed him. But when Gawain opens the door to reveal his wife, standing in her shift by the fire with her hair red-gold around her, he is forced to admit that there is no danger. The whole story is told and Ragnell asks the king to forgive Gromer, which he does. The poem ends by telling that Gawain and Ragnell had one son, Guinglain, and that Ragnell lived but five years after, and was much mourned by her husband.

Such is the substance of this extraordinary tale. The poem itself is a minor masterpiece, told with humour and wit. That it is also a very ancient and magical story is evident from the start when, as so often before, Arthur is found hunting in the forest of Inglewood and close to the Tarn Watheling – both enchanted places and the scenes of several other adventures – in search of a great stag. The sudden appearance of the stranger, Gromer Somer Jour, who immediately has power over Arthur, identifies him as an otherworldly personage. So also is Ragnell, who despite the efforts of the author to present her as an ordinary mortal woman who has been enchanted by her step-mother, is very obviously a creature of Faery, whose dramatic ability to change herself from hideous to beautiful derives from a far older and more significant story.

In the fragmentary ballad of *The Wedding of Sir Gawain* we first meet her sitting 'betwixt an oak an a green hollen [holly]', and later in the same poem we see her 'underneath a green holly tree'. The otherworldly significance of these trees hardly needs to be mentioned. Both were held to be sacred by the Celts, and the holly has continued to be associated with Faery. Turning to Ragnell's brother, Gromer Somer Jour, his name alone – usually translated as 'Man of the Summer's Day', though in fact 'Gromer' derives from an old Norse word *grom* meaning 'child' – identifies him as a kind of old nature spirit, perhaps the summer equivalent of the Green Knight of Gawain's most famous adventure. The two together form a pair whose every feature points to their faery nature.

Ragnell's name appears to derive from the Middle English

208 *Ladies of the Lake*

name for a minor demon. As such it appears in both the alliterative poem *Patience* and again in the Chester mystery play *Antichrist*. Sir Israel Gollancz, the original editor of *Gawain and the Green Knight* cites the name as originating in the apocryphal *Book of Enoch* where it was applied to an angel. However, its association with colloquial words such as 'ragamoffyn' caused it to become degenerated. The fact that it is applied to the Loathly Lady says something about the way she was understood at this point in the history of the tale.

In the text summarized above Ragnell twice refers to herself as an owl – despite which she can seek a mate. The owl in Celtic myth is associated the faithless Blodeuwedd ('Flower-Face') who was turned into an owl by the enchanter Math after she betrayed her husband Llew Llaw Gyffes. She had in fact been created by Math and his brother Gwydion from flowers, as related in Chapter 1, and there is in this a very ancient theme which reflects the relationship of humanity with the natural world – as well as the fact that Blodeuwedd is a type of the Flower Bride discussed in Chapter 3. The owl was anyway regarded as a chancy bird, often presaging ill-omen or disaster. That it was also a bird of the Otherworld goes without saying.

But what does this make Ragnell? It is notable that she is said only to have survived for five years after the incident of her wedding – long enough, indeed, to give Gawain a child who is destined to grow up a hero. It is likely that we are seeing here the last vestige of a story in which the king's nephew acquired a Faery Bride. Such were believed to enter the world of men, marry, get a family and then, at some moment known in advance only to them, disappear. The Lady of Llyn y Fan Fach, for example, of whom we have heard in Chapters 2 and 3, and who is herself a late resonance of the Ladies of the Lake, is just such a one.

In Chaucer's version of the story, the setting is different. Here an anonymous knight rapes an innocent woman and, as a punishment, set by Queen Guinevere herself, is sent forth to find the answer to the all-important question. This is interesting in itself as it suggests that at one time it may well have been a woman, rather than a man, who initiated the test. Another story, *Arthur and Gorlagon*, tells how Guinevere sent the king himself out on a quest to find out about the nature of women - though the outcome is somewhat different from that in *The Wedding of Gawain and Ragnell.*[1] In Chaucer's version, the knight encounters the hideous damsel, just as Arthur does, and she promises to save him if he agrees to marry her. Despite Chaucer's very different intentions, and the fact that the Loathly Lady remains unnamed and there is no mention of Gromer, the remainder of the story is much the same. But a notable detail shows that Chaucer saw the hideous dame as she truly was - a member of a faery band. For, as the nameless knights rides out in search of his answer, he sees a ring of 'four-and-twenty ladies' dancing in a circle on the greensward - yet when he approaches, they are gone, and only the hideous woman remains, waiting for him.

These facts alone are sufficient to indicate the antiquity of the story and the importance of Ragnell as a character. Another is the presence of Gawain. One of the earliest heroes to be attracted into the circle of Arthur and his Round Table fellowship, Gawain's roots are in the myths of the Celtic peoples. Though in later versions of the legends his character became degraded to that of a murderer and womaniser, he began life as Arthur's foremost hero and the Champion of the Goddess. His relationship to Arthur - that of sister's son - made him a figure of central importance in the Arthurian world and, since Arthur and Guinevere had no surviving children, the rightful heir to the throne. These facts in themselves may seem unimportant to our consideration of Ragnell, but in fact they point the way towards the central theme of her story - the question and its answer. The answer, that what every woman desires most is sovereignty, can, and indeed has, been interpreted in a number of different ways. There are those who would say that a more simple and direct way of expressing it would be to say that what every woman wants is her own way! But to reduce the answer to this level is a *reductio ad absurdum*. It misses the point entirely, and fails to take in a theme which is at least as old as history. It is at this that we must look next.

THE CHALLENGE OF SOVEREIGNTY

The descriptions of Ragnell in the poem *The Wedding of Sir Gawain* are quite horrific in their detail:

> Her face was red, her nose snotted
> Her mouth was wide, her teeth all yellow
> With bleared eyes, bigger than balls.
> Her mouth was not lacking,
> Her teeth hung over her lips,
> A lute she bare upon her back.
> Her neck was long and great,
> Her hair was clotted in a heap.
> Her shoulders were a yard across,
> Her hanging paps a horse's load,
> And like a barrel she was made . . . (lines 232–3)
> She had two teeth on either side,
> Like boar's tusks, I will not hide –
> In length a handful wide:
> The one went up, the other down.
> A mouth full wide, and very foul,
> With grey hairs many upon it.
> Her lips lay heavy on her chin,
> A neck on her was never seen . . . (lines 549–56)[2]

For another description as detailed and specific as this we must look to Irish myth, and in so doing discover the root of Ragnell's character and the reasons for her actions.

In *The Adventures of the Sons of King Daire* from *The Book of Ballymote* the following story is told. There was a prophecy that one of the five sons of King Daire Diontech would obtain the kingship of Ireland. As the name this son would bear was to be 'Lughaidh' each boy was given that name. One day the king asked his druid how he would know which son would be the successor, and the druid said that a golden fawn would come, which only the son destined to fulfil the prophecy would be able to catch.

When this duly took place, only the son known as Mac Niad was able to catch it.

Soon after a heavy fall of snow caused one of the Lughaidhs to seek shelter in a mysterious house. Within was a roaring fire, food, ale, silver dishes to eat from and couches of white bronze. The owner of the house was a hideous hag, who demanded what the youth sought.

'I am looking for a bed till morning,' he said.

To this she replied that he might have one but only if he shared it with her. The youth said he would not and returned to his brothers. As he left she remarked, 'You have severed yourself from sovereignty and kingship.'

One by one the brothers entered the house and were given the same offer. When the refused they received nicknames which concerned their part in the hunt for the fawn. Finally Mac Niad entered. The hag asked what he had won that day and he replied that he had taken the fawn when no other might do so. To him she gave the name Lughaidh Laidhe (the Fawn).

He raised no objection to her amorous advances, and as he joined her on the bronze couch found that at his side was the most beautiful maiden he had ever seen.

> It seemed to him that the radiance of her face was the sun rising in the month of May, and her fragrance was likened by him to an odorous herb-garden. And after that he mingled in love with her. 'Auspicious is your journey,' she said. 'I am the sovereignty, and the kingship of Erin will be obtained by you.'

She served him 'new food and old drink' and in due time sent him back to his father.

This is an archetypal story, in which the youngest son is the only one with the ability and perception required to pass the challenge of sovereignty, in this encounter with a living personification of the land itself. Significantly, the hag is hideous until Lughaidh accepts her without question, at which point she becomes beautiful. The two meanings attached to the word 'sovereignty' - which are, after all, perhaps one and the same -

are, according to the way they are interpreted, the foundation upon which both stories, that of Gawain and Ragnell and of Lughaidh and Sovereignty, are built.

The version of the Sons of King Daire story in the *Dindsenchas* follows the line of the version give here in most details. The variations occur when four of the sons have killed the fawn and have found shelter together in a hut. Then, as they are sitting together around the fire, the hag appears:

> As they were in the house
> The men within at the fire,
> A hag approached, ugly and bald,
> Uncouth and loathsome to behold.
>
> High she was as any mast,
> Larger than a sleeping booth her ear,
> Blacker her face than any visage,
> Heavy on each heart was the hag.
>
> Large her front-tooth, who could but see it –
> Than a square of a chess-board,
> Her nose projected far in front
> Longer than the plough's cold share.
>
> Larger than a basketful of ears of wheat
> Each fist; – in a woman it was unbecoming –
> Larger than a rock in a wall
> Each of her rough black knees.
>
> She was one continuous belly
> Without ribs, without separation,
> A rugged, hilly, thick, black head
> Was upon her like a furzy mountain.[4]

There can be no mistaking what this is. It is a description of the land, of Eriu (Ireland) itself, personified by the hideous woman. And she always appears first in this guise, because the hero, or the neophyte king, must prove himself worthy of the position he seeks by facing the dark aspect of the land, the wildness and sheer animality of Sovereignty's representative.

Once again, when Lughaidh Laidhe approaches her without reserve she assumes 'a form of wondrous beauty' and tells him that although he himself will not become king, his son will.

The third and final version we shall look at here is the eleventh-century Irish *Adventures of the Sons of Eochaid Muigmedon* which tells the story of the youthful deeds of the hero Niall of the Nine Hostages. In this, once again the meeting with the hag of sovereignty is much the same as in the previous texts, save that here she guards a well, always a significant factor in Celtic myth, since water brought not only life but inspiration. Again, the description of the loathsome hag is detailed:

> This was the hag: every joint and limb of her, from the top of her head to the earth, was as black as coal. Like the tail of a wild horse was the gray bristly mane that came through the upper part of her head-crown. The green branch of an oak in bearing would be severed by the sickle of green teeth that lay in her head and reached to her ears. Dark smoky eyes she had: a nose crooked and hollow. She had a middle fibrous, spotted with pustules, diseased, and shins distorted and awry. Her ankles were thick, her shoulderblades were broad, her knees were big, and her nails were green.[5]

Yet, when she is transformed by Niall's kiss, the details there are as precise:

> Like the end of show in trenches was every bit of her from head to sole. Plump and queenly forearms she had, fingers long and lengthy: calves straight and beautifully coloured. Two blunt shoes of white bronze between her little, soft-white feet and the ground. A costly full-purple mantle she wore, with a brooch of bright silver in the clothing of the mantle. Shining pearly teeth she had, an eye large and queenly, and lips red as rowanberries.[6]

The beautiful woman tells Niall that she is the sovereignty of Ireland. Her next words are important: 'As thou hast seen me loathsome, bestial, horrible at first and beautiful at last, so is the Sovereignty; for seldom it is gained without battles and conflicts; but at last to everyone it is beautiful and goodly.'[7]

Here is an important point indeed. Sovereignty must be fought for as in the story of *Pwyll*; and this can be interpreted in more ways than one. Women today, as perhaps always, have had to fight for their own sovereign rights; the modern battles and conflicts are well documented. But there is another kind of struggle also, which goes beyond the right to be recognized as beautiful in a particular way - it is the struggle for identity and it concerns men as well as women. Gawain, Lughaidh and Niall strive to be recognized as kings, to become themselves; Ragnell and the two sovereign women seek to have their own reality acknowledged, both physically and in a loving way.

What happens when the sovereignty question is *not* answered correctly is seldom dealt with. One text only, the fifteenth-century Irish tale *The Chase of Gleann an Smoil* preserves a possible answer.[8]

One day as the hero Fionn and his men are hunting they discover a marvellous doe, black on one side and white on the other. They give chase but cannot catch it. Then a beautiful woman approaches and invites them into the otherworldly house of the King of Greece. There is great feasting therein but as they are about to go to bed a loathsome hag appears, wearing a crown and a robe which is black on one side and white on the other. She declares that she was the doe they had pursued and angrily demands that Fionn marry her. When he refuses, she kills many of his men and rampages through the land for a long while before she is at last slain. She dies cursing her father, the King of Greece, who had put the *geasa* upon her to marry a great prince or remain a hag forever. If she had done so she would have been beautiful forever and born a son who might have ruled the world. The story is a confused one, but there is little doubt that the doe, the beautiful woman and the hag are in reality one and the same. It is after the pursuit of the miraculous deer that the events take place, just as in all the other versions of the Sovereignty myth we have looked at. The fact that the hag is the daughter of the King of Greece need not deter us - he, and his land, were long recognized as referring to the Otherworld in Irish myth, and in fact in other stories Fionn's wife is also a woman who periodically transforms herself into a deer. This time, however, the hero fails to make the right response, and though there is no sign of the all-important question, the effect of Fionn's failure is immediate and terrible. The hag deals out death and rampages through Ireland until she is herself finally killed.

The message here is not hard to read. If the beauty within Ragnell and her kin is not recognized, it turns to hatred and destructiveness. The love which results in each case in the birth of new life, whether this be seen as a child or as the reflowering of the land under a new king, can turn inward upon itself and become barren and destructive. The failure of the king to pass the test of sovereignty or the hero to give the right answer to the Loathly Lady results in more than just a personal loss - by implication the whole land is wounded, and in this we may catch a glimpse of the basis upon which the wasteland story from the Grail myth is founded.

The Grail of Love

There is a Gaelic variant to the story of 'what women most desire' which is entitled *An Aon Sceal* or 'The One Story Worth the Telling'. For many women this question of what women most desire has assumed equal importance with the Grail Question. In the Ragnell story the sovereignty test of the king is transferred entirely to Gawain's successful answer to the question 'What is it women most desire?' To overcome her predicament, Ragnell has to trust a man to get the answer right, otherwise she has to go on asking the question. While she gives the 'official answer' to Arthur, in order that he might overcome Gromer Somer Jour, she herself remains trusting that Gawain will find the right answer to disenchant her.

This final disenchantment of womanhood is of critical importance in our time and one into which Ragnell herself can initiate us. The essential freedom of womanhood has to be accorded by each man to each woman - and indeed, by each woman to each woman. One of the worst predicaments which modern womanhood faces is the distrust and unsupportive attitudes which women have towards one other. True freedom in womanhood is not about going one better than one's sister, any more than it is about being more powerful than men.

The balancing act is effected by Ragnell and Enid jointly. Enid's advantages - her youth, beauty and innocence - all serve as disadvantages in her attempt to love Gereint. Her love never wavers, though, despite the moods of her erstwhile lover. She constantly proffers the hand of friendship and support. And, like Ragnell, she first appears poorly clad and has to be 'recognized' by Gereint in the same way that Gawain must see the true beauty in his bride. Ragnell's ugliness and discourtesy are advantages in her pursuit of a noble answer to her question. No-one imagines that she will provoke the correct answer. Only in the unexpected beauty of Gawain's homage can she turn into herself again.

In both cases, love without conditions is required. The solvent of this answer is the water of the lake, the draught of the cauldron or the primal spring of truth. It is for this reason, perhaps, that Ragnell herself says, when Arthur is so clearly outfaced by her hideous appearance, 'Though I am ugly yet I am also full of life.' The life that runs so strongly in her is far more important than her outward appearance, and though Arthur hesitates to recognize it, Gawain does not. However we judge his motivation for accepting Ragnell - loyalty to Arthur or innate courtesy - the outcome is the same.

The question which Gawain answers is very much bound up with another important question which is found in the Arthurian legends, the so-called 'Grail Question': 'Whom does the Grail serve?' This, or its equivalent, is always asked by the destined Grail-winner and, as in the story of Ragnell, it brings change, healing, a kind of rebirth. In most of the Grail stories the asking of the question has a twofold effect: it sets in motion the healing of the Wounded King, and it restores the waste land.

For the answer, as it is usually given, is that the Grail serves everyone, in as much as they (we) serve it. In this radiant exchange love, true and unconditional, is born. The Grail of love, which is the most triumphant aspect of this most mysterious and ever-changing symbol, shines out suddenly and all too briefly before it is again withdrawn; yet in that brief moment is all the sunlight we find in the transformed Sovereignty:

> Her eyes were thus:
> They were not such as to cloud her face,
> Three sunbeams in each of them shone,
> Whatever she looked on grew bright.[9]

Ragnell is first and foremost an agent of transformation. Her presence transforms us to view what is despised as of worth. Despite her ugly appearance, Ragnell never despises herself. This is important in today's society, which views as ugly many female traits. It also encourages women to disown their own femininity, thus disempowering many from the source of their greatest strength.

Ragnell shows us the possibility of women turning from owls back into flowers. She counter-balances the terrible agony of Blodeuwedd, made from flowers but turned into an owl because she is not free to exercise her choice. Women will continue to manifest their owl-nature unless they are given the freedom of love. For them, this is the ultimate Grail – to become themselves as they really are, not to have to dissemble. Forced into false positions, living on someone else's terms is not the best of conditions in which to transform. But the free and generous allowance of a woman's partner to allow her to grow into herself is seldom offered.

Just as Blodeuwedd, the Flower Bride, stands at spring, awaiting the outcome of the struggle between the champions of winter and summer, so Ragnell stands at midwinter, awaiting the transformation that will take her out of the stasis of the dead time into burgeoning spring. It is this transformation which women most desire: the freedom to find who they are and who they can be. This possibility is ever-present within all women; it is achievable if they are steadfast in their Grail quest. Ragnell was required to wait, but women today have already begun to bring about the conditions by which freedom may be effected. No longer subject to enchantment, they are returning from the Lands Adventurous with the Grail, from which they drink for . themselves and the world's healing.

The Well in the Forest

All around you the forest is thick, stretching league upon league. But on every side paths lead away through the tangled undergrowth. Which one will you follow? As you wonder you hear a far-off singing that comes from somewhere amid the trees, and this you decide to follow. A track leads in the direction you want and you strike off from the safety of the clearing into the uncertain half-light of the forest . . .

After a while you are no longer certain of your direction, and the singing has faded until you can no longer hear it. Then, in the undergrowth to your left you hear a crashing noise and abruptly a large roe deer leaps out upon the path before you. It seems as startled as you, but after a moment it is away, running before you as though you were a pack of hounds . . .

Something prompts you to follow, though you know that you cannot catch the deer. In a few moments you emerge into another clearing, in the centre of which is an ancient crumbling well-head. There is no sign of the deer but standing by the side of the well is a veiled woman. One half of her cloak is black and the other white, and the veil which covers head and face together is made of black stuff shot through with silver. As you approach she addresses you.

'I am Ragnell. I guard the Well of Truth which shows even the most secret things of those who look within. All are welcome who approach my well, but only those with great courage choose to look within it, and of them few ever seek to drink thereof.'

As you stand by the side of Ragnell you are disturbingly aware of her eyes regarding you from behind the veil, yet you can see nothing more of her face, which may be fairly aspected or otherwise. You look towards the well, trying to decide whether to look into it or not . . . Give yourself time for this and if you do not wish to, give thanks and say farewell to Ragnell and return to the place from which you have come. If you decide to brave the test of the well then proceed . . .

Look down into the well. At first it seems filled with nothing but cloudy water; then the cloudiness becomes crystal clarity and you are able to see to the very bottom. In the water are bubbles and within the bubbles are scenes that appear now close, now distant . . . What you see there depends very much upon what you seek. The particulars property of the well is that it can cause transformations to occur, thus if you believe your spirit to be mostly white you may see its darker side; if you believe it to be dark, then it is light that you will perceive - the ugly may become the beautiful, or the beautiful seem ugly. That is the way of the well as it is the way of its guardian . . .

When you have looked your fill, consider whether you will drink from the waters. They too can cause transformations, changing the way you perceive yourself forever. Think very carefully before you decide one way or the other . . . If you decide not to drink, then proceed with the visualization; if you decide to attempt the test, then do so now . . .

When you have drunk, or if you have decided not to, look once again at Ragnell. You see that she is unveiled. How will she seem to you? Hideous or radiantly beautiful? It is up to you how you perceive her, for here as in all things it is how we *chose* to see that governs the *way* we see. And whatever you see, the true appearance of Ragnell remains unchanged . . . Look well and carefully and test what you see before you decide on its reality, even in this place . . .

Now it is almost time to depart, but before you do so you may ask the guardian one question. Perhaps it will be the one to which she long since gave Arthur the answer: 'What is it that every woman most desires?' Perhaps it will be another? Ask, and Ragnell will answer with complete truthfulness . . .

When the answer has been given it is time to depart. Take leave of Ragnell and slowly allow the image of the well in the forest to fade from your inner sight. In your own time re-establish contact with this world, letting the other depart from your consciousness.

REFERENCES

1. Alan Bruford, *Gaelic Folk-Tales and Medieval Romance.*
2. Our translation.
3. S. Eisner, *A Tale of Wonder.*
4. Trans. John O'Donovan, *Miscellany of the Celtic Society.*
5. Eisner, op. cit.
6. Ibid.
7. Ibid.
8. Ibid.
9. Ibid.

Envoi

When we look closely at the stories of the nine Ladies of the Lake, we see that a single theme unites them all. This is one of misunderstanding, of the inability of the world of men to read the signs aright.

Thus Igraine seeks to transmit her knowledge to Arthur and to her male kindred, and when this does not happen, due to her early separation from son and husband, she retires to the Castle of Maidens, where men must actively seek that knowledge. Guinevere is consistently portrayed as a betrayer, while she in fact represents the ancient Sovereignty of the land, which becomes her secret bower. Morgan mostly presents her dark face throughout the stories, only appearing in her complete form as the land's guardian and the agent of Arthur's inner transformation in Avalon.

Argante's role is never wholly revealed, for she remains within, guarding the secret motherland of the Lake. Her seclusion lends her the objectivity of a neutral otherworldly observer who has full knowledge of events and their patterns. Nimuë is seen as a sly and sexually-insatiable woman rather than as her true self: the opener of the ways and the true mate of Merlin. Enid is pitied as a poor, helpless victim, rather than as the delivering messenger of love who restores joy to shuttered hearts.

Kundry's harsh tongue is feared, but she speaks the words that will change the face of the land from waste land into abundant growth. Dindraine is spurned as a weak woman with nothing to offer the Grail quest, but she perceives the Grail's imminence and mediates its power to all. Ragnell is a compendium of all that the world has hated: she is ugly, she is old, she is a woman.

Yet she is the bright joy at the heart of all women that longs to be unchained.

Each Lady of the Lake has been misrepresented in her day. The time now comes to set the record straight. The signposts to the magical realm of the Lake have been boarded over too long and the old proscriptions about travelling thither are beginning to lose their authority. The vital waters are welling up within each of us and prompting us to seek out the realm of the Lake and the ladies who sit about it. They gather about the otherworldly waters just as the ninefold sisterhood of Celtic tradition stand about the cauldron, each gifting the brew with a unique gift. Without the unique ingredients which each of the Ladies of the Lake provides, the Arthurian legends would be impoverished and savourless.

These are figures as powerful as any from Classical mythology, each representing an archetypal quality which is accessible to us today. They are not, however, merely 'psychological' archetypes: their faithful abiding transcends such a narrow definition. Approach them with respect, learn to understand their message, give them grateful thanks. Those who have voyaged to the Lake or drunk of the cauldron will already know the truth and justice of this remark. We have followed a complex and often winding path to recover the stories of our ninefold sisterhood. We hope it will lead you to explore the inner life of the Arthurian legends and the vitality which the Ladies of the Lake bring to them.

We are contactable by writing to BCM HALLOWQUEST, London WC1N 3XX, but we cannot guarantee to reply to all letters, especially those without return postage. If you are writing from outside Britain, 2 international reply-paid coupons, available from post offices, are essential.

For details of courses, events and forthcoming books, please send six first class stamps (within the UK) or eight international reply paid coupons or $5 US dollars for one issue of the *Hallowquest Newsletter*.

Two tapes are available from us: *The Sacred Nine* gives visualizations from this book, while *The Initiations of the Lake* has further ideas and practical work which do not appear here.

Bibliography

All titles published in London unless stated otherwise.

Arden, John and D'Arcy, Margaretta, *The Island of the Mighty* (Methuen, 1974).

Bergin, O. and Best, R.I. (eds.), 'Tochmarc Etaine' in *Eriu*, XII, 1938.

Blaess, M., 'Arthur's Sisters' in *Bibliographical Bulletin of the International Arthurian Society*, 8, 1956, pp.69-77.

Bogdanow, Fanni, *The Romance of the Grail* (Manchester University Press, Manchester, 1966).

- , 'Morgain's Role in the Thirteenth-Century French Prose Romances of the Arthurian Cycle' in *Medium Aevum*, 37/8, 1968-9, pp.123-33.

Boll, Lawrence L., *The Relation of 'Diu Krone' of Heinrich von dem Tulin to 'La Mule Sanz Frain'* (Catholic University of America, Washington, 1929).

Bradley, Marion Zimmer, *Mists of Avalon* (Sphere, 1984).

Brown, A.C.L., 'The Esplumoir and Viviane' in *Speculum*, 20, 1945, pp.426-532.

Bruford, Alan, *Gaelic Folk-Tales and Medieval Romance* (Folklore of Ireland Society, Dublin, 1969).

Bryant, Nigel, *The High Book of the Grail (Perlesvaus)* (D.S. Brewer, Cambridge, 1978).

Butler, Isabel, *Tales from the Old French ('Melion' and 'Le Lai du Cor')* (Houghton Mifflin, Boston, 1950).

Carmichael, Alexander, *Carmina Gadelica* (Scottish Academic Press, Edinburgh, 1972).

Chaucer, Geoffrey, *The Canterbury Tales* (Oxford University Press, 1906).

Chrétien de Troyes, *Arthurian Romances*, trans. D.D.R. Owen (Dent, 1987).

- , *Arthurian Romances*, trans. W.W. Kibler and C.W. Carroll (Penguin, 1991).

Cross, T.P. and Slover, C.H., *Ancient Irish Tales* (Figgis, Dublin, 1936).

Curtin, Jeremiah, *Hero Tales of Ireland* (Macmillan, 1894).

- , *Irish Folk Tales* (Talbot Press, Dublin, 1944).

Eisner, S., *A Tale of Wonder* (John English & Co., Wexford, 1957).

Ellis, Peter Berresford, *A Dictionary of Irish Mythology* (Constable, 1987).

Eschenbach, Wolfram von, *Parzival*, trans. A.T. Hatto (Penguin, Harmondsworth, 1980).

Evans-Wentz, W.Y., *The Fairy Faith in Celtic Countries* (Lemma Publishing Co., New York, 1973).

Fletcher, Robert H., *The Arthurian Material in the Chronicles* (Burt Franklin, New York, 1906).

Fortune, Dion, *Aspects of Occultism* (The Aquarian Press, 1962).

Gilbert, Max, *The Fairies Melusine, Viviane and Aine* (Richard Madley, 1974).

Graves, R., *The White Goddess* (Faber and Faber, 1961).

Green, Miranda, *Symbol and Image in Celtic Religious Art* (Routledge & Kegan Paul, 1989).

Gregory, Lady, *Voyages of Brendan the Navigator and Tales of the Irish Saints* (Colin Smythe, Gerrard's Cross, 1973).

Grimm's Tales for Young and Old: the Complete Stories, trans. R. Mannheim (Gollancz, 1979).

Hall, L.B., *Knightly Tales of Sir Gawaine* (Nelson Hall, Chicago, 1976).

Hamp, E.P., 'Viviane or Ninian - A Comment' in *Romance Philology*, VIII, 1954, p.91.

Harf-Lancner, L., *Les Fées au Moyen Age* (Librarie Honoré Champion, Paris, 1984).

Holbrook, S.E., 'Nymue, the Chief Lady of the Lake in Malory's *Morte Darthur*' in *Speculum*, 53, 1978, pp.761-77.

Jarman, A.O.H., 'A Note on the Possible Welsh Derivation of Viviane' in *Gallicia: Essays Presented to J.H. Thomas* (University of Wales Press, Cardiff, 1969) pp.1-12.

Johnston, R.C. and Owen, D.D.R., *Two Old French Gauvain Romances* (Scottish Academic Press, Edinburgh, 1972).

Jones, Prudence and Matthews, Caitlín, *Voices from the Circle* (The Aquarian Press, Wellingborough, 1989).

Julius Caesar, *The Conquest of Gaul*, trans. S.A. Handford (Penguin, Harmondsworth, 1982).

Karr, Phyllis Ann, *The King Arthur Companion* (Chaosium Inc., Albany, 1983).

Keating, Geoffrey, *The History of Ireland*, vol 2 (Irish Texts Society, Dublin, 1908).

Kinter, William L. and Keller, Joseph R., *The Sibyl: Prophetess of Antiquity and Medieval Fay* (Dorrance and Co., Philadelphia, 1967).

Kitteridge, G.L., *A Study of 'Gawaine and the Green Knight'* (Peter Smith, Gloucester, Massachusetts, 1960).

Knight, Gareth, *The Secret Tradition in Arthurian Legend* (The Aquarian Press, Wellingborough, 1983).

Knott, E., *Togail Bruiden Da Derga* in Medieval and Modern Irish Series VIII (Dublin, 1936).

Korrel, Peter, *An Arthurian Triangle* (E.J. Brill, Leiden, 1984).

Krappe, Alexander H., 'Arturus Cosmocrator' in *Speculum*, 20, 1945, pp.405-14.

Lacy, Norris J. (ed.), *The Arthurian Encyclopedia* (Garland Publishing Inc., New York, 1986).

- , and Ashe, Geoffrey (eds.), *The Arthurian Handbook* (Garland Publishing Inc., New York, 1988).

Loomis, R.S., *Arthurian Tradition and Chrétien de Troyes* (Columbia University Press, New York, 1949).

- , 'Morgue la Fée in Oral Tradition' in *Romania*, LXXX, 1959, pp.337-67.

- , *Celtic Myth and Arthurian Romance* (Haskell House Publications, New York, 1967).

- , *Wales and Arthurian Legend* (Folcroft Editions, 1977).

Luke, Helen, 'The Return of Dindrane' in *At the Table of the Grail*, ed. John Matthews, q.v.

Lumiansky, R.M., 'Arthur's Final Companions in Malory's *Le Morte Darthur*' in *Tulane Studies in English*, 11, 1961, pp.17-18.

- (ed.), *Malory's Originality* (The John Hopkins Press, Baltimore, 1964).

McKay, J.G., 'The Deer-Cult and the Deer-Goddess Cult of the Ancient Caledonians', in *Folklore*, XLIII, 1932, pp.144-74.

The Mabinogion, ed. Lady Charlotte Guest (Ballantyne Press, 1910).

Malory, Sir Thomas, *The Morte d'Arthur* (University Books, New York, 1961).

Markale, Jean, *Women of the Celts* (Gordon Cremonesi, 1975).

- , *King Arthur, King of Kings* (Gordon Cremonesi, 1977).

- , *Le Graal* (Retz, Paris, 1982).

- , *Lancelot et la Chevalerie Arthurienne* (Imago, Paris, 1985).

Marie de France, *Lays*, trans. Eugene Mason (J.M. Dent, n.d.).

Masefield, John, *Midsummer Night* (William Heinemann, 1928).

Matthews, Caitlín, *Mabon and the Mysteries of Britain: An Exploration of 'The Mabinogion'* (Arkana, 1987).

- , *Arthur and the Sovereignty of Britain: King and Goddess in 'The Mabinogion'* (Arkana, 1989).

- , *The Elements of Celtic Tradition* (Element Books, Shaftesbury, 1989).

- , *The Elements of the Goddess* (Element Books, Shaftesbury, 1989).

- , *Voices of the Goddess: A Chorus of Sibyls* (The Aquarian Press, Wellingborough, 1990).

- , *Sophia: Goddess of Wisdom* (Mandala, 1991).

- , *The Celtic Book of the Dead* (St Martin's Press, New York, 1992).

Matthews, Caitlín and John, *The Western Way vol I: The Native Tradition* (Arkana, 1985).

- , *The Western Way vol II: The Hermetic Tradition* (Arkana, 1986).

- , *The Arthurian Tarot*, illus. Miranda Gray (The Aquarian Press, Wellingborough, 1990).

- , *Hallowquest: Tarot Magic and the Arthurian Mysteries* (The Aquarian Press, Wellingborough, 1990).

- , *The Arthurian Book of Days* (Sidgwick and Jackson, 1991)

Matthews, John, *The Grail: Quest for the Eternal* (Thames and Hudson, 1981).

- (ed.), *At the Table of the Grail* (Arkana, 1987).

- (ed.), *An Arthurian Reader* (The Aquarian Press, Wellingborough, 1988).

- , *The Elements of the Arthurian Tradition* (Element Books, Shaftesbury, 1989).

- , *The Elements of the Grail Tradition* (Element Books, Shaftesbury, 1990).

- , *Gawain: Knight of the Goddess* (The Aquarian Press, Wellingborough, 1990).

- , *The Celtic Shaman* (Element Books, Shaftesbury, 1991).

- , *Taliesin: The Shamanic and Bardic Mysteries in Britain and Ireland* (with additional material by Caitlín Matthews) (Mandala, 1991).

- , and Green, Marian, *The Grail Seeker's Companion* (The Aquarian Press, Wellingborough, 1986).

- , and Stewart, Bob, *Warriors of Arthur* (Blandford Press, Poole, 1987).

- , and Stewart, Bob, *Legendary Britain: An Illustrated Journey* (Blandford Press, Poole, 1989).

Monmouth, Geoffrey of, *History of the Kings of Britain* (Penguin, Harmondsworth, 1966).

- , *Vita Merlini*, ed. and trans. J.J. Parry (University of Illinois Press, Illinois, 1925).

- , *Vita Merlini*, trans. Basil Clarke (University of Wales Press, Cardiff, 1973).

Mookerjee, Ajit, *Kali: the Feminine Force* (Thames and Hudson, 1988).

Morris, John, *The Age of Arthur* (Weidenfeld and Nicolson, 1973).

Morris, L., *Celtic Remains* (J. Parker, 1878).

Nennius, *British History and Welsh Annals*, ed. and trans. J. Morris (Phillimore, Chichester, 1980).

Nitze, W.A., 'An Arthurian Crux: Nimue or Vivien' in *Romance Philology*, VII, 1953, pp.326-30.

- , 'The Esplumoir Merlin' in *Speculum*, 18, 1943, pp.69-79.

O'Donovan, John, *Miscellany of the Celtic Society* (Dublin, 1849).

Oxford Companion to the Literature of Wales, compiled and edited by Meic Stephens (Oxford University Press, Oxford, 1986).

Parry-Jones, D., *Welsh Legends and Fairy Lore* (Batsford, 1953).

Paton, L.A, 'Merlin and Ganieda' in *Modern Language Notes*, XVIII, 1903, pp.163-9.

- , *Les Prophecies de Merlin* (New York, 1926-7).

- , *Studies in the Fairy Mythology of Arthurian Romance* (Burt Franklin, New York, 1960).

Quest of the Holy Grail, trans. P. Matarasso (Penguin, Harmondsworth, 1969).

Rabten, Geshe, *The Essential Nectar* (Wisdom Publications, 1984).

Reinhard, John Revell, *The Survival of Geis in Medieval Romance* (Max Niemeyer Verlag, Halle, 1933).

Rhys, John, *Celtic Folklore* (2 vols) (Wildwood House, 1980).

Room, Adrian, *Room's Classical Dictionary* (Routledge & Kegan Paul, 1983).

Rosenberg, Samuel N., 'The Prose Merlin and the Suite Merlin' in *The Romance of Arthur*, ed. James J. Wilhelm (Garland Publications, New York, 1986).

Ross, Anne, *Pagan Celtic Britain* (Routledge & Kegan Paul, 1967).

Sir Gawain and the Green Knight, trans. Brian Stone, (Penguin, Harmondsworth, 1959).

Sir Lancelot of the Lake, trans. L.A. Paton (Routledge, 1929).

Skeels, D., *Romance of Perceval in Prose (Didot Perceval)* (University of Washington Press, Seattle, 1966).

Skene, William F., *The Four Ancient Books of Wales* (Edmonston & Douglas, Edinburgh, 1868).

Smyth, Alfred, *Warlords and Holy Men: Scotland AD 80-1000* (Edinburgh University Press, Edinburgh, 1984).

Smyth, Daragh, *A Guide to Irish Mythology* (Irish Academic Press, Blackrock, 1988).

Spence, Lewis, *The Mysteries of Britain* (The Aquarian Press, 1970).

Spenser, Edmund, *The Faerie Queen* (Oxford Standard Authors, New York, 1963).

Stafford, Greg, *Pendragon Game* (Chaosium Inc., Albany, 1985).

Stewart, Mary, *The Crystal Cave* (Hodder & Stoughton, 1970).

- , *The Hollow Hills* (Hodder & Stoughton, 1973).

- , *The Last Enchantment* (Hodder & Stoughton, 1979).

Stewart, R.J., *The Underworld Initiation* (The Aquarian Press, Wellingborough, 1985).

- , *The Mystic Life of Merlin* (Arkana, 1986).

- , *Living Magical Arts* (Blandford Press, Poole, 1987).

- , *Advanced Magical Arts* (Element Books, Shaftesbury 1988).

- (ed), *Merlin and Woman*, (Blandford Press, Poole, 1988).

- , *The Merlin Tarot*, illus. Miranda Gray (The Aquarian Press, Wellingborough, 1988).

- , *The Way of Merlin* (The Aquarian Press, 1991).

Sutcliff, Rosemary, *Sword at Sunset* (Hodder & Stoughton, 1963).

The Tale of Balain, trans. D.E. Campbell (Northwestern University Press, Evanston, 1972).

Tennyson, Alfred, Lord, *The Idylls of the King* (Penguin, Harmondsworth, 1983).

- , *The Lady of Shalott*, illus. Charles Keeping (Oxford University Press, Oxford, 1986).

Tierney, J.J., *The Celtic Ethnography of Posidonius* (Hodges Figgis & Co., Dublin, 1960) (*Proceedings of the Royal Irish Academy* 60, Section C, No. 5.)

Todd, J. and J.M., *Voices from the Past* (Reader's Union, 1956).

Tolkien, J.R.R., *The Lord of the Rings* (George Allen and Unwin, 1974).

Trioedd Ynys Prydein, trans. Rachel Bromwich, (University of Wales Press, Cardiff, 1961).

Villemarque, Hersant de la, *Chants Populaires de la Bretagne* (Didiet et Co., Paris, 1867).

Wace and Layamon, *Arthurian Chronicles*, ed. E. Mason (J.M. Dent, 1962).

Wainwright, F.T., *The Problem of the Picts* (Melven Press, Perth, 1980).

Watson, W.J., *The History of the Celtic Placenames of Scotland* (Irish Academic Press, Dublin, 1973).

Webster, K.G.T., *Guinevere: A Story of her Abductions* (Turtle Press, Milton, Massachusetts, 1951).

Weston, Jessie, *The Legend of Sir Perceval* (David Nutt, 1909).
- , *From Ritual to Romance* (Doubleday, New York, 1957).
White, T.H., *The Once and Future King* (Collins, 1952).
Zatzikhoven, Ulrich von, *Lanzelet*, ed. and trans. K.T.G. Webster
(Columbia University Press, New York, 1951).

Index